D0898156

TANKKILLING

IAN HOGG

TANK
KILLING

ANTI-TANK WARFARE BY MEN AND MACHINES

SARPEDON
New York

Published by
SARPEDON
166 Fifth Avenue
New York, NY 10010

First published in 1996 by
Sidgwick & Jackson
an imprint of Macmillan Publishers Ltd
25 Eccleston Place, London SW1W 9NF England

ISBN 1-885119-40-2

Cataloging-in-Publication Data is available from the
Library of Congress.

10 9 8 7 6 5 4 3 2 1

MANUFACTURED IN THE UNITED STATES OF AMERICA

CONTENTS

CHAPTER ONE

TANKS – AND HOW TO KILL THEM

The genesis of the tank can be said to be a thought which occurred to Lieutenant-Colonel Ernest Swinton of the British army who, driving across France in the winter of 1914 *en route* for England and mulling over the impasse caused by the two lines of trenches running from Switzerland to the North Sea when the mobile phase of the First World War (1914–18) had been replaced by static warfare, envisaged 'a power-driven, bullet-proof, armed engine capable of destroying machine-guns, of crossing country and trenches, of breaking through entanglements and of climbing earthworks'. He thought then of the contemporary Holt Caterpillar tractor, clad with armour and sprouting machine-guns; on his arrival in London he passed his ideas on, and the rest, as they say, is history.

Swinton's original inspiration was simply, as he saw it, to find a device which would break the German defensive line and allow the infantry to pass through and resume open warfare, something which unprotected infantry were unable to do in the face of machine-guns and barbed wire. But from that humble beginning, the tank took on a life of its own and moved in many different directions. Before the First World War was over the theorists had seized upon the tank as the salvation of mankind, and in the years that followed they expounded and extrapolated until their view of the ideal army of the future was of an entire force subordinated to the tank. This, of course, upset several people and did the theorists no good, but at least it made sure that the tank was not forgotten, and that there was a permanent interest, not to say dispute, over its correct employment. Moreover, if the tank was in one form or another to become the principal element of a new army, then of course the rest of the army had to keep up with it, and so the mechanization of armies tended to move rather faster than it might have done in the absence of the tank. And as long as there were people who were proclaiming the invincibility of the tank, then, not unnaturally, there were other people who saw their life's work as proving that the tank was not as invincible as thought by its protagonists. Thus, in one way and another, the pendulum began to swing. Today the tank was superior to all forms of defence; next day the defence had mastered the tank; then came a new and improved tank which restored its dominance on the field; and this was followed by a new and improved gun or rocket or grenade or mine which, again, swung the pendulum the other way and put the tank back in its proper place. In just this fashion, from 1916 to the present day, the pendulum has swung back and forth, in a varying rhythm to be sure, but it has swung inexorably and is still swinging.

The original tanks were of hardened steel, little better than boiler-plate, but they kept out ordinary rifle and machine-gun bullets, shrapnel balls and shell splinters reasonably well. Unfortunately the only way in which the occupants could see out, so as to manoeuvre the machine and acquire targets for their weapons, was by slits in the plating, and once the enemy realized this they had aiming marks. The chance of putting a bullet through such a slit was relatively small, given the stress under which the firer was operating and the movement of the target, but the firer was certainly able to put one or more bullets close enough to splash metal fragments through the slits and thus place the occupants at hazard. This led to the practice of wearing chain-mail visors, steel masks and similar protection. Then, as discussed below, came the use of reversed ball bullets and armour-piercing bullets, and suddenly the boiler-plate tanks were as vulnerable as anything else on the battlefield. The solution to this was to swing the pendulum back by making the tanks of thicker metal and producing proper armour (in the form of face-hardened steel) to counter the threat.

Until that happened, the soldier faced with a tank simply fired whatever he had at the bulk in front of him; wherever he hit, some good would come of it, he assumed. In fact, examination of one of those 1916 monsters reveals quite a lot of empty space inside it. When in action, this space was needed by the (by today's standards) enormous number of men forming the crew. The original figure for the British tank, the Tank Mk I, was nine men: commander, driver, two 'gearsmen' who manually changed gear on each track on signals from the driver, two side gunners manning

6-pounder (57mm) guns, and three machine-gunners each manning a Hotchkiss machine-gun (one in each side and one in the front). There was also a rear machine-gun, manned by anyone not doing anything better at the time. So the chances of hitting some member of the crew were rather higher than that of hitting some vital piece of machinery and bringing the tank to a stop. This, if one cares to think about it, is the whole purpose behind shooting at a tank: not to damage the tank, but to get at the crew and the machinery which is behind the armour plate. This may sound like stating the obvious, but it is surprising how many people are seduced by the problem of the armour and forget that the object is not the armour but the contents.

Artillery was an obvious answer to the tank, but the field artillery of the period had not been designed to deal with close-up moving targets: in order to track a tank it was necessary to heave the gun trail up and swing the gun bodily, something not always easy in the mud of the battlefield. If the tank could be stopped, however, then it became a stationary target and its life measured in minutes, provided the field gun was quicker into action than the machine-gunners and 6-pounder gunners inside the tank. Any contemporary field gun in 1916 could make mince-meat of a tank with a single high-explosive shell, provided it could get a clear shot at it, but the disposition of artillery was generally such that the guns were a considerable distance behind the front line. Bringing a single gun forward to deal with tanks meant putting it into a position where it was a fine target for the opposing machine-guns. If the tanks got through the forward line and into the artillery area, however, then the chances were that the gun would soon stop the tank.

Other methods were proposed and tried. Charges of explosive could be laid in the ground to be detonated should the tank run across them, either by the tank actuating some form of trigger device or by an observer firing the mine electrically as the tank passed over it. Ditches were not a success: the tank was designed to cross trenches, and unless the ditch was enormous, and therefore as much of an obstacle to the defenders when it became their turn to attack as it was to the current attackers, then it was of little use.

Grenades were another solution: the defender could let the tank get close and then lob a grenade on to the roof. When it detonated it would blow a hole in the roof and do a considerable amount of damage inside. But this was soon countered by sloping pent-roofs of wire netting which caused the grenades either to explode harmlessly some distance away from the armour or else simply to roll back off the netting and explode on the ground.

Statistically speaking, the greatest enemy of the First World War tank was itself: its mechanical unreliability, lack of power, lack of mechanical refinement meant that the tank often broke down, bogged down, or failed to overcome some obstacle, and thus halted and in the process became a stationary and therefore relatively easy target.

So when the war ended in 1918, the science of countering the tank was scarcely extant: it was simply a case of shooting at it with whatever you happened to have and hoping for the best.

Already the tank had begun to diversify. There were

now two kinds of tank: the 'infantry' tank which was heavy, unwieldy and as slow as the walking pace of infantry, and existed to fulfil the tank's original function, namely the punching of a hole in the enemy line to allow the infantry to walk through; and the 'cavalry' tank which was light, fast and designed to outmanoeuvre an enemy and thus set up a diversion to draw troops away from the point at which the infantry tanks and the major assault would be directed. The light tank was originally proposed as simply a method of concealing an infantry soldier behind armour: each crewed by a driver and a machine-gunner, large numbers of these vehicles would act in the same way that marching troops would act, but doing it on tracks and faster. This idea, proposed by the French, never really got off the ground, for the simple reason that it was obviously economically impossible. One could muster 5,000 infantry for an attack, but trying to muster 5,000 tanks and 5,000 drivers to take those 5,000 infantrymen forward was impossible. So the light tank assumed the 'cavalry' role, the heavy tank remained as the protector, and the infantry walked just as it had always done.

The development of the tank during the 1920s became a development of these two types, one of them heavy and the other light. The heavy tank got heavier: the turret was adopted, and if one turret was good, some reasoned, then two turrets must be better and this led to such tanks as the Vickers Independent and the Russian T-32 with main turrets, subsidiary turrets and machine-gun turrets, requiring the use of enormous crews. Experience on exercises soon showed that trying to control all the crew members of such a tank, direct their fire, instruct the driver, study the map, consider the tactical moves and co-operate with other tanks was beyond the grasp of a single commander, and the idea collapsed under its own weight.

The light tank divided again: the original two-man mobile infantryman concept still had its adherents, though they tended to see the two-man 'tankette' as a machine-gun carrier. The tankette was too small for the envisaged 'cavalry' role, however, and the new light tank became a bigger vehicle with a three- or four-man crew. Three was the preferred figure, allowing the tank to be suitably small and light, but again this threw too great a burden on to the commander: either he sat alone in the turret, his other two crewmen acting as driver and hull machine-gunner, which meant that he led, commanded, sought out targets, loaded and fired the gun, and went quietly mad trying to do everything at once, or he had a gunner in the turret with him and had to act as the loader as well as doing almost everything else.

While all this was going on, the opposite camp was looking at the way the tank was evolving and contemplating methods of stopping it. The anti-tank task was becoming harder, for almost yearly improvements in mechanical reliability, speed and agility meant that the moving tank was becoming an increasingly difficult target. Every specification for a new field gun now included the demand that it should have a split trail so as to allow greater traverse of the barrel before it became necessary to shift the whole gun bodily, and direct-fire sights were also a new requirement. The British had taken a bold step in 1918 and thrown a gun-wheel on the ground and then balanced an 18-pounder (83.8mm) field gun on it so that the wheels of the gun rolled on the rim of the grounded wheel, allowing the entire gun to be swung rapidly even on soft ground. The system worked in a primitive way, and it was the foundation of an idea which came to fruition with the 25-pounder (87.6mm) field gun in the Second World War.

Gradually, certain features of the tank's basic construction became apparent, features which might afford methods of attack to be developed. Firstly, because steel was heavy, the armour tended to be concentrated most thickly on the front face of the tank hull and turret, somewhat less thickly on the sides, and thinnest of all on the rear and top surfaces. This was in accordance with the tank designer's view of how his brainchild would be most likely to be attacked – generally from the front as the tank advanced towards the enemy, sometimes from the sides as it passed through the enemy lines, seldom from behind after it had passed through the enemy line since the accompanying infantry would mop up any likely attacker, and from above virtually never. Vision for the tank crew meant either opening hatches so that members of the crew could put out their heads, or closing the hatches and relying upon glass prism periscopes or vision blocks, so such vision devices became prime targets for rifles and machine-guns. Hatches themselves were weaknesses in the structure which could be breached by explosives, and the tracks and suspension were always open to attack since there was no way that they could be adequately protected. The tank carried inflammable fuel and ammunition, so that fire was an obviously dangerous threat, and it also carried men so that poison gas was a threat to the crew.

As detailed in later chapters, a variety of weapons and

theories developed during the 1919–35 period, but the first chance that most people had of seeing whether any of these theories and weapons were actually of any value came with the Spanish Civil War (1936–39).

Here the totalitarian powers backed their ideological companions, the Soviets supplying the Republican government side, and the Germans and Italians aiding the Nationalist insurgent side, and among the supplies delivered by each party were tanks. The Germans and Italians sent light tanks, for at that time light tanks were all they had; the Soviets began with light tanks but then sent a somewhat heavier model. Actions took place between tank forces, between tanks and infantry, and between tanks and artillery, and as a result everyone went home sure that they had extracted the lessons from their experience. About the only lesson they agreed on was that light tanks were useless: they had been easy targets for the 37mm and 45mm anti-tank guns of the time, they had fallen prey to Asturian miners with home-made dynamite bombs and bottles full of petrol, and they had even been shot up by armoured cars carrying better armament.

On the matter of tactical handling, however, everyone disagreed. The Germans felt that their experience showed the success of independent tank units, but the Soviets believed that such units were a disaster. The Germans did emerge from this testing ground of a war with one useful nugget of information: they had taken a few 88mm anti-aircraft guns to Spain and, in a small and otherwise unremarkable skirmish, had been compelled to turn these weapons on to a few approaching Soviet BT-4 tanks, and blew them apart. Some of the German gunners tucked this one away in their memories in the belief that it might come in useful one day.

As the Spanish Civil War died down, so the Second World War not only began but began with a dazzling display of armoured mobility and power as the German armoured (Panzer) divisions raced across Poland in a series of sweeping moves which partitioned and defeated the Polish army in three weeks. The Panzer divisions seemed unstoppable, but in factories and drawing offices around the world various people began applying their minds to the problem of defeating the modern tank, which was an altogether more difficult target than its predecessors. The reasons for this were varied and included, during the 1930s, the first applications of welded and cast armour plate and of 'ballistic shaping'. Hitherto the tank had usually been bolted together from flat slabs of armour and, when completed, presented a slab-sided appearance to the world. But there is an interesting parallel to be drawn here between the history of fortification and the history of the tank. At the time that artillery first appeared on the battlefield, castles from the previous era were protected by walls that were relatively narrow and generally vertical, and proved relatively vulnerable to artillery fire. The medieval builders soon appreciated, however, that if they presented a sloping or curved surface to the enemy, there was an excellent chance that his shot would bounce off, and therefore they began building castles with sloped walls, curved parapets and similar 'ballistic shaping'.

Thus too was it with tanks: as the 1930s progressed, tanks began to take on a rounded appearance in their hull and turret surfaces so as to deflect the steel shot which, at that time, was the only possible projectile to use against armour.

For as far as making hole in armour plate went, the ammunition makers knew just about all there was to know on that subject: they had been providing shot and shell for the attack of warships since the 1860s, and what happened when shot met plate was well understood. The only problem lay in converting technology developed around such things as 12in (306mm) calibre naval guns to suit more portable weapons in the 37–40mm range of calibres. The other side of the coin was that the makers of armour plate had just the same amount of experience in the opposite direction, developing different types of armour in order to protect the warships against the guns. Through the 1920s, when the worst they were expected to face was a 20mm projectile or an anti-tank rifle, simple rolled plates of hardened steel were quite sufficient, and 10mm of armour was considered adequate protection. By the mid-1930s there were appearing light anti-tank guns of 37 to 40mm calibre with considerably better armour-penetration capabilities, and the armourers accordingly responded with cast and curved plates, rounded and sloped turrets, sloped hull fronts, joints that were created by welds rather than rivets as these latter could be driven in by a lucky shot and become even more dangerous missiles for the crew than the original shot, and of course increased speed and better suspensions which made the tanks more difficult to hit.

The response from the gunmakers was simply to produce guns which would fire as heavy a charge as possible so as to achieve high velocity and thus cut down the time in which the tank could move after the gunner had fired.

High velocity also meant high striking velocity so that the shot would penetrate the armour plate by its own kinetic energy. As the guns got larger an unfortunate physical fact appeared: when a steel shot struck armour plate at a velocity in excess of about 750m (2,460ft) per second, the steel shot shattered from the sudden impact and the armour remained undamaged. This became more prominent when the armour experts began putting face-hardened armour on their tanks.

Armour is of two kinds: homogeneous – the same toughness all the way through – or face-hardened. The first steel armours, which appeared in the late 1870s, were all homogeneous and simply relied upon their thickness and the careful alloying of steel, nickel and other secret compounds to produce a slab of metal resistant to violent forms of attack. But the gunmakers simply built bigger guns – this was in the days of naval armour – and eventually began making holes in homogeneous plate. It was possible to temper a plate to a degree of hardness which would resist any attack, but as hardness increased, toughness decreased, and a really hard plate would be so brittle that it would shatter when struck by a shot.

So in the early 1880s the steel-makers developed 'compound' armour, in which a relatively thin plate, tempered to extreme hardness, was cemented to a thick, tough, homogeneous plate. The hard plate would resist the impact of the shot, while the thick and tough backing would resist the violence of the blow and prevent the facing plate from shattering. Then in about 1890 H. A. Harvey, an American engineer, invented a method of 'carburizing' the steel plate by piling charcoal on one face and keeping it at white heat for several hours or even days, so that carbon from the charcoal was absorbed into the structure of the steel and gave the plate a hard face without affecting the toughness of the remaining thickness. Finally, in 1895, came the 'Krupp Cemented Plate' in which Krupp turned everything upside-down and made a plate with a tough front and a hard rear face, so that the shot buried itself in the tough outer layers, slowed down, and was stopped completely by the hard rear face.

The thickness necessary for warships allowed the exploitation of the benefits inherent in Krupp's system, which was soon licensed by armourers all over the world, but the reduced thickness available in tank armour did not. So the tank builders of 1940 decided on simple face-hardened (carburized) armour plate, and this, with the high velocities being achieved now by guns of up to 75mm (2.95in) calibre, soon exposed the problem of 'shot shatter'.

The problem was solved by putting a soft metal cap over the nose of the hardened steel shot. This took the initial impact and spread it over the whole diameter of the shot instead of concentrating it in the nose, so avoiding the concentrated stress which caused shatter. And at the velocities involved, the soft steel melted as soon as it had transferred the shock and the molten metal thus offered the additional attraction of serving as a lubricant to help the steel shot penetrate the face-hardened plate.

The only trouble was that putting a cap on the nose upset the ballistic shape of the projectile and it would not fly accurately; so a second cap of the desired ballistic shape had to be put on in front of the piercing cap, to give the shot the desired smooth pointed shape which aided accurate flight.

Eventually the thickness and hardness of tank armour reached the point where even capped shot failed to penetrate. There were two courses now open to the gunmakers: either they could make bigger guns or they could try some original thinking about ammunition. The problem with making bigger guns was not technical: people who could make 16in (406mm) guns for battleships would scarcely find it difficult to make lesser calibres for shooting at tanks. The problem was therefore tactical: a vehicle had to pull the gun across country, somebody had to dig a pit to conceal it, somebody had to push the anti-tank gun into this position, and somebody had to lift and load the ammunition. A big gun demanded a big mounting and a heavy recoil system to take up the shock of firing, moreover, and all this meant tactically undesirable weight and bulk. So the gunmakers and the ammunition wizards were constrained to working within a very tight weight limit: the gunmakers were now at the limit, and it therefore became the turn of the ammunition designers to think up something new.

The problem was twofold: first was the need for more velocity so as to penetrate armour which thickened with each successive generation of tank, and second was the need to overcome the shot shatter problem. The latter appeared to be the easier: stop using steel and adopt some harder material. The harder material of choice (and probably the only harder material that existed in economic quantities) was tungsten carbide. Unfortunately tungsten carbide had a density of 1.6 compared to steel's 1.0 – in other words it is 60 per cent heavier than steel. So a 57mm shot which fitted the 6-pounder anti-tank gun weighed 6lb (2.7kg) in steel but about 9.5lb (4.3kg) in tungsten. A shot of this weight was slower to accelerate, so the propelling charge used with a steel shot could not be used with a tungsten shot; and the slow-moving shot would cause a build-up of pressure greater than the safe capacity of the gun, so that even if the gun did not burst the shot would never reach the same velocity as steel. And if the tungsten shot did not reach the same velocity as the steel shot there was no point in it.

Back in 1903 a German called Karl Puff had patented a design for a gun with a tapering barrel, gradually reducing in calibre between the breech and the muzzle. He also postulated designs for a suitable type of projectile in the form of a bullet with 'skirts', which fitted the large bore at the breech and were gradually squeezed down to match the bore as it reduced, until the projectile emerged from the muzzle with the skirts pressed into the bullet body so as to present a nice, smooth small-calibre projectile. His argument was quite reasonable: if the calibre at the breech end of the barrel was such as to give the base of the skirted projectile an area of, say, 1sq in (6.45cm²) and if the combustion of the propellant developed a pressure of, say, 20,000lb (9,072kg), then the impulse applied to the projectile was 20,000lb/sq in (1,407kg/cm²), resulting in a projectile velocity of x ft per second. In the taper-bore gun the bullet was decreasing in diameter as it went down the barrel, however, so when the base of the bullet had contracted to 0.5sq in (3.25cm²) the pressure remained the same 20,000lb (9,072kg) but the impulse was now 40,000lb/sq in (2,814kg/cm²) so the velocity would be increased to 2x. (Admittedly, this is a gross simplification of a complex piece of mathematics, but it is the fundamental reasoning underlying the taper bore principle.) Everybody agreed Puff was a clever chap but nobody could see a great deal of point in it, and what was more to the point, nobody was quite sure how they were going to drill a tapering hole or how they were going to make those peculiar skirted bullets. So Puff's patent stayed on the shelves of the patent office for a long time.

In the 1920s a German gunsmith called Herman Gerlich took another look at the Puff idea and decided that it would produce a good high-velocity hunting rifle. He finally mastered the tapering barrel and skirted bullet problems and, with his partner Friedrich Halbe, produced a number of rifles and cartridges under the trade name 'Halger'. Gerlich then began calling in military offices trying to sell the idea as a sniping rifle. He worked, at various times and with little success, with the Germans, British and Americans, and then returned to Germany where his idea was taken up by Rheinmetall and applied to a light anti-tank gun. Their interest was aroused because this important gun-making company suddenly saw in the concept the solution to the two basic problems of tank-killing. The taper bore would generate the high velocity that was required, and the use of a tungsten core inside a soft steel body and skirts would provide the desired penetrative effect, since the tungsten would only occupy a proportion of the projectile and thus the weight could be kept within bounds.

The system worked. The 28mm/21mm projectile left the bore at 1,400m (4,593ft) per second, which was a velocity that was otherwise only the stuff of imagination during 1940, and went through 60mm of homogeneous armour at a range of 550m (600 yards). So the Germans went to work on a 42mm gun which reduced to 29mm and on a 75mm gun which reduced to 55mm. The tank was about to be mastered at last.

The British had also appreciated the point about the hardness and density of tungsten but did not believe the taper-bore idea was anywhere near a solution and so did not waste time on it. Indeed, when a refugee Czech appeared with the idea he was sent away with a flea in his ear: 'This device is not within measurable distance of being used in war,' said the Ordnance Board, not knowing the Rheinmetall taper-bore guns were already at work in the North African desert.

So the British took a small core of tungsten and then built it up to the calibre they needed by using light alloy. The result, for the 57mm gun, weighed just under 4lb (1.81kg) and left the muzzle at 1,076m (3,530ft) per second. The projectile had a formidable performance at short range, but at longer ranges its lack of weight began to tell and its performance fell off rapidly. This was to be expected: it is a question of 'carrying power', which is best exemplified by the old question beloved of ballistics lecturers: 'If I throw a ping-pong ball and a billiard ball at equal velocities, with which would you rather be hit?' Striking energy is a combination of weight and velocity, so that at equal velocities the heavier projectile delivers the more useful blow. So as soon as the tungsten-cored 'AP

Composite Rigid' shot fell to the speed of a steel shot, its perforation performance fell a good deal below that of a steel shot. And the APCR shot fell off in velocity simply because it did not have the mass to create the momentum or 'flywheel effect' that sustained velocity in a heavier projectile.

By the time the APCR shot reached service early in 1943, the British had also captured specimens of the German taper-bore 28mm gun and tested it. They agreed that it was a clever solution, but the prospect of trying to make taper-bore gun barrels in the United Kingdom, in wartime, with every existing facility working full blast and with no spare machine tools available for experimental work, was daunting. At about this time, however, two scientists in the Armaments Research & Development Establishment at Fort Halstead in Kent remembered a report on something a French designer, Edgar Brandt, had been doing before the war in an endeavour to get more range out of the obsolescent French 75mm (2.95in) field gun. Brandt had taken a smaller-calibre shell, put light-weight collars around it to fit the 75mm bore, and fired it. The whole thing weighed less than the usual 75mm shell, so it left at a higher velocity, the collars were arranged to fall off outside the gun, and as a result the small shell flew off at a much higher velocity than the 75mm gun could usually produce and thus went to a greater range. Brandt had done some work on his idea, but the collapse of France put a stop to further efforts in this direction. The two British scientists, Mr L. Permutter and Mr S. W. Coppock, had no interest in extra range as such, but knew that the gain in velocity was worth having, and thus they began designing a projectile containing a tungsten core, surrounded by a light alloy 'sabot' of bore diameter, skilfully designed with weak spots which would break during the passage up the gun barrel but be retained in place until leaving the muzzle, after which the centrifugal action of spin would throw them aside and leave the tungsten core flying to the target at very high speed. After some experiments with a 20mm barrel to prove their theory, they developed an 'Armour Piercing Discarding Sabot' (APDS) shot for the 6-pounder gun. It weighed 3.25lb (1.47kg) on loading, reached a muzzle velocity of 4,050ft (1,234m) per second and went through 146mm of armour at a range of 1,000 yards (915m). This was issued in June 1944, just in time to be of use in the Normandy battles.

This was just as well for the British, because by 1944 tank design had come a long way from the level of 1939. Tank armour was thicker (the German Tiger II had 100mm on its hull front and 150mm on its turret, while the Jagdtiger had 250mm on its front and 150mm on its turret), and the vehicles were also considerably better armed. The Tiger II was fitted with an 88mm (3.465in) gun which could destroy any tank at over 1,500m (1,640 yards) and the Jagdtiger with a 128mm (5.04in) gun which could penetrate 200mm of armour at 1,000m (1,095 yards). Both of these capabilities were achieved without benefit of tungsten as the Allied blockade had so severely curtailed German imports of wolfram, the tungsten ore, that in 1943 all supplies were earmarked for machine tools and the use of tungsten in ammunition was ended.

The UK was under no such restriction, and therefore went on to develop APDS for the 17-pounder (76.2mm) anti-tank gun while the Americans began working on APCR and APDS designs for their 76.2mm (3in) and 90mm (3.54in) guns.

By this time, too, there was a better understanding of the vulnerability of tanks, mostly discovered by practical experience. Gunners were still trained to aim 'at the centre of the visible mass' of the target, rather than try to be clever and aim at some particular point on the tank, but an experienced gunlayer familiar with his gun, sight and ammunition could often, at short ranges, pick and choose his point of impact, provided the target was obliging enough to present him with a view of a vulnerable area. If the tank came head-on he had little choice, but a side or rear shot allowed him some selection. The first choice, if it was available, was the engine compartment, which was relatively thinly protected at the sides and rear: a shot here could immobilize the tank. A stationary tank was still a dangerous tank, since the turret could move and the gun could fire, but it was a much easier target, and once it was stopped a second shot had a better chance of penetrating the hull and either disabling the crew by splinters or hitting the ammunition and exploding the whole vehicle. Alternatively, and this was a delicate choice, the gunner could aim for the turret ring, where the turret revolved on top of the hull. Any blow in this area was liable to jam the turret, and even a glancing shot could strip off a splinter of metal which would be sufficient to disrupt this delicate area. Once the turret had been stopped, it became easy for an infantryman to sneak up behind in the blind area and plant a charge, or for the attacker to manoeuvre and get in another shot which would finish the matter.

German troops on the Eastern Front against the Soviets discovered the vulnerability of the turret ring of the T-34 and soon developed a suicidal tactic which almost always worked, though the attacker was risking his life. A soldier would prepare a charge of explosive, comprising a demolition charge or something as simple as a hand grenade with half a dozen more hand grenade heads tied around it, wait until the tank was past, and then throw the prepared charge on to the engine deck so that it wedged underneath the turret overhang at the rear. The subsequent explosion would always jam the turret and could, if things were just right, lift the turret partly off the tank, killing the crew by the blast through the opening so caused.

If the tank commander had his hatch open to offer better observation – as most did – then he was vulnerable to almost anything. After the initial British landings in Italy during July 1943, Sergeant Evans of the Dorset Regiment was commanding a platoon positioned across a main road where it passed through a slight cutting in a hill. A German armoured car platoon appeared on the road and Evans stood up alongside the leading car and neatly lobbed a hand grenade down the open turret, killing the crew. The vehicle stopped, blocking the road, and the rest of the German force turned about and retired. Evans received a bar to his Military Medal.

The tracks, of course, were always vulnerable to mines, and generally to gunfire and explosives, though there was often so much space between the wheels and the tracks that an explosive charge thrown in that area could detonate without doing a great deal of damage. Gunfire was rarely aimed at the track area, largely because the tank was often in such a position that the tracks could not be clearly seen, but if the gunner did take a shot at the tracks, then if he missed the machinery he would inevitably hit the hull and penetrate, so there would always be a result. But, as mentioned above, attacking the track or wheels or suspension led only to a stationary tank: it was still dangerous and still had to be dealt with to silence the armament.

Other methods of attack beyond gunfire, mines and grenades had been explored. Flame was a popular suggestion, because tanks carried fuel and ammunition, and flame reaching either of these could produce some conclusive results. Moreover, of course, there is the psychological effect: a man sitting inside a metal box is not likely to retain his peace of mind when threatened with a jet of liquid fire. But provided the tank was closed down and well constructed, and the crew kept their heads, fire might have little immediate effect. The flaming substance could stick to the outside, but if the driver kept going and the gunner opened fire at the source of the flame, there was every chance the tank would emerge the victor. If the flaming liquid was sufficiently viscous, there was the chance that it would stick to the tracks and wheels and set fire to the rubber tyres and track elements, but this would hardly stop the tank immediately.

Many wartime texts recommended throwing incendiary grenades on to the engine deck in the hope of igniting the fuel supply; it may well have worked, but incendiary grenades were not a common issue (except for the notorious British No.76 grenade, of which more elsewhere) and they frequently burned themselves out on the engine deck without having had much effect on the engine. Petrol-filled bottles — 'Molotov cocktails' — were also recommended: the official manual *Tank Hunting and Destruction: Military Training Pamphlet No.42* of August 1940 said: 'These bombs should be directed above the louvres or vents so that burning liquid may be sucked into the tank to make it uninhabitable or possibly to set the vehicle on fire ... The first inclination to throw the bomb hard at the tank must be avoided; an underarm lob will often be the best method of throwing, unless the bomb can be dropped from the windows of a house or some other position above the tank ...'

Gas was another weapon mentioned frequently in the period from 1938 to 1940. Again, provided the crew put on gas masks and kept their heads, there was no particular danger, for the gas certainly could do nothing to the tank. The difficulty lay in getting the gas inside the tank in the first place. Here the Germans struck on an ingenious idea; inside the 7.92mm (0.312in) bullet for their anti-tank rifle there was, as well as the armour-piercing core, a tiny capsule of tear gas. It is supposed, nobody ever having found an official German statement on the matter, that the object was for the bullet to penetrate the armour and break up inside the tank, liberating the tear gas, whereupon the crew would succumb to uncontrollable sneezing and weeping and lose control of their vehicle sufficiently to permit some more lethal weapon to be brought to bear. If that was indeed the idea, then it failed, for nobody ever remarked on the tear gas effect of being hit by German anti-tank bullets, and it was not until 1941, when specimens of this ammunition were captured, that an examination of the bullet revealed the presence of the gas capsule.

Anti-tank obstacles were still fashionable in 1944, and these served two purposes. Firstly, a large enough obstacle encouraged the tank to go somewhere else, to find an easier route, and that easier route could be covered by a anti-tank weapon lying in ambush. Secondly, an obstacle not large enough to deter the tank would certainly slow the vehicle which, in crawling over the obstacle, would probably expose the under-belly section that was always the weakest part of the hull. A well-aimed shot as the tank was cresting a pile of logs or rocks, and that was that for the target tank.

The war ended in 1945 with the Allies conscious that it had been a near-run thing and that they were fairly deficient in the anti-tank weapon inventory. Their existing anti-tank guns had only just managed to master the German tanks, and with thicker, well-sloped armour and higher speed the tanks of the new Soviet generation were far harder targets. The anti-tank guns which had been under development as the war ended all turned out to be monstrous engines of war which were all but impossible to manhandle in the field. There were hopes that a new generation of tanks might redress the balance, though there were plenty of people as late as 1949 who were opining that the gun was now master of the tank and that the tank's day was therefore over. The invasion of South Korea in 1950 saw the end of that particular song, and it also revealed what a lot of American soldiers had been saying since the summer of 1944, that the standard 2.36in (60mm) Bazooka was no longer man enough for the job.

The drawings of the planned 3.5in (89mm) weapon were hurriedly taken down and dusted, and the 'Super-Bazooka' appeared in Korea in 1951.

To many people, salvation appeared to lie in the recoil-less (RCL) gun. The conventional gun had become too big to be tactically possible, but the recoil-less gun, which was far lighter for the same calibre, offered a manoeuvrable large-calibre weapon. True, it had negligible velocity, so that APDS and other kinetic energy attack projectiles were useless, but the shaped charge was by now fairly well understood, and the British development of RCL guns had also revealed a totally new type of ammunition which the British called 'squash-head' or HESH (for High Explosive Squash-Head). Put simply, it delivered a chunk of plastic explosive to the exterior of the tank and then detonated it, blasting off a large slab from the interior face of the tank's armour. This slab ricocheted around inside, dealing out death and destruction to anyone or anything for which the shock wave of the detonation had not been sufficiently lethal. Like the shaped charge, HESH was independent of velocity. Provided one could get it to the tank and make it stick, it did not matter how it was delivered.

So it became a natural partner to the RCL gun as well as being developed for field artillery as a self-defence weapon and for tank guns as an attack weapon. The Americans accepted the idea from the British and called it HE/P (for HE/Plastic) but appear to have had more faith in shaped charges.

Postwar examination of German experimental establishments, and interrogation of their staffs, revealed all sorts of interesting things to the Allied investigation teams.

While the public's imagination was stimulated by the V-2 rocket and similar grandiose weapons, the imagination of some weapons scientists was more taken by something a good deal smaller: three missiles called X-7 (or 'Rotkäppchen', Red Riding Hood), Steinbock and Pfeifenkopf. They were all designed as anti-tank weapons, and X-7 is without doubt the ancestor of all anti-tank missiles. These are discussed in greater detail below, but once the feasibility of a missile had been appreciated several projects were begun. The UK took no official notice whatever, and all its early missile development was due to private enterprise. The USA also took little notice. France took a good deal of notice, however, had a design team at work as early as 1948 and thus had the first anti-tank missiles in service during 1955 and used in action by the Israelis in 1956. The Americans bought some prototypes in 1954, realized what they were missing and began their own developments. The Australians, despairing of interesting British officialdom, set about their own missile programme in 1951 and had a serviceable weapon by 1956. The Soviets started about the same time (a precise starting date is unlikely ever to emerge) and had a working missile ('Snapper') in the field by the early 1960s, since the Egyptians were using it against the Israelis in 1967. And since then there has been no let-up, with improved weapons coming along at regular intervals.

The advantage of the missile is twofold: firstly, it can be steered more or less precisely to impact with the target; and secondly, it can carry a massive warhead, far more explosive than any gun which could be brought to an equivalent position on the battlefield. There are, of course, some fairly sizeable disadvantages: there is the firing signature (a loud explosion and flash as the missile is launched) though it has to be said that this is common to almost all anti-tank weapons; there is a delay while the missile flies to its target, during which time the operator has to grit his teeth, stay at his post and steer the missile, irrespective of whatever the enemy might be throwing at him; and there is the staggering cost, something like $15,000 per missile, which does tend to inhibit practising with real missiles and leads to far too much reliance on training the operator with simulators and arcade games. Nevertheless, on balance the missile is worth it: $15,000 in exchange for over $1 million dollars' worth of tank is not a bad rate, and the other drawbacks can be overcome by careful training.

Malkara, the Australian missile, was unique in using a HESH warhead: it was a big missile and it carried a big warhead, guaranteed to reduce any tank in the world to rubble. After that, though, the shaped charge has been the universal choice of warhead, since it was possible to assemble large-diameter heavy charges of enormous capability: MILAN, for example, can go through 1m (39.4in) of homogeneous armour plate. The missile was really beginning to master the tank, and it was time for the tank armourers to shake themselves and start having some ideas.

Before they could manage that, another threat appeared. In the 1960s the Soviets, intent upon extracting as much velocity from a gun as they could, took the unusual step of arming a tank with a smooth-bored gun. The argument ran that a great deal of the energy of the propelling charge was absorbed by the friction arising from the driving band of the projectile being engraved in the rifling of the gun and having to turn as it moved up the bore. With the cause of the friction removed by eliminating the rifling to create a smooth-bore gun, more of the propelling charge's energy would be converted into projectile velocity. There was, of course, the slight problem that firing elongated projectiles out of a smooth-bore gun was a grossly inaccurate pastime, which was why rifling had been invented in the first place, but there had been a few advances in ballistics and aerodynamics since the invention of rifling, and finstabilization was the answer. In fact, as the Soviets discovered, it was not quite so easy as it had first seemed: their first attempt was a failure and the guns had to be given a short length of slow rifling to induce a stabilizing roll to the projectiles. The Soviets got it right with their next attempt.

It meant, also, that they had to redesign all their projectiles. A smooth-bore gun was ideal for shaped charge, since this always worked better when there was no spin stabilization present. To make APDS work without spinning was a much greater problem, but it brought another advantage in its train. The solution was to use a long, fin-stabilized dart as the sub-projectile (containing a tungsten core, of course) and built a sabot around it to fit the gun bore. A long dart was necessary to achieve accurate stabilization but it also added to the weight of the core. This was acceptable, because the reduced friction allowed a greater charge to be used and the velocity achieved was more than adequate. But the bonus was that adding weight to the existing diameter gave the core a greater punch over the same impact area, so that penetration was improved.

Within ten years every country using tanks had adopted the fin-stabilized round, now known as APFSDS (Armour-Piercing Fin-Stabilized Discarding Sabot), even those who still used rifled guns. In a rifled gun it proved possible to have a slipping sealing ring on the sabot which trapped the propellant gas behind it and spun with the rifling but transferred very little spin to the fin-stabilized sub-projectile.

At much the same time, during the 1970s, came the use of depleted uranium as a core material instead of tungsten carbide. Depleted uranium is a scrap by-product of the nuclear industry: it is barely radio-active but it has a density similar to that of tungsten carbide and is somewhat better in its physical properties, being rather more resistant to side shear. It is also pyrophoric, so that the tiny dust particles which break off when it shatters ignite spontaneously. This gives a bright flash which indicates a hit, and it also sets fire to anything in the neighbourhood capable of being easily ignited.

By this time the armour manufacturers were being pursued by the tank builders to come up with something capable of stopping these new missiles and projectiles, since ordinary old-fashioned steel armour was rapidly succumbing to the new weapons. In fact, the armour manufacturers had not been entirely idle. As early as 1945 the British had been investigating methods of countering the shaped charge by using a layer of heat-absorbing chemicals between two layers of armour, but the constructional difficulties of making a double-skinned tank and then filling the space between the skins with crystals was beyond a practical solution.

In the early 1970s, however, the British announced their

adoption of 'Chobham Armour', named after the experimental establishment where it had been developed. Precisely what goes into Chobham armour is still an official
secret, but sufficient other 'compound' armours have been
talked about to enable us to get a broad idea of what this
modern defence involves. Briefly, it is steel armour into
which is embedded such things as tungsten rods and
blocks, interlayered with plastic and ceramic materials.
Any APFSDS core that enters the steel will probably strike
a piece of tungsten, which is hard enough to deflect it from
its course so violently that the long rod will shear and thus
lose much of its mass and therefore momentum. A shaped
charge will pierce the steel but the heat will be drawn off
by the plastic and the weakened jet of vaporized metal and
gas will then be arrested by the ceramic layer. And so
forth, and so on. Any type of projectile, said the armourers, will be defeated by the combination of obstacles.

Shortly after this the Israelis invented ERA (Explosive
Reactive Armour), which is armour that actually attacked
the attacking projectile or missile. This involves covering
the tank, or at least the front surfaces and other vulnerable
parts, with metal boxes containing explosive in carefully
calculated amounts. If struck by a projectile or by the jet
from a shaped charge, the explosive is detonated and the
resulting blast disrupts the shaped charge jet, or deflects or
shatters the kinetic energy projectile. ERA has been widely
adopted during the 1980s by almost every major power. It
is, though, not thoroughly proven in battle: Soviet tanks
fighting in Chechnya during 1994 found that their reactive
armour was doing far too much damage to the tank when
it went off; it is all very well deflecting the enemy

projectile, but a trifle profitless if one's own radio equipment is destroyed in the process. Another point of contention is the possible effect on ERA of a low-power fuel/air explosion over the tank.

The armourers having had their say, it was the turn of the ammunition designers again, and they now focused their attention on an aspect scarcely thought of before: the top surface of the tank. True, this had already been the target for attack from the air, but generally speaking tank designers discounted this: they always assumed that their own side would have command of the air. In the 1980s Bofors, the leading Swedish munitions company, introduced an infantry missile which was programmed to fly across the top of the tank and fire a shaped charge downwards into the top of the turret, which is the thinnest part of the tank and one which is difficult to up-armour because of the hatches, periscopes and other devices built into it. 'Top attack' became the buzzword of the 1980s and a number of other systems have appeared to take advantage of this weakness. SADARM (Seek And Destroy ARMor) is an American warhead which can be fired from a gun or rocket and which deploys a parachute-suspended bomb with an optical seeker. This scans the ground below, finds a tank, steers itself towards it and then fires a 'self-forging fragment', a variation of the shaped charge, straight down into the turret. And there, or thereabouts, the state of the art rests, each side watching the other warily, alert for any improvement.

There is, of course, one other way of dealing with the tank threat, and this is what one might call the 'strategic option': on the first day of the conflict, one launches a number of strategic missiles at the other side's tank factories, arsenals and storage areas, thus depriving him of reserves, repair facilities and construction plants. The enemy is then left with only his tank force in the field, and we have just seen how this can be decimated. Once the tanks of the force in the field have been used and either destroyed or crippled, the enemy has no more tanks. This sounds so simple as to be ridiculous, but there is a certain amount of logic in it. Most countries have only two or three facilities for manufacturing tanks: it is, after all, a highly specialized business using very heavy and expensive machinery, and the economics of the country define the number of plants they can afford to keep running. Equally, repair and refurbishment is a specialized business, usually concentrated in one or two locations. Thus a dozen missiles would probably do sufficient damage to put a complete stop to tank production for several months. It would be impossible to set up new construction plants at a moment's notice, and very difficult to set up heavy repair facilities. So the 'strategic option' is not to be dismissed out of hand.

After this thumb-nail sketch, it is time to examine in more detail the various methods of killing tanks.

CHAPTER TWO

ONE-MAN ANTI-TANK WEAPONS

In 1903 Georg Roth, the Viennese ammunition manufacturer, patented the first AP (Armour-Piercing) bullet for use with rifles and machine-guns. This bullet had a hard steel core inside a lead sleeve and a cupro-nickel jacket: everybody thought it was a jolly smart idea, but nobody could imagine what Roth thought it would be fired against. The only armoured warlike structure was the warship, and what use was a rifle against a warship? Perhaps old Georg was getting a bit past it.

In 1915, while the tank was still a basis of discussion, infantrymen on both sides of the lines in Flanders and Russia were collecting pieces of scrap steel plate and using them to mask the firing slots in their trenches; snipers were going further and demanding (and getting) sheets of armour steel with slots cut in them. Some unsung hero discovered that taking the bullet from an ordinary ball cartridge and reversing it, putting it back in the case mouth and then firing it base first, produced a projectile with greater piercing power than the right-way-round bullet. This was probably due to the fact that the lead core was exposed at the base of the bullet and therefore able to pass through the target plate while the jacket was stripped off and left on the outside. This may sound peculiar, and in those days was certainly thought peculiar, but later experiments have shown that plain lead balls will pass through quite considerable thicknesses of steel provided they are given sufficient velocity, and since much of this 'trench armour' was little more than boiler plate, the reversed bullet was quite enough to pierce it.

Then, of course, somebody remembered Roth's patent and AP bullets began to appear in German hands. At much the same time development of AP bullets began in the UK and France, so that by the early part of 1916 AP bullets were at least known and available, if not actually common.

The tank first appeared in the autumn of 1916, and after the initial shock of its appearance and capabilities had worn off the AP bullet fired from rifles or machine-guns became the foot-soldier's anti-tank weapon. Given the fact that the armour of these early tanks was of relatively poor quality, these primitive AP projectiles were sufficient to make life unpleasant for the tank crews. 'Bullet splash', the delivery into the tank of fragments of bullet shattered on striking a loophole or after piercing the plates, became a serious hazard and British tank crews adopted chain-mail visors to protect their faces when using the vision slots and loopholes.

As the armour plating gradually improved, the German reaction was to look for a heavier weapon to project bigger

AP bullets, and this was provided by Mauser with the Tank Gewehr, which was a heavy 13mm (0.512in) calibre single-shot bolt-action rifle which was little more than the action of the contemporary Gewehr 98 service rifle scaled up to take a bigger and more powerful cartridge. The bullet weighed 51.65g (1.82oz) and had a muzzle velocity of 792m (2,598ft) per second: it had a steel core with hardened tip and could penetrate 28mm of armour plate at a range of 50m (55 yards), which was more than sufficient to deal with any tank of the period. The core, it was discovered, tended to break during penetration, and in the middle of 1918 the design was changed to use a core which was hardened throughout, which changed the bullet weight to 52.49g (1.85oz) and the charge was adjusted to retain the same velocity and penetration.

The Tank Gewehr was effective enough, but slow in action: firing a 13mm cartridge meant that the soldier required a few seconds to collect his wits after each shot, operate the bolt and re-aim. So a heavy Maxim machine-gun was developed to suit the 13mm cartridge, and in this form became the 'Tank und Flieger' (TuF) because it was also contemplated as an aircraft weapon, but in the event the war ended before the design could be brought into production. It left its mark, though: Browning's development of the 0.5in (12.7mm) heavy machine-gun was based on a cartridge derived from the 13mm TuF. (There was also some work done on an 18mm/0.71in version of the TuF, but this got little further than a prototype.)

Another German wartime development was the Becker 20mm aircraft cannon, patented as far back as 1913 and intended as part of the trainable armament for Zeppelin airships and, later, for bombers. Final design and development were slow, however, and by the end of the war fewer than 200 had been produced by the Becker company. The Becker company, seeing the end of the First World War fast approaching and under few illusions about what would happen afterwards, acquired a Swiss machine-tool company, the Maschinenbau AG Seebach, and transferred the drawings and patents for the Becker gun to Switzerland. But by 1924 both companies had collapsed, and the remains of the Seebach firm, together with the Becker cannon rights, were acquired by a Swiss firm, the Oerlikon Machine Tool Company. The new owner improved the gun design and promoted it not only as an aircraft gun but, on suitable mountings, as an anti-aircraft or anti-tank weapon. From there on, the Oerlikon development really belongs to the story of the anti-tank gun, but it is mentioned here because it was the reason for the development of 20mm cartridges carrying solid armour-piercing projectiles, and once these were available it was not long before somebody began contemplating their use in a one-man portable weapon.

Meanwhile, during the early 1920s, people began looking at anti-tank rifles. In the UK Vickers developed the 0.8in (20.3mm) Elswick rifle, and one or two commercial rifle-makers made some tentative experiments. In the first place the soldiers were not entirely certain of what they wanted, as the precise course of the tank's development was uncertain, and in the second place they had no money. This was the period when the commandant of the Tank School was allotted the princely sum of £50 for a year's development of a tank machine-gun, and even in those far-off days one was unlikely to get much of a custom-built rifle for that sort of money.

By the mid-1930s, though, a number of anti-tank rifles had appeared, and these fell broadly into three classes. First were those which fired a conventional but powerful cartridge, such as the British Boys 0.55in (13.97mm) rifle. This was a bolt-action magazine weapon firing a steel-cored bullet weighing 47.6g (1.68oz) at 990m (3,250ft) per second to penetrate 21mm of armour at a range of 300m (330 yards).

Second were those rifles which fired an unconventional cartridge, usually a massive case sharply necked down to take a normal calibre bullet. In this class was a Polish bolt-action magazine rifle, the Karabin Przeciwpancerny wz.35 Maroszek which launched a 7.92mm (0.312in) bullet at 1,280m (4,199ft) per second to defeat 20mm at a range of 300m (330 yards); and the German Panzerbüchse (PzB) 38, a single-shot rifle which fired a 7.92mm (0.312in) steel-cored bullet at 1,210m (3,970ft) per second to defeat 33mm of armour at a range of 100m (110 yards). Both these weapons took the original Mauser T-Gewehr cartridge case and necked it down to the standard 7.92mm (0.312in) rifle calibre: the Poles had the edge because of their adoption of a tungsten core, while the Germans wasted some of their effort by incorporating a tiny capsule of tear gas in the bullet (see Chapter One).

Third was the adoption of one of the existing 20mm cartridges from the Oerlikon gun (or one of its imitators) and the design of a rifle to use it. This produced some potent weapons, but it would be stretching things slightly to call them one-man devices. One of the best of this breed was the Swiss Solothurn s18-1100, a recoil-operated semi-automatic firing a sizeable base-fused piercing projectile at 750m (2,461ft) per second to penetrate 27mm at a range of 300m (330 yards). This was a fine weapon with good performance, but it weighed 54.7kg (120.6lb), which is hardly something an already-laden soldier could manage single-handed. The Japanese 20mm Anti-Tank Rifle Type 97 was even heavier at 67.5kg (148.8lb), but this was a monster of a weapon, gas-operated and capable of firing fully-automatic when required, and it demanded a four-man crew just to carry it.

It is fashionable today to deride the Boys and all the other anti-tank rifles as being futile. But in their day, which could be considered as the period from 1935 to 1940, they were a definite threat to the contemporary tanks, few of which had more than 12mm of armour. Indeed, the Soviets did not introduce anti-tank rifles until 1941, when they produced two weapons, the Degtyarev PTRD 1941 bolt-action and Simonov PTRS 1941 semi-automatic rifles, each firing an extremely powerful 14.5mm (0.57in) cartridge capable of defeating 25mm of armour at a range of 500m (545 yards). The Soviets retained these weapons throughout the war, long after such weapons had been abandoned elsewhere. Further details of these weapons are given below.

The principal deficiency of all these weapons, however, was simply that they were designed to defeat armour. Thus they did very little damage inside the tank unless the bullet happened to strike some vital part of the engine, the ammunition or the crew, and this was an unlikely occurrence. The small bullets could find lots of paths through a tank which hit nothing of any significance, for the tanks of those days were not so packed with equipment as those of later years and had plenty of empty space in which a bullet could divert itself relatively harmlessly. It should be remembered, though, that these rifles had to be adopted simply because there was nothing else which a single soldier could possibly use which could damage an armoured vehicle.

What sealed the fate of the anti-tank rifle was the rediscovery of the shaped charge. Like so many weapons, especially in the anti-tank field, this had been discovered many years previously when technology was in no fit state to take advantage of it. It had therefore become a rather recondite parlour trick and generally forgotten until events took a sudden lurch forward in 1938.

In the 1880s an American scientist, one Monroe, was experimenting with gun-cotton: the slabs of gun-cotton had the words US NAVY impressed into one surface, and Monroe found that if he laid this surface on a steel plate and detonated the gun-cotton, the words were impressed into the surface of the plate somewhat deeper than the dent caused by the explosion. By laying a leaf on the plate and laying the plain side of the gun-cotton above it, he could impress the vein pattern of the leaf into the surface of the plate. This was all good fun, but of no apparent practical value.

Various people played with the idea from time to time, and in the early 1900s a German experimenter, Neumann, discovered that if he made a conical or hemispherical cavity in the face of the explosive, there was a considerable indentation in the plate, and if he lined the cavity with steel, the plate was pierced. He spent some time during the First World War trying to devise some way of adopting this phenomenon to a warhead for a torpedo, but without success.

Late in 1938 two Swiss gentlemen, Matthias and Mohaupt, announced that they had developed a new and powerful explosive which could defeat armour plate, and that they would hold a demonstration for interested military parties in January 1939 near Zürich, after which they would entertain offers for their patent. With the war clouds visibly gathering over Europe, the military attachés and their experts hurried to the appointment and watched Matthias and Mohaupt as they placed various projectiles (which they kept carefully concealed from close inspection) in front of armour plates and proceeded to detonate them and blow holes in the plates. Reading the reports submitted by observers, one gets a glimpse of what must have been furious activity by stealthy characters around the Zürich area early in 1939: 'Examination of the targets showed yellow traces, suggesting the use of picric acid; however, we have discovered that they have purchased TNT from Dottikon ... and this must therefore be seen as an endeavour to lay a false trail.'

However, most of the experts gathered at Zürich were quick to realize that what they were seeing was a demonstration of the Monroe Effect, as it was then known, and that if two unknown entrepreneurs from Zürich could do it, so too could they. They all scuttled off home to their workshops and laboratories, and began designing and testing. Matthias and Mohaupt got nothing out of their demonstration, though Matthias turned up a few years later in the USA, helping them to design an anti-tank grenade.

The first shaped charge device to see combat was, in fact, a German demolition charge which was used to good effect in capturing the fort of Eben Emael in Belgium. The first projectile using the shaped charge was the British No.68 rifle grenade, a small cylinder with fins intended to be fired from a cup discharger on the muzzle of a service rifle, using a special blank cartridge to provide the necessary power. Once this grenade became known, and introduced the shaped charge to people who had never heard of it before, ideas began to flow thick and fast, and before long the shaped charge was being applied to virtually every possible type of projectile, most of which failed to materialize. The basic research which underpins most types of weapon simply had not been done on the shaped charge at that time: nobody knew much about it, and design was entirely empiric, or 'suck it and see' as the phrase of the period put it. As a result many applications failed through simple lack of knowledge. Slowly a body of experimental knowledge was put together, however, and people began to understand why (if not always how) the shaped charge worked. After long attempts to make gun shells which worked, it was eventually discovered that a spinning shaped charge simply dispersed the explosive jet because of the centrifugal force, so that it gouged a wider but shallower hole and generally failed to penetrate the armour.

This, though, did not stop designers from producing gun shells, as detailed below. But it did cause a number of designers to look elsewhere for a method of delivering a shaped charge without spinning it, and the only practical alternative was to put fins on it, after which the problem arose of how to project it through the air.

During the First World War the trench mortar had become an important weapon, and *en route* to the final perfected designs various oddities were tried. One of them was the 'spigot mortar': instead of a barrel through which the projectile was fired, this had a steel rod mounted on a baseplate. The bomb had a hollow tail, inside which was the propelling charge. The tail was slipped over the steel rod (or 'spigot') and the cartridge exploded, generating gas and blowing the bomb off the rod and into the air. The rod was long enough to support the bomb and give it initial direction. It was also a great deal easier and cheaper to make than any sort of gun barrel, which made it an attractive proposition for trench mortars, which had a short life at the best of times.

A Lieutenant-Colonel Blacker of the Royal Artillery became fascinated with the spigot idea and in the early 1930s began experimenting with the idea, hoping to produce a lightweight platoon mortar which the British army had decided it required. In the event, his design (known as the 'Arbalest') was turned down and a Spanish design accepted, but Blacker continued with his experiments. He thought of an anti-tank weapon, but was handicapped because his spigot idea was incapable of generating the high velocity which was demanded in order to smash through armour. He eventually came up with a spigot device on a swivel which fired a 9.1kg (20lb) bomb full of high explosive to a range of about 91m (100 yards): the detonation was sufficient to do severe damage to the contemporary tanks, even if it did not actually succeed in piercing the armour, and the 'Blacker Bombard' became a standard weapon of the British Home Guard in 1940. Deployed in fixed positions around road-blocks, it would have proved a formidable weapon against tanks and vehicles.

But when the shaped charge appeared, Blacker saw his salvation on the horizon because the great advantage of the shaped charge is that it relies upon the energy contained in the projectile and not on velocity or smashing power. One can walk up to a tank carrying a shaped charge and detonate it, and it works in exactly the same fashion, although rather less successfully in most cases, as when one fires it at high velocity.

Blacker therefore designed a shaped charge bomb with a hollow tail and a shoulder-fired launcher which was simply a metal casing containing a huge spring and a steel rod. At the front was a trough into which the bomb was laid. Pulling the trigger released the spigot to ram into the tail of the bomb and ignite the cartridge. The subsequent explosion blew the bomb off the spigot and out to a range of perhaps 140m (150 yards) with reasonable accuracy. The explosion also arrested the forward motion of the spigot and blew it backwards against the spring, which helped to soak up some of the very powerful recoil. Blacker called his idea the 'Baby Bombard' and in 1941 offered it as a one-man anti-tank gun.

The weapon was tested in June 1941 and the report on it was rough:

The mounting is flimsy and unlikely to survive rough usage . . . the firing mechanism is unreliable . . . the fuse is unreliable . . .

the sights are inadequate . . . No bomb detonated on the target, so its anti-tank performance cannot be assessed, but in view of the light weight of the bomb the anticipated performance would not be formidable. The Baby Bombard . . . would prove ineffective as an anti-tank weapon under any conceivable conditions of employment . . .

Blacker was working for MD1, a peculiar and surreptitious design establishment which developed clandestine weapons for guerrilla use and for supply to resistance groups inside occupied Europe. Shortly after this inauspicious trial, he was posted to other duties, and left the 'Baby Bombard' with another MD1 officer, Major (later Major-General) Mills Jefferis, who redesigned the fusing of the bomb, and made a few improvements in the weapon, and in February 1942 it was tested once more, this time with results that were so much better that a month later the War Office was asking Jefferis if he could design high-explosive anti-personnel and screening smoke bombs, as well as anti-tank bombs, for his new weapon. Though this idea was played with for some time it was later dropped, however, and the weapon now received the title of PIAT (Projector, Infantry, Anti-Tank), which is the sort of uninspiring name which only the British army can achieve. By the end of August 1942 the PIAT had been approved and was in production, and it was to remain the British infantry's personal anti-tank weapon for the next ten years.

The PIAT could never be said to have been popular: it was ungainly, heavy, cumbersome and idiosyncratic, and it demanded some considerable faith by the user. As an infantry soldier put it:

The PIAT was really nothing but a steel tube with a damn great spring and a huge firing pin inside it. The spring drove the firing pin forward to fire the bomb, and it had to be a damn great spring because it then had to take the recoil of the firing pin being blown backwards. And it had to have somebody behind it because otherwise the whole lot would have gone backwards and the firing pin wouldn't have caught on the trigger and been cocked for the next shot. So you had to hold the thing into your shoulder very tightly so it didn't kick you to death, but on the other hand you didn't dig your toes in because you had to be able to move a little bit with the recoil. The instructors used to scare us with tales about the bloke who braced his feet against a tree and broke his back and stuff like that; I don't think any of it was true, but we were young soldiers.

But, you see, you couldn't do anything with the PIAT until that massive spring had been cocked ready to fire the first shot. After the first shot it cocked itself on the recoil, but for the first shot you had to cock it, and that was murder. You put it on the ground, butt first, put both your feet on the shoulder pad, gripped the body of the thing and gave it a half turn. This unlocked the body from the butt and locked the firing pin to the butt. Then you bent over, got a firm grip of the trigger guard with both hands, and pulled the body upwards. Because you were standing on the butt, and the firing pin was fixed to it, so it pulled back the spring as you raised the body, until you got it up far enough for the firing pin to click on to the trigger. Then you could simply lower the body back to the butt and give it the half turn to lock it again.

This was OK if you were a big man. But a little man couldn't get the lift, you see, and he would get the body up against the spring almost to the cocked position, but he couldn't get it up that little bit extra and you'd watch him going redder and redder and in the end the spring simply pulled him back down again. And of course, if you were in the line, you had to do all this lying on your back in a slit trench, with the butt between your feet and your arms around the damn PIAT stretching out on your back until it clicked. I should think that there's a fair number of old chaps walking around with sticks today that can blame it on cocking a PIAT a bit carelessly.

And then you fired it and looked up and saw the bomb lolloping along dead slow and you thought, 'My God the tank'll be gone before the bomb gets there', but when it struck, you rang the bell all right. You had to keep your head down, too, because it wasn't unusual for bits of the bomb to be blown back at the firer, because the range was only about a hundred yards with any reliability.

Perhaps the most famous episode with the PIAT was in May 1944 when Fusilier Jefferson dashed forward in Italy and fired one from the hip to take out a Tiger tank and then calmly reloaded and fired a second shot from the hip to take out a second tank. He was awarded the Victoria Cross, and the general opinion among the soldiers was that he deserved it for firing the PIAT from the hip, never mind taking out two tanks.

By early 1942 the US Army was beginning to realize that they needed a short-range anti-tank weapon. Until then, its faith had been pinned to the 0.5in (12.7mm) Browning machine-gun, but tank armour was getting thicker and therefore impenetrable by the AP projectile fired by the excellent Browning. The US Army's first idea was a shaped charge rifle grenade to be launched from the

Browning machine-gun, and Matthias of Switzerland was retained as a technical adviser on the design. Although the grenade worked, it was a cumbersome device and not particularly accurate, so the idea was shelved.

As it happened, there was a Colonel Skinner of the US Army who had a lifelong interest in rockets and had amused himself in his spare time for several years in making and firing various devices of his own invention. In 1940 the US Army suddenly took notice of this, brought him back from Hawaii, gave him a soldier to do the fetching and carrying, and told him to try to make some sort of a rocket weapon. Within a year he had designed, built and tested a simple rocket, fired from a tube on a man's shoulder. All that it lacked was some sort of warhead which would produce a worthwhile result, and it was at this point that the US Army found it had a growing pile of grenades and nothing from which to fire them. Early in 1942 Skinner found out about this stockpile and began adapting the grenade to his rocket. In fact, he adapted the rocket launcher to the diameter of the grenade and then rebuilt his rocket to suit, ending up with a 2.36in (60mm) diameter tube with a simple electrical firing circuit powered by two dry batteries and connected to the rocket by a trailing wire and a paper-clip. Having fired a dozen dummy rockets to prove it worked, Skinner took his device to Aberdeen Proving Ground in Maryland to try out his few live warheads.

Skinner discovered, when he arrived, that there was a demonstration in progress, as some other device was being tried against a moving tank target. So without announcing his presence, Skinner and his soldier tacked themselves on the end of the firing line. The launcher had no sight, so a rough sight was made up from a piece of bent wire and the soldier fired the first round, hitting the tank. Skinner then took the launcher, fired again, and scored another hit. The high-powered audience assembled to watch the other device, which was not working very well, left their places and rushed down to see what this new weapon was. Several of them fired rockets and scored hits, before the supply of rockets was exhausted. There and then the weapon was ordered into production, since one of the audience (and the first to try the weapon) was General Barnes, Chief of Army Ground Forces Development.

Introduced as the 2.36in Rocket Launcher M1, the weapon was soon given the name which has stuck to it, and its descendants, ever since: the Bazooka. The name came from a home-brewed wind instrument 'played' by a popular radio and vaudeville comedian of the day, Bob Burns. His bazooka was a well-known gimmick, and the name seemed appropriate for this tubular device hoisted on to a man's shoulder and 'played' to good effect against tanks.

The bazooka was a very simple weapon: a steel tube through which the rocket was launched. A shoulder rest or wooden stock was provided along with two grips for aiming. The rear grip included the trigger group. The rocket was fired electrically, but unfortunately in low temperatures not all the propellant was consumed before the rocket left the launcher. This meant unburnt powder was blasted into the firer's face. To prevent this a small circular wire mesh screen was fitted just behind the muzzle. It was later improved into the M9, which came in two pieces, joined by a bayonet joint, so that it was a little less cumbersome to carry. It was then greatly improved by the War Department, which developed a much more powerful 3.5in (88.9mm) calibre model. But the Army Service Forces, which had overall responsibility for military equipment, could see no point in replacing the original model, which worked perfectly well, and the 'Super Bazooka' was put on the shelf. There it stayed for the rest of the Second World War, even though by 1945 the 2.36in model had been outstripped by German armour and was by then only marginally effective.

One of the virtues of the bazooka was its use against a variety of targets, such as pillboxes and barbed-wire obstacles. It could even be used against targets such as vehicle parks, to clear combat lanes through minefields, and there are even reports of bazookas being used against artillery pieces at close range. By the time the war ended no fewer than 476,628 bazookas of all types had been produced, together with 15,603,000 rockets of all kinds.

Many bazookas were sent to the USSR as part of the considerable quantity of munitions supplied by the Western Allies, and of course it was not long before one fell into the hands of the Germans. They rapidly appreciated the effectiveness of this weapon, for their Panzers had already encountered it in North Africa and been suitably chastened, and went on to develop their own version, the Raketenpanzerbüchse 43, otherwise known as the Panzerschreck (Panzer terror). This was very similar to the American model in that it was a one-piece tube firing a rocket, but was of 88mm (3.465in) calibre and therefore rather more effective at the target since it fired a heavier warhead. The Germans then went on to develop a more complex version called the Raketenwefer 43, otherwise known as the Püppchen (dolly). This was a smooth-bore 88mm barrel on a light wheeled carriage, so that it resembled a conventional gun. It even had a conventional breech and cartridge case, but the cartridge launched the same 88mm rocket, which then ignited in flight, giving it rather more range and considerably better accuracy since it was fired from a more stable platform than a man's shoulder. Fortunately for the Allies, the Püppchen took some time to perfect, and only a relatively small quantity were produced before the war ended.

Two problems faced the Germans in 1942: one was the sudden discovery that the Soviet army had tougher tanks than the Germans had expected, and the other was that the Germans themselves had so many different kinds of weapon, all relying upon nitrocellulose propellants, that they were beginning to face a propellant shortage. So instead of developing more rocket weapons, which gulped propellant in large quantities, the German army went to the munitions makers and asked for a shaped charge weapon capable of being fired by one man, but using the least possible amount of the cheapest propellant available.

Dr Langweiler of the Hugo Schneider company took up the challenge, and before the year was out had produced the Faustpatrone (fist cartridge), which was a 355mm (14in) tube carrying a small gunpowder charge in its centre and a hollow charge bomb at one end. This was grasped, held at arm's length and triggered, whereupon the gunpowder charge fired, blowing the bomb forward: the rearward blast from the other end of the tube balanced the thrust of the bomb and the tube was practically recoil-less. The weapon worked, but it was scarcely practical since, holding it at arm's length, the firer had no way of aiming it. So the tube was lengthened and sights were fitted: the bomb was redesigned to have a warhead much greater than the diameter of the tube, but a simple wooden tail boom carried four flexible fins which wrapped around the boom and slipped into the tube. Now the firer tucked the tube under his arm, took aim, squeezed the trigger, and the over-sized warhead was launched to a range of about 30m (33 yards). So it was called the Panzerfaust 30 and in October 1943 went into production at a rate of 200,000 per month.

Panzerfaust (Armoured Fist) was the first 'disposable' weapon; you fired it, and threw away the tube, then went and got another one. It could penetrate 140mm of armour, striking at 30 degrees from normal – which would be enough to give a lot of modern armour a worrying time – and it was devastating against the tanks of 1943. The only real problem was in the range; it took a very courageous soldier to lie still in the face of an advancing tank until it was within 30 metres, then stand up and launch a charge of high explosive at it. So the next objective was to increase the range. By mid-1944 Langweiler had adopted a thicker launching tube and a more powerful gunpowder propelling charge and introduced the Panzerfaust 60 – for 60 metres range. Then came a version using two propelling charges, slightly separated so that they fired in succession to give a more sustained shove to the bomb and thus attained even more range; that was the Panzerfaust 100.

Finally, because the economics people were getting

concerned about the tonnage of steel tubes being flung away on the battlefields in 1944, came the reloadable Panzerfaust 150. This had the propellant charge attached to the tail of the bomb, and the firing system used a strip of ignition caps. The idea was to permit the tube to be reloaded up to ten times before being thrown away. The bomb was also redesigned to use less explosive while retaining the same penetrative power (people were beginning to understand the shaped charge by this time) and it also had a fragmentation sleeve around the bomb so that it became a useful anti-personnel weapon as well as an anti-tank device. Production of this version began in January 1945, and about 100,000 were made before production ended in April, but very few of them ever reached the front line because of transportation problems.

Although the Soviets had been given bazookas, and had captured Panzerfausts and Panzerschrecks from the Germans, they appear to have had no urge to develop similar weapons of their own. This was partly due to production policy: the Soviets were reluctant to expend energy on developing weapons which would demand a disproportionate amount of research time and an entirely fresh manufacturing technology. It was doubtless also due to their enormous strength in artillery, which regardless of basic classification (field, divisional and medium) was provided with anti-tank ammunition and expected to engage any tank which came within sight. It may also have resulted from the availability of two exceptionally powerful anti-tank rifles, weapons which they kept in service for many years after everyone else had abandoned them.

The Soviets began looking for an infantry anti-tank

weapon as early as 1932. In 1936, after an unsuccessful period with a 37mm recoil-less weapon, a number of designers were given the task of developing an anti-tank rifle, and between then and 1938 no fewer than fifteen designs were built, tested and rejected. The testing authority came to the conclusion that before anything more could be done a new type of ammunition was needed and they set another design team to work. This produced a powerful 14.5mm (0.57in) cartridge, the bullet carrying a tungsten core, which was guaranteed to go through 20mm of armour at a range of 500m (545 yards) after striking the armour at 30° angle. This specification of the angle of impact is important: if a piece of armour is 20mm thick and a bullet approaches it exactly at right angles, then it will have to go through 20mm. But if it approaches at an angle, it has to go through a greater thickness, since it is travelling obliquely through the plate: the exact thickness it has to go through in this case is 20mm × Sine 30°, or about 34mm. Designers now set to work to produce a suitable rifle: the Rukavishnikov was accepted, but then came a decision not to make small anti-tank weapons. As a result, when the German army invaded the USSR in 1941, the Soviets had no anti-tank rifles at all.

In July 1941 the two well-known designers Vasiliy Alekseyvich Degtyarev and Sergey Gavrilovitch Simonov were given a rush order to produce a 14.5mm rifle. Degtyarev produced a self-loading design within a month, then modified it into the PRTD 1941 single-shot rifle in which the bolt was automatically opened on recoil. Simonov produced the PTRS 1941 self-loader using gas action to reload from a five-round magazine. Both weapons were approved and were issued by November 1941, something of a record for weapons design and production. Their first action was with the 1075th Rifle Regiment near Petelino, where eight rifles were used at ranges of 150 to 200m (165 to 220 yards), and two medium tanks were crippled and subsequently destroyed. Such was the pace of Soviet production that in 1942 almost a quarter of a million of these rifles were made.

So with two perfectly good weapons the Soviets saw no need to complicate their manufacturing system, which was sufficiently stretched already, by trying something new. By the middle of 1943, by which time the older and less well-protected German tanks had all been knocked out or withdrawn, the Soviets were finally compelled to admit that the rifles made less impression. Their manufacture was stopped late in 1944, but the 14.5mm cartridge made such a favourable impression on the Soviets that one of their first postwar tasks was to develop a heavy machine-gun to fire this round as an anti-aircraft weapon.

So the Second World War ended in 1945 with the various armies in possession of a handful of one-man anti-tank weapons, all of which had been hastily conceived under pressure and none of which was really satisfactory. But because they had nothing else, and because there was an immediate cutback in funds for arms development and procurement, and because every penny, cent or ruble that could be found was being flung at missiles and nuclear warheads, nothing new appeared for some years. The Korean War (1950–53) was fought with more or less the same weapons that had been used in 1944–45, though the Americans, confronted with the T-34 Soviet tank in North

Korean hands, found that the 2.36in bazooka was ineffective and that the drawings for the 3.5in model had to be got out of the cupboard in a hurry. For the sake of simplicity in ammunition supply the British troops in Korea also got the 3.5in bazooka, and it was such an obvious improvement over the PIAT that it was forthwith taken officially into British service.

Which brings in my own particular bazooka story. Early in 1952, a sergeant in an artillery regiment, I was presented with a 3.5 inch bazooka, the training manual, and a large wooden box on which was printed ROCKETS, HE/AT, 3.5INCH 4. Large lead and wire seals were on the fastenings of the box, and when I requested permission to fire a rocket to try the thing out, it was refused; only to be opened in time of need. So I went down the road to a nearby American outfit and practised with a 2.36 inch model. Some weeks later the word came that an enemy tank was moving in our direction. My assistant gunner and I ran with the bazooka and our precious four rockets to a previously chosen position. I lay down and assembled the launcher. He took his boot to the lead seals and opened the box. 'Christ, Sarge!' he shouted, 'it's full of bloody hand grenades!' It was, too; and they weren't even primed. Thank God, the tank never appeared.

The postwar years did see some activity in rifle anti-tank grenades; probably because they were comparatively cheap. The Energa grenade became popular with several armies: this was a Swiss invention, manufactured by a Belgian firm, and slipped over the muzzle of a rifle to be launched by a powerful blank cartridge. It carried a shaped charge, detonated by a base fuse and was moderately effective to about 140m (150 yards), though nobody in his right mind would expect it to defeat a tank in frontal attack. It was better than nothing, one supposes, but not a lot better.

It seemed as if inspiration was lacking in the light anti-tank field: much work was being done by the late 1950s on anti-tank missiles and heavy weapons, but soldiers might have been forgiven for thinking that the design staffs had given up on the problem of providing something for the foot soldier to carry. But in the early 1960s two designs appeared which showed that some people had been doing some original thinking.

The first step was the appearance of the Soviet RPG-2 launcher in the late 1950s. This appeared to have been inspired by the German Panzerfaust, for it was a tube which launched a finned over-calibre shaped charge grenade by means of a recoil-less charge. The weapon had a maximum range of 150m (165 yards) and could penetrate 180mm of armour when conditions were favourable. The design was copied by the Chinese, who managed to develop a HEAT warhead which could defeat up to 250mm of armour at right angles, though it was inferior to the Soviet design at an oblique attack angle.

So far, so good: Western observers nodded, looked wise and said 'Ah, well, it's simply an improvement on the original Panzerfaust and with not much better performance' and left it at that. But in the early 1960s the Viet Cong began damaging American light tanks and APCs in Vietnam with the RPG-2, and the observers then realized that even a copy of a German design was not to be despised. Then in about 1966 the Viet Cong appeared with a totally new weapon, the Soviet RPG-7. Here the designers had taken a major step by adding a rocket motor to the tail of the grenade. The recoil-less charge now merely launched the grenade from its tube and ignited a short delay. This allowed the grenade to coast for a few yards before the rocket ignited far enough away from the launcher to avoid damaging the firer with the blast, and accelerated in the direction of the target. If it was motionless, the target could be up to 500m (545 yards) away and still be in danger, while moving targets were picked off up to 300m (330 yards) or more. The increased range of the weapon was matched by the increased lethality of the warhead: this would defeat 320mm of armour plate and do severe damage inside the tank or APC. The success of the warhead, it was found, resulted from the practical application of a technique known as 'wave shaping'. In a simple hollow charge the detonation of the explosive crushed the inner liner and propelled it forward in a rather haphazard manner; but now by incorporating dense blocks of plastic in the explosive charge it became possible to control, slow or guide the detonating wave so that the collapse of the liner and its acceleration were more precisely controlled, and this produced a penetration capability well above anything previously thought possible.

At much the same time Hesse Eastern, an American company, had been doing some experimenting of its own and now produced a revolutionary weapon, the 66mm (2.6in) M72 rocket launcher. This consisted of two concentric tubes, the inner made of aluminium alloy and the outer of fibreglass. Inside the inner tube was a 66mm shaped charge warhead with a rocket motor, while the outer tube carried a trigger and a simple sight. To use the weapon the soldier simply grasped the two tubes and pulled the ends apart, so that the outer tube slid over the inner and the two extended like a telescope, at the same time automatically cocking the firing mechanism and erecting the sights. The soldier then put the tube on his shoulder, took aim and squeezed the trigger. The rocket was ignited and had burned out before it left the tube, which is why this type of weapon gives off a sharp explosive noise rather than the long-sustained swish which most people expect of rockets. By having the rocket all burnt before it left the tube, there was no need to protect the firer against back-blast. The M72 had a maximum range of 1,000m (1,095 yards), but its sights were fairly rudimentary and it was at its best at a range of about 300m (330 yards), and the warhead could defeat 300mm of armour.

These two weapons were rapidly adopted all over the world, the M72 by NATO and other Western-aligned nations, the RPG-7 by those aligned with the Soviet bloc. What was more important, the two weapons stimulated designers in several countries to begin work on more advanced one-man weapons. Many fell by the wayside: few people now remember the Canadian 'Heller', the American 'Viper', the British 'Red Planet' and similar shoulder-fired weapons which appeared, showed promise, then showed problems, and finally faded into oblivion. The French produced the LRAC (Lance-Roquette Anti-Char), which was a variation of the bazooka which showed original thought. It came in two parts: the launching tube with its sight, and a short sealed tube containing the rocket and ignition system. One man carried the launch tube and a couple of rocket tubes, the rest of the section carried a few more rocket tubes. When the need arose, one rocket tube was clamped to the rear end of the launch tube by a simple bayonet joint; the soldier fired his rocket, then unscrewed the expended rocket tube and threw it away and screwed on another, ready for the next tank. The warhead was a shaped charge, 89mm (3.5in) in diameter, which had a maximum range of 2,300m (2,515 yards), though the 'effective anti-tank range' was only 600m (655 yards). Even that was better than that of any other shoulder-fired launcher, however, and the warhead could pierce 400mm of armour or 1m (39.4in) of reinforced concrete. The LRAC appeared in the late 1960s and remained in use until the early 1990s.

West Germany took the old Panzerfaust and from it developed a new Panzerfaust which it called Lanze (lance), and then went in exactly the same direction as the Soviets by adding a rocket motor to the warhead tail. Apart from the fact that the warhead was much less in diameter and the whole thing rather better engineered, the Lanze greatly resembled the wartime Panzerfaust, but the rocket gave it an effective range of 400m (440 yards), and modern technology gave the warhead the ability to punch a hole through 370mm of armour.

It was the peaceable Swedes, however, who produced the most unusual one-man weapon. This was the 84mm (3.31in) Carl Gustav, which is a shoulder-fired recoil-less gun firing a shell from a cartridge case. The shell is a shaped charge projectile, oddly shaped with a flat head from which protrudes a long forward probe carrying the fuse, and a plastic driving band which engages the rifling of the gun but which skids on the body of the shell so that it gave it a degree of spin but not enough to upset the shaped charge jet. The cartridge case is of light alloy with a thick plastic base. The gun is loaded by swinging the breech to the side, inserting the round, and swinging the breech back into position. The breech had a venturi in the middle and a conical nozzle behind it, and the loader must take care to crouch at one side of the firer, and not directly behind him. The venturi is a nozzle which first narrows and then widens out; as gas passes through, the sudden expansion after it enters the widening portion causes an accelerated gas flow, and this helps to produce the combination of velocity and gas mass which counter-balances the momentum of the shell leaving the barrel. On firing, a proportion of the propellant gas blows the shell out forward, while the rest is exhausted to the rear and due to the venturi gives the gun its recoil-less characteristic. The Carl Gustav has a range of 1,000m (1,095 yards) and can defeat 400mm of armour with the armour-piercing projectile, which is complemented by high-explosive fragmentation, smoke and illuminating shells, all helping to make the Carl Gustav gun a very versatile weapon. This was proved in the Falklands War (1982), when a young Royal Marine first shot down a helicopter and then damaged a submarine with his 84mm (3.31in) artillery.

Bofors, the developer of the Carl Gustav, next bowed to fashion and produced a one-shot, throw-away device called the Miniman. This was little more than a fibreglass tube containing a round of Carl Gustav shaped charge ammunition. One put it on one's shoulder, took aim through a simple peep sight, fired, and threw away the tube. Maximum range was only about 200m (220 yards) as the propelling charge had to be somewhat less than that of the Carl Gustav since the 'gun barrel' was no longer of steel, but the penetration was still close to 400mm of armour.

There were two objections to the shoulder-fired rockets and shells which the 1960s and 1970s produced. Firstly, they could make little impression on the frontal armour of the heaviest tanks, and secondly they had to be positioned fairly carefully, because they inevitably threw out a formidable back-blast. This could be dangerous: at best it kicked up stones and dirt and gave away the firer's position, and at worst the back-blast washed round and fried the firer if the weapon was used inside a closed space such as a room or pillbox. So once more the designers got to work.

The first problem to be solved was the back-blast problem. The West German Armbrust was a shoulder-fired recoil-less gun, but instead of using a blast of incandescent gas to the rear to give the recoil-less balance it reverted to a much older idea, that of the 'countershot'. Briefly, the idea is to put the propelling charge in the centre of the firing tube, put the shell in front of it and put an equal weight behind it. Ignite the charge and the shell goes forward, the countershot goes backward, both at the same speed, and there is no recoil. In the Armbrust the propelling charge sat in the centre between two piston heads. The shaped charge projectile sat in front of the front piston, and behind the rear piston was a countershot composed of strips of flexible plastic. On firing, the explosion blew the two piston heads apart. The forward piston threw the projectile out of the front of the tube while the rear piston ejected the countershot out of the rear. But, and this is the crucial bit, when the two piston heads reached their respective ends of the tube they were stopped and locked. So no gas, no flame and very little noise ever escaped from the tube. The counter-shot, being flexible plastic, soon fluttered to the ground, and if the firer was inside a closed room then all that happened was that he might be flicked gently by a piece of rebounding plastic strip. The shell went forward to a maximum of about 300m (330 yards) and could penetrate about 350mm of armour. Unfortunately Armbrust had some teething troubles, and though several NATO armies tried it, none was sufficiently impressed to adopt it. It was later perfected and the design sold to Singapore, where it has been made in the 1990s. But the countershot idea has been taken over by other designers and will appear again.

Defeating the heavy tank (the Soviet T-72 was usually the indicated target and this has 200mm of sloped laminated armour on the hull front and 280mm of cast armour on the turret front) proved to be more difficult. The obvious answer was to increase the size of the shaped charge, but this meant increasing the diameter and there comes a point where the weapon is too big to be easily carried or operated by one man, and that point is usually reached long before the desired performance is met.

Improved shaped charge technology has enabled some weapons to come close to the ideal, however, and one that well exemplifies the current state of the art is the British LAW 80, a 94mm (3.7in) rocket with an advanced shaped charge warhead. The effective range is 500m (545 yards) or so, the warhead can defeat over 700mm of armour, and the weapon incorporates an aiming rifle. This is a simple self-loading 9mm rifle using a special cartridge which has a tracer and explosive bullet which duplicates the trajectory of the rocket. The soldier puts LAW 80 on his shoulder, takes aim, and presses the trigger to fire the rifle. If he gets a hit, well and good: he presses a selector switch and pulls the trigger again, firing the rocket which should strike at the same point as his aiming bullet. If he misses with the spotting rifle, he takes another point of aim and tries again; and again, until he hits, and then he fires the rocket.

One neglected idea which has surfaced in the 1990s is that of the 'follow-through grenade'. This was first developed in the UK during the Second World War, and the idea was to have a thin tubular projectile filled with poison gas or explosive or marzipan – whatever took one's fancy – and mount this behind the shaped charge in some sort of projectile. The theory was that the shaped charge would blow a hole in the armour and the momentum of the tubular projectile would carry it through the hole to burst inside the tank and thus deal with the crew. The theory turned out to be correct, and one or two experimental projectiles performed exactly as predicted, launching their 'follow-through grenade' through the hole and into the tank. Unfortunately, rather more projectiles failed to do so. Much of the trouble was due to the fact that in 1944–45 the exact mechanics of how the shaped charge worked were not entirely understood, and the hole being blown by the shaped charge was frequently not wide enough to admit even the narrowest sub-projectile. So the idea was knocked on the head late in 1945 and more or less forgotten.

It was left to the Spaniards to revive it in 1991 as a new projectile for their C-90 shoulder-fired launcher. The C-90 is a conventional one-shot, fire and throw away launcher which in normal form launches a 90mm (3.54in) shaped charge rocket with a range of 400m (440 yards) and the ability to defeat 400mm of armour. But in the 1980s this class of weapon began to be looked at with a view to defeating field fortifications, 'bunker busting' being the fashionable phrase. Several countries developed variations on the theme of the shaped charge for this purpose, but the Spaniards produced a follow-through grenade warhead which shows a great deal of promise. Others have taken up the idea, and the late 1990s should provide us with some very interesting new devices for enabling a single infantry soldier to give a severe shock to even the heaviest tank.

CHAPTER THREE

THE ANTI-TANK GUN

The immediate solution to any new weapon appearing on the battlefield is to direct a large gun at it, presuming one has one handy. Yet this was a course that the Germans could not adopt in 1916, for no one in his right mind put guns in the front line, and this was the only place in which they could have tackled the first tanks. This, then, was the cause of the rush for armour-piercing bullets and the Mauser anti-tank rifle. As the tank began to appear more often, however, it found itself confronted with a gun, and provided the gunners got over their initial shock before the occupants of the tank, the result was a foregone conclusion. A 77mm (3.03in) shell from the standard German field gun could demolish a tank with one shot, and it was not necessary to take any pains about where to put it: a hit anywhere on the tank would detonate the shell and the tank was simply not built to resist direct artillery fire. From this fact, no doubt, came the gunner's maxim of 'aim at the centre of the visible mass'.

As tank crews gained experience, though, they could usually manage to put a burst of machine-gun fire into the gunners and at least put them off their stroke for long enough for the tank to either get a shot in from its own main gun, or retire rapidly to a safer position. It was neither convenient nor conducive to good discipline to have the gunners try and manhandle their gun into a fresh position to take another shot for there were, of course, various other people around the battlefield who would regard such a manoeuvre as a fine target, and shifting an artillery piece plays havoc with the artillery's own affairs.

So with these various things in mind, the idea of a dedicated gun for anti-tank operations began to take shape. It needed to be light and easily manhandled by its crew, and at that stage of the tank's development it was not necessary for it to be very large in calibre or weight of fired projectile. The gun also needed to be as inconspicuous as possible so that the gunners could conceal it and thus be able to wait until a tank presented itself in the best position.

As it happened, though there was no suitable gun in existence there was a suitable round of ammunition, namely that for the 37mm Hotchkiss revolver gun. This had been developed in the 1880s and was popular with navies for clearing the upper decks of enemy ships, and it was also used in a number of continental armies as a fortress weapon. In effect, it was rather like the better-known Gatling gun, a multi-barrel machine-gun operated by a hand crank, but it fired a useful little high-explosive shell. So, taking the shell as his starting point, Lieutenant-Colonel Fischer, a Bavarian in the German army, set about designing a light single-shot cannon which could be easily moved around the front line. The result weighed about 80kg (176lb), had a semi-automatic breech which opened on recoil and was thus ready for reloading as soon as the gun stopped moving, could reach a rate of 35 rounds per minute with a trained crew of two men, and could be mounted on a machine-gun tripod. The Army Test Commission approved, and set about improving the ammunition. The Germans eventually came up with a new cartridge and shell that increased the velocity and penetrated up to 16mm of nickel-steel armour plate, which was a lot more than any Allied tank carried. Some fifteen of the guns were built and sent to the front for field test. This was successful, and a contract for 2,000 was placed, the first guns to come off the production line in January 1919. But, of course, the Armistice came along in November 1918 and other than the trials weapons none of the guns ever got into service.

Meanwhile, others had been at work. Krupp and Rheinmetall, the principal German gunmakers, had both been handed the problem. Krupp was slow and did not get very far, but Rheinmetall produced what is generally considered to be the first serviceable anti-tank gun, the 37mm Tankabwehrkanone. This started with the same ammunition as had Fischer, but the result was a low-set wheeled carriage, with a 37mm gun and a seat on the trail for the gunner. He sat there, his legs astride the trail and the gun in front of him, taking aim by high-set open sights, while his assistant knelt to one side to operate the breech and load. Rheinmetall also worked on the ammunition once more and finished up with a shell fired at a muzzle velocity of 650m (2,133ft) per second and capable of piercing 21mm of armour. The whole equipment weighed about 135 kg (297lb) and could be easily manhandled into position by its two-man crew. Development completed, the Army decided to set Krupp, Rheinmetall, and a third firm, Henschel, to the task of producing the gun. The contract was given on 29 October 1918 but, needless to say, no production ever occurred beyond the initial trials weapons.

The 37mm round found favour with the French, which was not unreasonable as they had invented it. They had, for some time, used a small 'trench cannon', a single-shot 37mm gun which was, frankly, of little use other than as a morale-raiser for infantry in the front line. Now the gun appeared to have a useful role, and the French quickly adapted it to the anti-tank role. But since the German tank strength could practically be counted on the fingers of two if not one hand, there was very little practical use made of the gun. A similar weapon was used by the Austro-Hungarian army, and it too made some gestures in the anti-tank direction, but since it saw even fewer tanks, again there was not a great deal of practical experience to be gathered from its use. So when the First World War ended in 1918 there was a certain amount of theory flying around, some limited trials experience, but not a lot of hands-on, soldier-type experience of anti-tank warfare.

In the 1920s the tank occupied the minds of many people: theories of its employment were assembled, discussed, dismantled and rebuilt monthly, and since most of these theories postulated fleets of tanks swarming all over the battlefield and beyond, the question of stopping them was also examined. As early as 1920 the British had developed a circular ground platform for their 18-pounder (83.8mm) field gun: this was carried on the ammunition limber and dropped on the ground; the gun was then run on to it so that the wheels sat on the flat perimeter of the platform, and a boss in its centre connected to the gun. Now the whole gun could be swung round rapidly on a firm and smooth path to track a tank or make a wide switch in direction to confront a sudden target. Having shown that the idea worked, because it was the only way that a gun with limited traverse could be made to engage dispersed or moving targets, the concept was then shelved: no money was currently available for the production and deployment of a service version, but the concept was none the less put away and still borne in mind.

Since money was short and small guns cost less than big ones, small guns were attractive and seemed to have all the power necessary to deal with the contemporary tanks. Moreover, there was a strong argument, particularly in the UK, for further economy by using the same gun to arm the tank and to counter the tank. After all, the argument ran, they both had the same target, in the form of an enemy tank, and one gun to do both jobs would certainly simplify things. What this argument suggested was that the tank supporters had the bit between their teeth and were anxious to prove that the tank was the best weapon for dealing with other tanks, and that the initial reason for the tank's existence (to accompany the infantry, deal with obstacles and assist them on to their objective) was being forgotten. It was a persuasive argument and it eventually won the day in the UK.

One of the small guns which attracted attention was the Oerlikon 20mm cannon. This began life as the Becker aircraft cannon, developed in Germany during the First World War as armament for Zeppelin airships and Gotha bombers, but relatively few had been made before the war ended. The patents and rights were then bought by See-bach, a Swiss firm, which mounted the gun on a light two-wheeled carriage and offered it as an anti-tank weapon. The company went bankrupt in 1923 and the remains were bought by the Oerlikon Machine Tool Company, which overhauled the design and managed to interest several armies in the weapon. But although many tried, few bought, and the reason was probably that nobody could see the point of a fully automatic weapon against tanks. One or two shots were quite sufficient to damage the contemporary tank, and a stream of ten to fifteen shots appeared to be over-egging the pudding. It was also wasteful of expensive ammunition. There was also some doubt as to whether or not the 20mm gun would have much of a life in front of it, for the next generation of tanks would surely have thicker armour. One way or another, therefore, the Oerlikon cannon made little progress as an anti-tank weapon, though fortunately for Oerlikon it did better when sold as an anti-aircraft gun and aircraft cannon. The Oerlikon-developed ammunition was also attractive to one or two designers of anti-tank rifles, but again 20mm was a peculiar calibre as it was really too much for a shoulder-fired rifle and not enough for an artillery piece.

So the designers moved upwards and settled on the 37mm calibre. As seen above, this calibre was well understood, having been pioneered by Hotchkiss and Maxim in the 1880s. The reason for this was the St Petersburg Convention of the late nineteenth century, which outlawed explosive projectiles weighing less than 400g (14.11oz). The smallest explosive projectile which weighed above this lower limit was of 37mm calibre and that settled the question, since both designers wanted as small a cartridge as possible in order to make their heavy machine-guns work. Hotchkiss produced the revolver cannon and Maxim the 'Pom-Pom', and 37mm became a recognized calibre. But neither of the rounds developed by the two 'old masters' had sufficient power for modern warfare, so while the calibre was kept, the cartridge was lengthened to a considerable degree and made more powerful.

The Russians appear to have been the first in this field. During the First World War they produced the Rosenberg 37mm gun, which was a small, wheeled affair with a shield set so far forward that it sat slightly in front of the muzzle and must therefore have been uncomfortable for the crew, reflecting a fair amount of the muzzle blast back at them. Little appears to have been done with this design during the war, but after the Communist revolution it was put into production and several thousand remained in service until the early 1930s. Another little known Russian design was the Maklen 37mm cannon, a gas-operated automatic gun firing from a five-shot magazine. This was on a wheeled and shielded carriage resembling a field gun in appearance and fired a 480g (16.93oz) shot at 650m (2,133ft) per second. This also remained in service until at least 1930, albeit in lesser numbers than the Rosenberg, and was probably the best anti-tank gun in the world at the time, though very few people outside the USSR ever heard of it.

Perhaps the most important 37mm designs were the two guns which appeared in the middle 1930s from Bofors of Sweden and Rheinmetall of Germany, since they were widely used, copied and licensed. Bofors made a few experimental models before it got the design right. One of these experimental models was a most novel weapon, for it was a gun with two barrels in the form of one 81mm (3.19in) unit for infantry support with high-explosive shells and, mounted above it and coupled to the same recoil system, a 37mm anti-tank barrel firing solid shot. However, novelty never sells guns and by 1934 Bofors had settled on a neat two-wheel split-trail carriage with a steeply sloping shield and a 45-calibre barrel. This fired a 700g (24.69oz) shot at 800m (2,625ft) per second to penetrate 20mm of armour at a range of 1,000m (1,095 yards), which was a quite satisfactory performance given the tanks of the time. The weapon was adopted by Sweden, Denmark and Finland almost immediately and sales were made to many places after that: the British army in Egypt acquired some and put them to use in the North African desert in 1941–42, the Danes and Poles built the type under licence, and some later Japanese and Soviet designs suggest that the Bofors might have been an unacknowledged source of inspiration.

The Rheinmetall design was, of course, made difficult by the provisions of the Versailles Treaty (1919) which ended the First World War. Under the provisions of this treaty the company was severely restricted in the number and calibre of the guns it made. Nevertheless it seems that work on a 37mm design began some time in the 1920s. A prototype was built by 1930 and trials indicated areas which could be improved. In 1933 a fresh design was begun and this duly appeared in 1936 as the 3.7cm Panzerabwehrkanone 36, generally abbreviated to PaK 36. A carriage with two pneumatic tyres and a split trail carried the gun and its shield, which traversed together across a 60° arc, giving the gun excellent tactical coverage before the trails had to be moved. The PaK 36 fired an AP shell weighing 680g (23.99oz) at 762m (2,500ft) per second to defeat 48mm of armour at a range of 500m (545 yards). A quantity of these guns went to Spain with the Condor Legion, which was the German expeditionary force sent to the aid of the Nationalist insurgents in the Spanish Civil War (1936–39), and the weapon was tested against the current Soviet tanks being supplied to the Republican government side. Such was the success of the PaK 36, moreover, that the Soviet army bought several hundred guns between 1937 and 1940. Over 20,000 were made for the German army and the type remained in use until 1945, though by that time its original ammunition was no longer very effective and the guns had to resort to other methods as described below.

In addition to these two major users, the PaK 36 was bought by Czechoslovakia, Estonia, Finland, Greece, Japan, Spain and Turkey, and the design was copied by the Netherlands and the USA. It was probably the most widely distributed and used of any anti-tank gun in the period up to 1945.

Attractive as the 37mm calibre seemed to be, there were other contenders. Hotchkiss of France produced a useful

25mm wheeled gun, the Canon Leger de 25 anti-char
SA-L modèle 1934, firing a 320g (11.29oz) AP shell at
950m (3,117ft) per second to defeat 40mm of armour at a
range of 500m (545 yards), and this was also used by
Finland, Poland, Spain and, in small numbers, the UK. The
French army, however, decided that while the 34 SA was a
handy weapon for infantry battalions (it weighed only
496kg/1,093lb and was easily manhandled), something
with a little more authority would be required for divisional anti-tank regiments, and they encouraged the
Puteaux Arsenal to develop a 47mm design, the Canon de
47 anti-char SA modèle 1937. This had a formidable
performance, firing a 1.725kg (3.8lb) AP shell at 855m
(2,805ft) per second to go through 70mm of armour at a
range of 800m (875 yards). It was a very well-designed
gun, with the barrel set very low between the wheels, a
split trail allowing 68° of traverse, and an all-up weight of
1,070kg (2,359lb). Like so many French weapons of the
period, however, production began slowly and took its
time in accelerating, so that when the German army
descended on France in May 1940 there were only 1,120
of these guns in service. This may sound a lot, but split up
between 94 divisions it means under 12 guns per division.

The British looked at the various weapons being developed elsewhere and then applied their usual solution: they
asked Vickers-Armstrong for an anti-tank gun. They also
pointed out that they required guns in tanks as well, and
that the same weapon would be required to do both jobs.
This, of course, immediately put a limit on the size, for the
required weapon had to fit inside a tank turret, and in that
period tank turrets were not very large. So the answer was

the 2-pounder weapon of 40mm calibre. The Ordnance, QF, 2-pounder anti-tank gun for use by the infantry was probably the most luxurious model of any in existence: it had a two-wheeled carriage with three trail legs which opened to form a firm platform. The wheels were raised from the ground and the gun could then be traversed through 360°; a two-speed traversing gear allowed very fast movement to pick up a target and then a slower and more precise movement to track and aim; a semi-automatic breech allowed a high rate of fire; and a demand to fire in poor light gave it an excellent optical sight. As for performance, the 2-pounder fired a 1.08kg (2.38lb) AP shot at 792m (2,616ft) per second to defeat 42mm of armour at 915m (1,000 yards) at 30° angle of impact.

The only problem was that the whole thing weighed 832kg (1,848lb), almost twice the weight of the German PaK 36 and the Hotchkiss 25mm guns, yet offered much the same performance. It was really too heavy to be pushed around by three or four laden infantrymen, and in 1938 responsibility for anti-tank defence was taken from the infantry and given to the Royal Artillery, which could provide the necessary manpower and whose tactical doctrines meant rather less manhandling.

Although the 2-pounder of 1938 could master the contemporary tanks, there were those who foresaw that tanks would probably improve in the future, and in the same year the British Director of Artillery demanded a 6-pounder gun of 57mm calibre as a future replacement. Designs were agreed and a prototype tested, but financial restrictions meant that available funds were being spent on weapons today, rather than weapons tomorrow, so the 6-pounder gun went on the shelf until it was needed.

Those with lesser financial restrictions found the same problem only slightly easier to solve. The German army demanded the successor to its 37mm gun in 1938, and Rheinmetall developed the 5cm PaK 38 in reply. This was really the first anti-tank gun to lift the weapon out of the two-men-and-push-it category into the full-sized artillery piece that it later became. The gun was of conventional design, with an efficient muzzle brake, a split-trail carriage with two solid rubber-tyred wheels, and an all-up weight of 986kg (2,174lb). The PaK 38 may have been large and heavy by the standards of the day, but it fired a useful 2.25kg (4.96lb) piercing shell at 825m (2,707ft) per second and could defeat 60mm of armour at a range of 1,000m (1,095 yards). Just as important, moreover, was the ability of the shot not only to penetrate this thickness of armour, but also to do some considerable amount of damage.

At this point it might be as well to take a closer look at what these guns were shooting. In 1938, except for one or two eccentrics scratching away in secret, there were only two recognized projectiles which offered any chance of defeating armour: the armour piercing (AP) shot, and the AP shell. Both had a long history, dating from the 1870s when ironclad warships first appeared, and each had its supporters. The AP shot was a solid projectile of steel, generally with a carefully heat-treated tip of extreme hardness and a body of less hard but tougher constitution. The difference is significant: a hard steel tip is excellent for punching a hole in plate, but hardness also generally means a degree of brittleness (glass being an extreme example) and since a shot very rarely impacted the target at a perfect 90° strike, there was bound to be some sideways stress placed on the body of the shot during its passage through the plate. Therefore the body needed to be less brittle and more able to absorb these side-stresses. Really, the tough body of the shot is only there to add weight to the blow of the hardened tip. The tip punctured the plate, the momentum of the shot carried it through the plate, and the damage inside the tank was done by splinters of armour peeling off the inside of the tank and possibly by the shot shattering as it went through.

The AP shell, on the other hand, had a similar hardened tip but had the body bored out from the rear for a short distance to make a cavity which was filled with explosive, the hole at the rear being sealed off with a base fuse. The sequence of operation now became firstly the penetration of the plate by the hard tip; next the initiation of the fuse due to the sudden shock of deceleration as the shot hit the target; then a short delay in the fuse's action while the shell passed entirely through the plate; and finally the detonation of the shell behind the plate, so as to damage the crew and interior of the tank.

In favour of the shot was the indisputable fact that being solid it weighed more, for a given calibre, than the shell, and therefore had greater momentum and a more smashing effect at the target. Against it was the fact that the only damage it did inside the tank was incidental to the piercing effect, and relied entirely on splinters of metal.

In favour of the shell was the explosive effect inside the target, which was more devastating than mere fragments. Against it was the lesser weight and lesser momentum, which meant that it would rarely defeat as much armour as a shot; its complicated manufacture; the difficulty of designing a fuse which would infallibly wait until the shell was through the armour before it detonated; and the distortion of the shell by side-stresses due to the somewhat lesser strength of the hollow part, a distortion which could sometimes squeeze the fuse out like a cork from a bottle before it had a chance to detonate the explosive. There was also the problem of finding an explosive inert enough to ignore the enormous shock of impact but sensitive enough to be detonated by the fuse, and the argument that since the explosive usually made up less than 4 per cent of the shell's weight, there really was not enough of it to make the exercise worthwhile.

In the days of AP shell versus battleships, much of this was irrelevant: with 16in (406mm) guns and shells weighing upwards of 1,000kg (2,205lb), a low percentage was still a reasonable amount of explosive and the results were satisfactory. But in the small calibres of anti-tank guns, the complications of the AP shell were often held not to be worth the trouble. While continental armies, by and large, went for the AP shell, the British ignored it and relied upon the AP shot.

Whether it was shell or shot that was fired, the only way to punish the tank was to fire at as high a velocity as possible: this gave the necessary momentum to penetrate the target, and also reduced the time of flight of the shot so that a moving target could not move very far while the projectile was in the air and the problem of aiming-off to hit a moving target was reduced. To achieve this velocity demanded a powerful cartridge and a long barrel, so that increases in performance were inevitably going to lead to increases in the size of the gun.

This is precisely what happened during the Second World War. Rheinmetall took a bit longer than it had expected in getting the 5cm PaK 38 into production: the campaigns in Poland and France were fought using the 37mm PaK 36, and it was not until late in 1940 that the new and bigger PaK 38 appeared. However, the PaK 36 was enough to see off the Polish armour in 1939, which was entirely light tanks and tankettes, and it saw off a fair amount of the British and French armour in 1940. By that time the British and French did have some very well-armoured tanks, notably the British Matilda II and the French Char B, and the German 37mm anti-tank gunners were somewhat dismayed to see their shot bouncing off these thick-skinned vehicles. The Germans had their worst fright at Arras on 21 May 1940, when a scratch Anglo-French force with the British 1st Tank brigade (Matildas with 78mm of armour), the French 3rd Light Armoured Division (SOMUA 35s with 40mm of armour) and a battalion of Durham Light Infantry sliced through General Rommel's 7th Panzer Division, cutting it in two, shattering two German rifle regiments and causing the 3rd SS Division to panic and run. Rommel managed to get some semblance of a defence together and, seeing that his anti-tank guns were doing no good, seized on an anti-aircraft regiment which was standing idle and got its men to depress their 88mm (3.465in) FlaK 18 anti-aircraft guns and thus managed to halt the Allied armour. It is generally supposed that this was the first time the 88mm gun was used against tanks, but in fact a similar panic-stricken moment had visited the Condor Legion during the Spanish Civil War and it had responded in the same way, using the guns as anti-tank weapons. In that affair they fired high-explosive shells, since that was what AA guns always fired. But the incident was reported home and considered, and as a result the 88mm gun was allocated a secondary anti-tank tasking which resulted in the introduction of proper direct-fire sights and an AP shell. It was this ammunition which came out of the lockers on 21 May 1940 and stopped the Matildas.

Even before the 5cm PaK 36 had entered production, the German army was looking to the subsequent generation and in 1939 they issued a demand for a 75mm (2.95in) anti-tank gun. The demand went to Krupp and Rheinmetall, and the solutions of the two companies could scarcely have been more different. Rheinmetall took the simple route: it scaled up the 5cm PaK 38 and produced the 7.5cm PaK 40, which was thus virtually the large brother of the PaK 38. The gun weighed 1,500kg (3,307lb) and fired a 6.8kg (14.99lb) AP shell at 792m (2,598ft) per second to defeat 116mm of armour at a range of 100m (110 yards). With a few improvements in ammunition, this was to remain the standard German anti-tank gun for the remainder of the war, though by 1945 it was rather past its prime. The only fault the German soldiers could find with it was its size and weight; in the muddy thaws of the Russian spring the PaK 40 often got left behind because it was too heavy to manhandle out of the mud and too dangerous to bring a vehicle in to drag it out.

Krupp took an entirely different route, and an explanation of this fact requires the backtracking of a few years to study a completely different line of development, namely the taper-bore gun. Mention has already been made of the German engineer, Gerlich, who dug up an old patent which led him to develop a rifle with a gradually tapering bore to give him a weapon with a very high muzzle velocity. Attempts to interest various nations in applying this idea to military sniping rifles had no success, and in the middle 1930s Gerlich returned to Germany where he managed to interest both Krupp and Rheinmetall in his taper-bore ideas. Rheinmetall simply took the idea as it stood, scaled it up, and produced the 2.8cm schwere Panzerbüchse 41, whose barrel tapered from 28mm to 21mm and launched a tungsten-cored projectile of 124g (4.37oz) weight at 1,400m (4,593ft) per second to penetrate 66mm of armour at a range of 500m (545 yards). The weapon, on a light wheeled carriage, weighed only 229kg (505lb) and, introduced in 1941, did a good deal of damage to British armour in the North African desert. Rheinmetall followed it up with a heavier version, the 4.2cm leichte PaK 41 with a barrel tapering from 42mm to 29mm, firing a 336g (11.85oz) shot at 1,265m (4,150ft) per second to defeat 87mm of armour at a range of 500m (545 yards). The gun was mounted on the same carriage as the 37mm PaK 36 and it was and still is difficult to distinguish the 4.2cm le PaK 41 from the conventional weapon except in close-up pictures.

Krupp took a different view of the taper-bore concept: it thought that it was too much of a technical problem to taper-bore a large gun, and therefore devised a modified system called the 'squeeze-bore' for its new 7.5cm PaK 41 gun. The gun barrel started out at 75mm (2.95in) calibre, but after a moderately short distance there came a sharply tapered section which squeezed the skirted projectile down to 55mm calibre, after which there was a short smooth-bore section to stabilize the shot before it reached the muzzle. The result was that the 55mm shot, weighing 2.59kg (5.71lb), left the muzzle at 1,125m (3,691ft) per second and could go through 124mm of armour at a range of 2,000m (2,185 yards), which was very formidable performance. The gun itself was innovative in that the shield formed a structural member, rather than being simply a piece of steel hung on as an afterthought: the trail legs were hinged to it and the gun itself was mounted in a ball-and-socket joint in the shield. The whole thing was very low-set, weighed 1,356kg (2,988lb) and was undoubtedly the best anti-tank gun in existence. The taper-bore barrel had only a short life of about 400 rounds, however, so production was limited to 150 weapons of this type, whose carriages were adapted to other ordnances after their barrels had worn out.

The success of the tungsten-cored shot in the 28mm s PzB 41 led to a rash of designs to incorporate tungsten into projectiles for other guns, and the 'arrowhead' shot was the result. This was a sub-calibre tungsten slug built up to the correct calibre by a lightweight pointed nose section and a similar full-calibre rear section, so that a side view gave the impression of a short finned arrow. Known as the Panzergranate 40, the 50mm calibre projectile weighed 850g (29.98oz), left the gun at 1,200m (3,937ft) per second and could go through 84mm of armour at a range of 1,000m (1,095 yards); and in 75mm calibre for the Rheinmetall PaK 41 it weighed 3.18kg (7.01lb), had a muzzle velocity of 990m (3,248ft) per second. and defeated 133mm of armour at a range of 1,000m (1,095 yards).

By late 1941, therefore, the Germans had a formidable armoury of anti-tank guns which could take on any tank then in existence. They were well ahead in the race, and it behoved the Allies to do something very rapidly to catch up with them.

From the collapse of France in June 1940 to the German invasion of the USSR one year later, the UK was on her own and the top priority was to re-equip the army after the disastrous losses of weapons during the retreat to and evacuation from Dunkirk. Among the losses were no fewer than 509 2-pounder guns and 50 25mm Hotchkiss guns, which left the army with almost no anti-tank guns at all. This put an end to the Hotchkiss, for there were not enough guns left to make ammunition manufacture worthwhile, and it also put paid to the hope of introducing the 6-pounder in 1940. It had been intended that this weapon should go into production in the summer and enter service as the Ordnance, QF, 6-pounder, but the shortage of guns posed a difficult question. With the German army apparently poised on the French coast preparing to invade, was it more important to deliver quite quickly a larger number of the 2-pounder gun with which the army was familiar, or more slowly a smaller number of the 6-pounder gun which was an unknown quantity and would require some fresh training? The decision obviously went in favour of the 2-pounder weapon, which therefore continued in production until the army had at least a reasonable number of the weapon with which it was familiar and which was still moderately effective. Then the production lines were closed down, changed to suit the 6-pounder gun, and started up again. Thus it was not until November 1941 that the first 6-pounder gun came off the line.

This left the army in North Africa dependent upon the 2-pounder, and while this had been good enough against the Italian light tanks in 1940, it was a different story when the Deutsches Afrika Korps appeared in 1941. By this time the Germans were fielding the PzKpfw III with up to 60mm of armour, and the PzKpfw IV with 50mm of armour. What was more threatening was that the Germans had also improved the guns carried by their tanks. The original PzKpfw III which went into Poland were mostly armed with the 3.7cm gun, the same gun as the anti-tank gun, though a few had a short 5cm gun for infantry support. The PzKpfw IV had a short 75mm (2.95in) gun, also primarily for infantry support. But in the desert, in 1941, the PzKpfw III had a longer 5cm gun, the PzKpfw IV a long 75mm (2.95in) gun, and with these they could stay out of range of the British 2-pounder guns and bombard them into silence using high-explosive shells.

The only salvation for the British army came from using the 25-pounder (87.6mm) field gun/howitzer as an anti-tank weapon. This was provided with a 20lb (9.07kg) solid AP shot and a special 'super-plus' propelling charge which gave the shot a velocity of 533m (1,750ft) per second. Compared with the muzzle velocity of a 'proper' anti-tan gun this was not very fast, but the 25-pounder made up for it in weight of shot. This shot could pierce 70mm of armour at a range of 400m (440 yards), and the impact, even if the shot failed to penetrate, was sufficient to lift the turret off some tanks. Moreover, if the tank decided to stay out of AP shot range, the 25-pounder could send a high-explosive shell to 12,250m (13,400 yards), and when such a shell hit a tank the result was usually fatal. So the 25-pounder gun found itself sited less for indirect support fire than for direct anti-tank and local defensive fire, and had it not been for that capability the British army in the Western Desert would have been in a very difficult position.

The Western Desert also brought the German 8.8cm FlaK gun to the fore again, most famously at the Halfaya Pass on the Libya/Cyrenaica border during Operation 'Battleaxe' in July 1941. German PzKpfw III and PzKpfw IV tanks manoeuvred in front of the pass, drawing the attention of the British armour, largely composed of various cruiser tanks and a number of heavier Crusader tanks with 30 or 40mm of armour. Imbued with cavalry dash, they immediately chased after the German tanks, which retreated into the pass. As the British followed and entered the pass they fell victim to several 88mm guns which had been concealed in ambush positions. Very few of the British tanks escaped.

By the end of 1941 the first British 6-pounder guns were in action, but even before they had been put into production the next generation of anti-tank gun was on the drawing boards. In November 1940 a conference had been held to decide on a heavier weapon, the result of which was the 17-pounder gun of 76.2mm (3in) calibre. This appeared in May 1942 and was a potent tank-killer. With its standard 17lb (7.71kg) AP shot it had a muzzle velocity of 884m (2,900 ft) per second and could defeat 109mm of armour at a range of 915m (1,000 yards) and the provision of a capped shot increased this armour-penetration capability to 118mm.

But 1942 saw a sudden change in the balance between the Allied and the Axis powers. The British blockade of Germany was effective in keeping out almost all their imports of wolfram, the basic ore from which tungsten was refined, and by early 1942 a decision had to be made in Germany: was the available tungsten to be used for ammunition or for machine tools? There were inadequate supplies to satisfy both needs, and tungsten used for ammunition was, once fired, lost for ever, whereas tungsten machine tools when blunt could be refurbished.

The fateful decision was taken in favour of machine tools. With this decision, the use of tungsten carbide cores for anti-tank ammunition ended in Germany once the current stock of ammunition had been fired. The taper-bore guns were withdrawn, and it was obvious that if more powerful anti-tank defence was needed, then more powerful conventional guns firing conventional AP shot or AP shell would be the only answer.

No such problem affected the UK. Though tungsten was scarce, there was enough for both tasks, and the Armaments Research Department had already begun exploring ways of using it. A Czech refugee called Janacek had proposed a taper-bore muzzle attachment for the 2-pounder gun and a special shot which would be squeezed down as it went through this adapter. After some misgivings he was given a contract and, with the BSA company, developed the 'Littlejohn Adapter'. Unfortunately, by the time the idea was perfected the 2-pounder had been relegated to the scrapyard as far as towed service went, but the device was used with some guns on armoured cars and gave their guns a useful boost in penetrating ability. Work had also been done on providing a full-calibre projectile composed of a tungsten core made up to size by a light alloy external body: this weighed rather less than a comparable steel shot, so it left the muzzle with a higher velocity, but lacking weight and therefore momentum this projectile soon lost velocity in flight and except at short ranges was no more effective than steel shot.

Finally, ARD began studying the 'sabot' principle in which a sub-calibre slug of tungsten carbide was sheathed in a light steel shell and then locked into a four-piece alloy 'sabot' which brought it up to full-calibre diameter. In the case of the 17-pounder gun, the APDS (Armour Piercing Discarding Sabot) shot weighed 3.45kg (7.6lb) instead of the 7.71 kg (17lb) of the steel shot: this allowed the APDS projectile to accelerate much more rapidly, and it therefore left the muzzle at 1,204m (3,950ft) per second. Once out of the gun, centrifugal force threw the components of the sabot away from the sub-projectile, which continued to the target. As a result of its small cross-section and considerable weight it had good momentum, did not lose velocity so quickly, and could go through 231mm of face-hardened armour at a range of 915m (1,000 yards) at 30° impact angle. In fact, APDS arrived for the 6-pounder gun first, in June 1944, and then for the 17-pounder gun in August.

With development of the 17-pounder gun under way, in 1942 the British made their final choice for the next generation of anti-tank gun. Their initial decision was to take the barrel of the 4.5in (114.3mm) anti-aircraft gun to fire a 24.95kg (55lb) shot at 800m (2,625ft) per second, but fortunately wiser councils decided against it. After all, the barrel alone weighed 2,794kg (6,160lb), and a weapon with such a barrel would have only very limited tactical mobility. Instead, and almost taking a leaf from the German book, the choice was the barrel of the 3.7in (94mm) anti-aircraft gun mounted on a two-wheeled carriage to become the 30-pounder gun. In fact, it became the 32-pounder gun since a 14.52kg (32lb) shot gave a better ballistic performance. Only two prototypes were ever built, however. They proved, beyond any argument, that the conventional anti-tank gun had reached its maximum, indeed it had gone over the top. The 32-pounder was about the same size as a 5.5in (139.7mm) medium gun and weighed something in the region of 9,145kg (20,160lb), and was quite impossible to manhandle by its six-man crew on anything other than a hard, smooth surface. Its armour-piercing performance would have been colossal, especially as it had been designed with a view to firing an APDS shot at 1,219m (4,000ft) per second, but this was never made and very few piercing trials were ever made with the prototypes before they were relegated to museums.

Germany went through a similar progression. The invasion of the USSR in 1941 exposed the German army to the T-34 tank, often considered to be the best of any wartime tank. This was armed with a potent 76.2mm (3in) gun and protected with 45mm of well-sloped armour which was rapidly upgraded to 70mm. The 7.5cm PaK 40 gun was stretched to its limit to deal with this tank, and the obvious answer was to adapt the 8.8cm FlaK gun barrel to a more convenient mounting. The result was the 8.8cm

PaK 43, which went in an entirely new direction for wheeled carriages. It actually used a four-legged mounting similar to that of the anti-aircraft gun but with the gun set much lower since it did not need to be elevated to high angles. It could be dropped into action and the wheels removed very quickly, or in an emergency it could be fired off its wheels. It fired a 10.4kg (22.93lb) AP shell at 1,000m (3,281ft) per second to defeat 159mm of armour at a range of 2,000m (2,185 yards) at 30° impact angle, and this capability was more than enough to see off any Soviet tank. There are cases on record of turrets being blown off and engines being blown out of the T-34 tank at ranges of up to 2,000m (2,185 yards). Production of the mountings was slow, however, and as an interim measure the 8.8cm PaK 43/41 appeared as the combination of existing components (the PaK 43 barrel was mounted into the two-wheeled carriage made up from the trail legs of the 10.5cm leichte Feldhaubitze 18, and the wheels of the 15cm Feldhaubitze 18) with a few specially made parts to link it all together. It was a cumbersome beast weighing 4,380kg (9,656lb) and the German troops on the Eastern Front nicknamed it the 'Barn Door' because of its awkwardness, but for all that it was as deadly a weapon as the PaK 43.

Having got these into production, the Germans started to consider their next generation of anti-tank guns and the result was a pair of 128mm (5.04in) guns, one design from Krupp and the other from Rheinmetall but both known as 12.8cm PaK 44 weapons. These used four-legged platforms in a similar manner to the PaK 43, and fired a 28kg (61.73lb) AP shell at 1,000m (3,281ft) per second to penetrate 173mm of armour at a range of 3,000m (3,280 yards). The weapons each weighed some 10,000kg (22,046lb), however, and in spite of their fearsome performance very few were actually used in towed form. Like the British 32-pounder, they had gone over the top and soldiers were incapable of handling them nimbly enough to survive as anti-tank guns in the field.

The Soviets, of course, were confronted with the PzKpfw V Panther with up to 110mm of armour in later models, the PzKpfw VI Tiger with 100mm of armour, and finally the Tiger II (or Königstiger) with 150mm of armour. At the start of the war on the Eastern Front in June 1941 the Soviets had their 37mm Rheinmetall guns and also an indigenous 45mm Model 1932 gun which was more or less a scaled-up version of the Rheinmetall design. In 1942 the Soviets produced a 57mm gun on a lightweight two-wheeled carriage which could defeat 140mm of armour at a range of 500m (545 yards), and this 57mm Model 41 weapon was quickly followed by a 76.2mm Field Gun Model 1942 which was actually planned as a field gun but given anti-tank ammunition: with steel shot it could defeat 69mm of armour at a range of 500m (545 yards), which was not very good anti-tank gun performance but indicated the way the Soviets were thinking. Their view was that any gun was an anti-tank gun if it got a tank in its sights, and they issued either AP shell or shaped charge shells to virtually every gun below 150mm (5.91in) calibre that could be expected to see a tank. Even so, the Soviets went on with the development of anti-tank guns which could, when nothing better offered, function as field guns. The 85mm (3.35in) D-44 fired a 5kg (11.02lb) tungsten-cored arrowhead shot to defeat 113mm of armour at 500m

(545 yards), but also threw a useful high explosive shell for several miles, while the 100mm (3.94in) DS-3 of 1944 fired a 10kg (22.05lb) tungsten shot to defeat 185mm of armour at a range of 1,000m (1,095 yards).

The Americans came late to the tank-killing business, but had enough sense to take a critical look at the anti-tank battle before they decided on their new armament. The US Army Ordnance Department obtained an example of the German 37mm Pak 35/36, and proceeded to design a similar weapon in the same calibre. Their entry weapon was the 37mm Anti-Tank Gun M3A1 which could beat 64mm of armour at 500m (545 yards) on a good day. The first versions were fitted with a muzzle brake in an attempt to reduce the recoil forces on the carriage, which was even lighter than the German original. However, it was soon discovered that the muzzle brake was unnecessary and it was removed. A small flat shield was provided for the gun crew and the breech mechanism was copied direct from the German gun and remained a vertical drop block. It was an unremarkable weapon, though it stayed in service throughout the war. It was rarely used in Europe, but it was quite sufficient to deal with the less well-armoured Japanese tanks and therefore saw considerable use in the Pacific theatre.

The M3's shortcomings were illustrated at the Battle of Kasserine (14–25 February 1943) in North Africa. Rommel's attack in western Tunisia caught the US II Corps off balance. The resulting series of engagements cost the Americans dear. In particular, the M3 anti-tank guns proved wholly incapable of stopping the tanks of the 21st and 10th Panzer Divisions (the latter had received deliveries of Panzer VI Tigers, which had 100mm (3.9in) of front armour) despite fighting courageously. By the time the Afrika Korps had been halted II Corps had lost 7,000 men (of whom 4,026 had been captured), 235 tanks and 110 self-propelled guns and reconnaissance vehicles. The M3's shells had literally bounced off the heaviest German tanks, which did little for the morale of the guns' crews.

When, in 1941, the US Army decided to look for a new anti-tank gun it decided that its quickest solution would be to adopt something already designed, and in November 1941 approved the adoption of the British 6-pounder gun as the 57mm Anti-Tank Gun M1. The only difference was that the American gun was 406mm (16in) longer than the British weapon: the British design had originally been of the same length, but availability of gun lathes was a critical factor in the UK in 1941 and 406mm (16in) was lopped off the length of the barrel in order to allow production by smaller lathes. The Americans had no such problem so they opted for the original 50-calibre length. This gave them an additional 33m (100ft) per second of muzzle velocity, although it made no practical difference in penetration at fighting ranges.

In September 1940, though, the US Army had demanded an anti-tank gun capable of stopping any tank then in existence. The Ordnance Department considered the matter and decided that the quickest solution would be to take the existing barrel of a 3in (76.2mm) anti-aircraft gun and marry it to the breech mechanism of the 105mm (4.13in) howitzer and put the result on the 105mm (4.13in) howitzer carriage. All this went together quite well and in December 1941 the 3in Anti-Tank Gun M5 was standardized.

The gun turned out to be a first-class piece of equipment, but the ammunition was a different story. For various reasons the ammunition design was deficient and the gun never achieved the performance expected of it. The principal problem lay in the fuse: the Americans were using an AP shell and the base fuse design gave problems, bursting the shell before penetration was complete or failing to burst it at all. All this led to evaporation of any confidence in the gun, and it was shelved in favour of a self-propelled gun design. When this project collapsed, the Americans turned again to the towed gun, managed to get some workable, if not perfect, ammunition, and sent it off to war. Firing a 7kg (15.43lb) AP shell, the M5 could defeat 100mm of armour at a range of 915m (1,000 yards), and it could also fire a useful high-explosive shell to a range of 14,700m (16,075 yards).

Work also went forward on developing 3in (76.2mm) and 90mm (3.54in) guns, but though prototypes on towed carriages appeared, both these weapons eventually ended as tank guns, and it was not until after the end of the Second World War that the towed versions were actually perfected and put into production.

Finally, of course, in line with everybody else, the Americans looked at a heavy anti-tank gun and settled on a 105mm (4.13in) design. A massive piece of equipment, this fired a 17.5kg (38.6lb) AP shell at 950m (3,115ft) per second to defeat 210mm of armour at 915m (1,000 yards), but its size, like that of the British 32-pounder and German 128mm (5.04in) weapons, was its undoing and only two prototypes were built in 1946. After testing they were sent off to museums.

As the war entered its final year the anti-tank prospect looked rather poor: the only way to conquer tanks seemed to be to hurl things at them at high velocity, and as the tanks got thicker so the guns had to get bigger to cope with their heavier armour. Now the size of the required guns had gone beyond the bounds of practicality. What was to be done now?

In 1941, during their airborne invasion of Crete, the Germans revealed a recoil-less gun. The principle of the recoil-less gun is quite simple: the barrel is open at each end, and in this one places two equal weights in the form of a shell or shot to go forward and a counterweight to go backward. The propelling charge is located in the middle, and its initiation drives the shell forward and the counter-shot backward, leaving the gun still as the recoil of each projectile cancels that of the other. This is fine in theory but ridiculous in practice, for no one wants a countershot screaming back into his own lines. So the Germans had carried the idea to its logical conclusion: if, for argument's sake, one fired a 10kg (22.05lb) shot forward, one could also balance the recoil by firing a 5kg (11.02lb) shot backward at twice – or a 2.5kg (5.5lb) shot at four times – the velocity of the 10kg (22.05lb) shot. If one goes on in this way, one arrives at the point at which one can discharge a relatively light weight of gas to the rear at very high velocity and still obtain 'recoil-lessness'. This is what the Germans did. The advantage of all this is that one no longer needs a massive and heavy carriage and recoil system to withstand the recoil of the gun. All one requires is something strong enough to tow it and support it while one fires it.

To obtain the necessary stream of rearward gas, one has to increase the propelling charge by about five times, and four-fifths of this is designed to stream to the rear as gas with only about one-fifth actually propelling the shell. This means that one cannot hope to extract much muzzle velocity from such a weapon, and need therefore not consider the use of piercing projectiles dependent on velocity for their effectiveness: and it also presents a rangefinding problem, because the shell is moving slowly and in a high looping trajectory, so that misjudging the range means missing the target. With a high-velocity gun firing on a flat trajectory, misjudging the range by a hundred yards or so is no great problem because the shot will still land somewhere on the tank. There is also the question of hitting a moving target with a low-velocity gun. At the beginning of the Second World War there were solutions to most of these problems except that of defeating the armour that was the primary target of such a weapon; but then the shaped charge began to make itself known.

This, it appeared, was the answer to the anti-tank gun designer's prayer. A shaped charge shell is independent of range and velocity, and so long as one can get it to the target it will defeat its designed thickness of armour. With the revelation that the Germans could actually make a recoil-less gun work, and with the promise of armour defeat at low velocity by the shaped charge, a lot of designers reached for their pencils. This meant that by the time the ghastly truth about the heavy anti-tank guns – the simple fact that they had become too cumbersome to be practical weapons of war – had made itself known, the designers were ready with some recoil-less designs which might just save the day.

The British were first off the mark, because they had begun even before they knew about the German weapons. A private individual, Commander Sir Denistoun Burney, was behind it. Burney was a gifted designer who had invented the paravane naval anti-mine device in the First World War, had been involved in the design of the R100 and R101 airships, and had developed a streamlined car in the 1930s among many other things. He had reasoned out the recoil-less gun problem, using the First World War Davis gun (a genuine countershot weapon) as his starting point, and developed a recoil-less four-bore shotgun as his demonstrator. He then made a 20mm weapon to convince people, and then went on to design an 87.6mm (3.45in) '25-pounder shoulder gun', a 94mm (3.7in) anti-tank weapon and a 95mm (3.74in) gun/howitzer. In the process of designing these prototype weapons, he also made another fundamental discovery.

Burney was not entirely happy with the shaped charge, and he looked at the ballistics of the recoil-less gun and decided that, since the acceleration up the bore was less violent than with a conventional gun, the stresses on the shell would be less. So he could design a shell with thinner walls and more high explosive. He then made a wire mesh liner for the inside of the shell, and filled it with plastic high explosive and a base fuse. When this was fired against a hard target the thin steel wall peeled away like a banana skin when it struck, the wire mesh bag held the explosive together and allowed it to plaster itself tightly against the target, and the fuse then detonated it. The result was an explosion that drove a pressure wave into the target: this rebounded from the inside surface and in so doing caused the inner surface of the target to fail, thereby blowing off a massive 'scab' at high velocity. Burney's objective at the time was concrete (he was designing a 182.9mm/7.2in RCL gun for the assault on Hitler's Fortress Europe), so he called the shell his 'Wallbuster'. It was well named: tried against reinforced concrete 1.5m (5ft) thick, it blew fragments off the back for 55m (60 yards), cut the reinforcing rods and severely bulged the wall. The success of the trial suggested that such a warhead might be effective against armour, and the type was tested against armour 305mm (12in) thick. The warhead's detonation blew a 53kg (117lb) scab, measuring 480mm by 620mm (18.9in by 24.4in), off the back at a velocity of 200m (655ft) per second and also generated a cloud of high-velocity splinters from the point at which the scab had torn free. A new anti-tank projectile had arrived.

None of the Burney guns ever reached service. A handful was made and the weapons were issued to selected units for evaluation shortly after the war, but there were too many technical problems to be overcome before they could be considered acceptable for service. So the responsibility passed from Burney to the Armaments Research & Design Establishment, who sat down to do some elementary research to solve some of the problems before going on to design a 120mm (4.72in) gun which utilized some of Burney's ideas. The principal visible difference lay in the cartridge: Burney had used a normal brass cartridge but bored large holes in the sides and then lined it with brass foil. This cartridge sat in a false chamber, which also had large holes in it, surrounded by another chamber which led forward to the bore and backward to two or four venturi jets alongside the breech block. On firing, the pressure burst through the brass foil and the gases filled the chamber, a portion driving the shell forward, the remainder passing back through the venturis to give the recoil-less effect. The trouble was that as the gases wore away the venturi throats unevenly, so the recoil-less effect varied from jet to jet, and the gun could move slightly sideways or up and down, ruining the accuracy.

The Germans, in their original design, had used an ordinary metal cartridge case but cut out the base and replaced it with a round slab of plastic material. They then put a single venturi in the breech block. When the cartridge was fired, the plastic held long enough to allow the shot to start moving up the bore, then collapsed and allowed the gases to pass through the venturi. And when the venturi wore away, and the gun started recoiling forward, it was a simple job to unscrew the jet unit and screw a new one in.

So the British 120mm (4.72in) Battalion Anti-Tank (BAT) gun used a plastic-based cartridge and a fat squash-head shell which could drive a slab off the inside of the armour of any tank in existence and reduce the inside of the tank to a shambles. The weapon went into service in 1954 and remained in service until the late 1980s, by which time its place had been filled by the MILAN missile. It was the last British anti-tank gun.

The Americans began by copying a German design, a 105mm (4.13in) short gun using a plastic-base cartridge, but when they saw Burney's system they realized it had some ballistic advantages and adopted the perforated cartridge case, though using many more, and much smaller, perforations. Instead of the large venturis adopted by Burney they used four slots in the breechblock, through which the gases could eject from the exterior chamber, and instead of Burney's wallbuster shell they preferred to use a shaped charge, which they understood, because they wanted to use the result before the war was over. The result was two 'Kromuskit' guns, so called from the names of the designers, Kroger and Musser: the 57mm T15 and the 75mm (2.95in) M30. The 57mm weapon weighed 20kg (44.1lb), was fired off a machine-gun tripod or a man's shoulder, and launched a 1kg (2.205lb) shaped charge shell at 370m (1,215ft) per second to a maximum range of 4,500m (4,925 yards). The projectile could defeat 76mm of armour at any range within that distance, and the weapon also fired a useful HE shell and, unusually, a canister shot. This last was a tinplate case filled with steel slugs which were ejected from the gun in the manner of a shotgun, and was a useful anti-personnel round for the defence of the infantry post. In order to reduce the friction in the barrel and thus demand less propellant, the driving band on the shell was pre-engraved, and when loading the gunner had to make sure that the rifling engaged correctly with the grooves inside the gun bore.

The 75mm (2.95in) gun was somewhat heavier, weighing 75kg (165.3lb), and fired a 6.5kg (14.33lb) HE shell to a range of 6,360m (6,950 yards), or a 6kg (28.65lb) shaped charge shell, capable of defeating 92mm of armour, to 6,675m (7,300 yards).

Both guns were issued early in 1945 and were first used on Okinawa on 9 June 1945. In Europe, they were used by the US 17th Airborne Division near Essen in the final days of the war. In general they were well received, the only complaint being the limited amount of ammunition which had been supplied: the authorities were reluctant to order large stocks until they knew whether or not the guns were successful.

Their success, particularly that of the 57mm weapon, far exceeded anyone's expectations. In the fraught postwar world they were adopted by several armies, among them Brazil, Austria, Japan, China, Yugoslavia, France and Spain. Even today, fifty years after the introduction of the original weapons, copies are still being used by Brazil and China, and ammunition is still being made to the original Second World War specifications.

Unknown to anyone else, the USSR had developed a recoil-less gun in 1936–38 and actually used it during the 'Winter War' (1939–40) against Finland. Very few details are known about this weapon except that it weighed about 200kg (441lb), had a barrel about 2.3m (7.55ft) long and had a single jet at the rear of the breech-block. The weapon appears not to have been successful, since it is not known to have been used against the Germans in 1941, and no specimen was ever captured. No further work on recoil-less guns was done until after the war, when three weapons were developed, probably in the early 1950s.

The 82mm (3.2in) B-10 was tripod mounted, weighed 91kg (201lb), and fired a 4.5kg (9.92lb) high-exposive shell to a range of 4,470m (4,890 yards), or alternatively a 3.6kg (7.94lb) shaped charge shell capable of defeating 240mm of armour. It was closely followed by the 107mm (4.22in) B-11 gun firing an 8.5kg (18.74lb) HE shell to a range of 6,650m (7,275 yards), or alternatively a 7.5kg (16.53lb) shaped charge shell capable of defeating 380mm of armour. Finally came the 75mm (2.95in) SPG-9 gun, which appears to have been chiefly intended for use by airborne troops, firing a 1.3kg (2.87lb) rocket-assisted shaped charge shell which could defeat 300mm of armour. The enormous difference in penetrative power between these guns and the wartime weapons indicates the amount of research which had gone into the shaped charge projectile in the years immediately after the war.

The Americans were satisfied that the recoil-less gun was a sound idea, but they were not satisfied with its penetrative power, and they too put a lot of work into basic research into the shaped charge before they set about replacing the wartime recoil-less guns. The result was the 105m (4.13in) M27, which, although adopted by the USA and some other countries, was not a particularly good design. The weapon was overhauled and its defects corrected, but rather than calling the revised weapon the M27A1, the Americans preferred to dissociate themselves from the earlier model and called the revised weapon the 106mm (4.17in) M40, even though it was still a weapon of 105mm calibre. This was a much better weapon, weighing only 220kg (485lb) and firing a 7.7kg (17lb) shaped charge shell at 498m (1,635ft) per second to defeat 450mm of armour. The M40 was adopted or used by just about every army outside the Soviet bloc.

Another country which showed a great deal of initiative with recoil-less guns was Sweden, and here as in the UK much of it was due to one man. An engineer named Hugo

Abramson devised and demonstrated a 20mm RCL gun in 1941. It used a single venturi in the breech block and had a very long barrel, developing a high muzzle velocity for this class of weapon. Adopted by the Swedish army in 1943 it was followed by a 37mm weapon, but this was abandoned as being too small in calibre, and in 1946 work began on what was to become famous as the 84mm (3.31in) Carl Gustav gun. This is a short-barrelled shoulder-fired gun with a simple single-venturi breech similar to the design first put forward by Abramson. It uses a cartridge case with a blow-out disc in the base, and the percussion primer is fitted into the side of the case, so that it has to be loaded very precisely in order that the primer falls beneath the firing pin: this is achieved by having a notch cut in the cartridge rime to engage with a lug in the chamber. The projectile is drag-stabilized, though the weapon is rifled and has a driving band: the band slips on the shell so that little spin is taken up, since spin tends to disperse the shaped charge jet. The shell is capable of defeating over 400mm of armour at any range. The gun is also provided with high explosive and illuminating shells so that it becomes a useful defensive weapon for the infantry section and can also lob illuminating shell to the far side of a tank at night so as to silhouette it for a shot with the shaped charge munition.

Though the recoil-less gun replaced the conventional gun for anti-tank use in most countries, the wartime 85mm (3.35in) and 100mm (3.94in) guns remained in service in the USSR and Warsaw Pact countries, and are still in use with a number of countries. Moreover, they have been upgraded by adopting various types of ammunition developed for use with tank guns, and in the USSR the 125mm (4.92in) tank gun has been adapted to a wheeled carriage, although few details are known. Smaller guns have also been developed, adopting tank gun ammunition technology in order to extract a much higher performance than might otherwise be expected. Mecar of Belgium has developed a 90mm (3.54in) Kenerga gun firing a modern fin-stabilized APDS round (APFSDS) at 1,200m (3,937ft) per second to defeat 100mm of armour at a range of 1,500m (1,640 yards) at an impact angle of 60°. It also fires a shaped charge shell capable of defeating 350mm of armour or 1m (3.25ft) of concrete.

Israel has developed a useful 60mm weapon known as the HVMS (Hyper-Velocity Medium Support) gun, firing an APFSDS shot at 1,620m (5,315ft) per second, which is probably the record gun velocity for the present time, and the projectile penetrates 120mm of armour at 60° impact angle at a range of 2,000m (2,185 yards). The development of the gun itself has been completed, but the final form of carriage has yet to be decided so the weight is not currently known, though it will be comparable with that of the British 6-pounder gun in 1942, for that carriage was used for the first prototype gun.

So as the century approaches its close, it becomes apparent that the obituary of the anti-tank gun has yet to be written: modern ammunition developments promise startling performance from conventional weapons of smaller calibre than the 1945 monsters, and even the most complex gun ammunition is a good deal less expensive than a missile and could even be cheaper than some unguided rocket weapons.

CHAPTER FOUR

TANK DESTROYERS

There are two principal schools of tactical thought on the subject of killing tanks: the first is to sit in ambush and wait for the tank to come to you, the other is to go out hunting for the tank. These are in effect the passive and active schools of tank killing, one might rightly think. There are profound arguments advanced for both points of view, but what it really boils down to is that one does not always know where the enemy tanks are, so hunting for them can be frustrating, whereas one can be fairly certain of where they will approach to attack you, so an ambush will usually pay off. But there is also what one could call an intermediate course: set up ambushes, but be prepared to move rapidly to set up another ambush somewhere else once the first has been unmasked. It is for the active and intermediate schools that the tank destroyer was designed.

The tank destroyer is no more than a dashing name for a self-propelled anti-tank gun, and, as you might expect, it was first coined in the USA, though it must be admitted that the idea itself appeared in various places at more or less the same time as the tactical situation made it an obvious course of action. In addition, and particularly the case in Germany and the USSR, there was an economic factor: self-propelled guns, whether anti-tank or for any other purpose, were cheaper and quicker to make than tanks, and they could be employed on many tasks for which tanks were perhaps misemployed.

It can be argued that the father of the tank destroyer was the assault gun, and there is little doubt that the success of these weapons led people to contemplate putting anti-tank rather than field guns into the chassis. The assault gun was devised by Germany as a means of getting a piece of artillery right up with the advancing infantry so as to blast away anything which looked like checking the infantry, and the best way of doing this seemed to be to put a field piece on to a tank chassis, put some armour plate around it to protect the gunners, and let it trundle along just behind the forward troops. The idea worked and various models were developed. The guns carried by these assault artillery vehicles were given shaped charge ammunition, in the first instance for their own defence should they be unlucky enough to encounter an enemy tank, but later for offensive purposes once battle experience had showed that they could also sneak into ambush positions and give the enemy tank the surprise. Thus dedicated anti-tank self-propelled guns began to appear.

The American approach was rather different. In 1940, when the Americans began looking at what was happening in Europe and overhauling their armed forces, American industry was not geared to the production of munitions. It was, however, well geared to the production of motor vehicles, and it occurred to somebody that perhaps it would be better to take the few anti-tank guns available and put them on wheels so that they could move rapidly from one threat to another. As a result of lessons drawn from the 1940 Louisiana Maneuvers, the War Department came to the conclusion that the towed anti-tank gun would be the last line of defence, and that the cutting edge would be a swarm of mobile guns which would, in their phrase, 'seek, strike and destroy'. In 1941 the first Tank Destroyer Battalions were formed and the TD Center was established at Fort Meade, Maryland, and then moved to Fort Hood, Texas. All this led to some astonishing machinery, some of which reinforces the idea that the designers simply had no conception of what warfare was actually like.

Take, for example, the Gun Motor Carriage T8. Before the Second World War the Ford Motor Company had expended some time on making a 'Swamp Buggy', a somewhat basic four wheels and an engine on a simple platform which could be used in the Florida and other swamps. This, with a 37mm anti-tank gun attached to a pedestal mounting, became the T8. The T27 was similar but larger, the Swamp Buggy in this case being a Studebaker design and the gun a 75mm (2.95in) field gun. The T1 Gun Motor Carriage was a 3in (76.2mm) anti-tank gun mounted on top of the hull of a Cletrac agricultural tractor: this at least had tracks so its cross-country performance would perhaps be improved over that of the Swamp Buggies, but once you had the driver on board and planted the gunner and his mate on the two seats provided on the gun mounting, there was no room for anybody else and very little room for ammunition. There appears to have been no sort of stabilizing device, so the whole contraption must have bucked like a bronco every time the gun fired.

The T55 was a monstrous eight-wheeled armoured hull with a 3in (76.2mm) anti-aircraft gun pointing out of the front. The T2E1, at the other end of the scale, was a 37mm gun firing out of the back of a jeep, while the T2 was the same thing but firing forward, past the driver's ear.

Some of the ideas, though, had a modicum of merit: this was sufficient at least to get them into manufacture and given a standardization number. Unfortunately, by the time the designs had been perfected, the standardization completed and production put in hand, the war had moved on and the equipment was obsolete before it ever reached combat.

Such a weapon was the Gun Motor Carriage T48. This was the marriage of the M3 half-track combat car (an excellent piece of machinery of which the US Army made particularly wide use) and the 57mm anti-tank gun. The idea may well have been partially British in concept: certainly the British approved of the equipment as soon as they learned of it, for it appeared to be just what the British needed in North Africa, namely a reliable, fast, tracked and armoured vehicle carrying a gun with sufficient punch to deal with the German tanks of 1942. The British had something of this nature already, a locally invented equipment nicknamed 'Deacon', which was simply the standard 6-pounder gun in an armoured shield on the back of a 3-ton truck. This was used as a divisional anti-tank reserve, to be rushed to whatever point it was required, but it was cumbersome and difficult to conceal, so a less bulky replacement was welcomed. But it was 1943 before manufacture of 1,000 T48s had been completed and they were delivered to the UK. By this time the desert war was over, German tanks had become somewhat tougher, and there was little or no scope for such a weapon in Italy or, so far as the British were concerned, anywhere else in the foreseeable future. So they were all hoisted back onto ships and sent to the USSR. What the Soviets made of them we will never know, since the communists took good care that no mention of foreign equipment, or any photographs, ever appeared in their wartime press releases if they could help it. Possibly the only one to survive is that in the Polish army museum in Warsaw.

Eventually it became obvious that thin-skinned vehicles might be nimble, but it really needed something heavy to protect the crew and be able to carry some worthwhile gun into battle. There were some false starts: the T20 which placed the 3in (76.2mm) anti-aircraft gun on to the M3 light tank, the T53 which put the 90mm (3.54in) anti-aircraft gun firing to the rear from a much-modified M4 Sherman tank chassis, and the T72 which put the 3in (76.2mm) anti-aircraft gun into an open-topped turret on an M4 Grant tank. Quickly enough, however, there did appear some combinations that made good sense, and these were soon standardized and put into production. Among the first of these, and the best, was the Gun Motor Carriage M10, which was the 3in (76.2mm) gun in an open-topped turret on a modified Sherman tank chassis. (There has always been some debate about why self-propelled anti-tank guns had open-topped turrets: one argument advanced by gunners was that if the turret 'had a lid on it' the vehicle became a tank and the armoured forces would claim it from the gunners, and thus as long as it was open it was a self-propelled gun and therefore the rightful property of the artillery. There is another point of view, which is discussed below.)

The only trouble with the M10 lay in the gun and, as noted in the previous chapter, the only trouble with the 3in (76.2mm) gun lay in its ammunition, which was not up to its job. But over 6,500 M10s were built between June 1942 and December 1943. By that time the defects of the 3in (76.2mm) gun were manifest and in November 1943 a design study had been started into the feasibility of replacing it with the 90mm (3.54in) anti-aircraft gun modified for anti-tank use. This took some time and the improved design, known as the M36, did not appear off the production lines until the summer of 1944, but eventually 2,324 were built by May 1945: of this total, 187 were new and the remainder converted M10s.

With this, the US Army finally had something which could go into the field and mix it with any tank it found. The 90mm (3.54in) gun, with its standard 11kg (24.25lb) AP shell, could defeat 122mm of armour at a range of 915m (1,000 yards), and by the end of 1944 it was provided with a tungsten-cored composite rigid shot which almost doubled that armour-penetration capability. The 702d Tank Destroyer Battalion, part of the US 2d Armoured Division in the advance to Germany in late 1944, was equipped with the M36 and in the course of one two-week period destroyed one PzKpfw III, eight PzKpfw IV, 15 Panther and one Tiger II tanks as well as two assault guns, two self-propelled anti-tank guns, two pillboxes and two half-tracks.

At the time the M10 went into service during mid-1942, the tank destroyer concept was running at full speed in the US Army, and the tank destroyer battalions were demanding something faster and less bulky with which they could put the 'seek, strike and destroy' idea into fully effective practice. The first result was the T49 Gun Motor Carriage, which put the 57mm gun on to a new lightweight chassis using Christie large-wheel suspension. Testing of the first pilot model revealed that it was too much vehicle for too little gun, and the Ordnance Department was sent back to rework it, using the same 75mm (2.95in) gun that was already in use on the M4 Sherman tank. This was duly tested and, again, the Ordnance Department was asked to go back to its drawing boards and produce a vehicle mounting the 76.2mm (3in) anti-tank gun. This time the department got it right, delivering a 17,690kg (39,000lb) vehicle with torsion-bar suspension for a speed of 90km/h (56mph) and an open-topped turret mounting the required gun; this was little more than a redesigned 3in (76.2mm) gun resulting from demands for a more capable weapon to replace the 75mm (2.75in) gun as tank armament, as the 3in (76.2mm) weapon was too bulky to go into the existing turrets. The new gun used the same ammunition and had the same performance, but its breech mechanism was smaller and the balance such that it took up less turret space. Nevertheless, the combination of high-speed purpose-designed chassis and 76.2mm (3in) gun proved successful, and some 2,500 such M18 'Hellcat' vehicles were made before production ended in late 1944.

In service the M18 proved to be one of the best examples of the American tank destroyer concept. It weighed half as much as the M10 and was much smaller, but it had a more powerful gun and was much faster – it was the fastest tracked vehicle to be used in action during the war. The M18 looked like a tank, even to the extent of having a 360-degree traverse turret. However, its armour protection was much less than would be expected in a tank, and the M18 relied upon its mobility and striking power to defend itself. The engine was positioned to the rear of the hull, and was powerful enough to give the M18 good power-to-weight ratio to provide excellent acceleration and agility. Despite its success in action, the M18 was gradually switched from the tank destroyer battalions as the enthusiasm for the exclusive tank destroyer concept dwindled. By 1945 many M18s were serving with conventional armoured formations within the US Army, and they were used more and more as assault guns and self-propelled artillery.

The M18 remained in service until the 1960s, and numbers were distributed to various friendly armies after the end of the Second World War.

The British, who had also received a quantity of M10s, decided not to wait for the arrival of the 90mm (3.54in) gun, but shortly after D-Day in 1944 withdrew the M10s piecemeal, refitted them with 17-pounder (76.2mm) guns, rechristened them 'Achilles', and sent them back into action. This was probably a better combination than the M36, because by that time the British were using APDS ammunition, and with that Achilles could defeat 230mm of armour at a range of 915m (1,000 yards) at 30° impact angle: the 90mm was straining to penetrate the same thickness at 90° impact angle. In actual combat, the difference was probably negligible.

In fact the British already had some experience with the 17-pounder gun on tracks. In 1944 they had taken the obsolescent Valentine tank, stripped off the turret, built up the hull into an armoured cupola, and mounted the 17-pounder gun into this, firing back over the engine compartment. This became known as 'Archer', and while it may not have been quite so impressive a vehicle as the M10 and M36, it did just as much execution. Whatever else was said about the Valentine tank, it at least had the virtues of being reliable and manoeuvrable. Being somewhat lighter than the basic Valentine, the Archer inherited these virtues and made use of them. It was a nimble weapon and, being low-set, easy to hide, which is always a primary virtue for the ideal tank destroyer. Its only defect was that it was somewhat cramped inside, so cramped indeed that after driving into position and then reversing the vehicle into its firing location, the driver was out of his seat like greased lightning, because the breech of the recoiling gun would decapitate him if he stayed there.

Actual combat experience was to show that the American concept of the tank destroyers moving en masse and devastating German armoured formations did not happen, just as the pre-war British idea of fleets of cruiser tanks moving around the battlefield like fleets of ships also did not happen, except on occasion in the atypical conditions of North Africa. What actually happened was that fleets of enemy tanks never materialized, and actions were one-on-one (to use a later phrase) with individual tank destroy-ers taking defensive areas and dealing with whatever came their way. The pre-war theory was that tanks supported infantry, while anti-tank guns shot at tanks. War showed that tanks shot at tanks more often than they supported infantry, and the dedicated role of the tank destroyer failed to materialize.

This change in tactics led to some misapprehension on the part of tank destroyer commanders: they thought they could go into action and mix it with tanks as if they were tanks. This is the root of the other theory about not putting tops on turrets, for it served to remind tank destroyer commanders that their vehicles were not tanks and were a good deal more vulnerable than tanks. The reversal of opinion can be seen by referring to General Patton's instructions to the US 3d Army: 'Towed anti-tank guns should be well to the front and located to cover likely avenues of enemy tank approach. They must be emplaced so that they cannot be seen beyond their lethal anti-tank range. Self-propelled anti-tank weapons should be held in reserve to intervene against enemy armoured attacks. They should locate routes to and firing positions from probable sites of future activities. All anti-tank guns should be trained to fire as field artillery and be provided with a large proportion of high-explosive shells.' As a result, many tank destroyer battalions spent the last few months of the Second World War serving as support artillery more often than they actually went looking for tanks.

The British point of view was somewhat different, as a wartime anti-tank officer explained:

We were given the Archer before D-Day so that we would have one troop of self-propelled 17-pounders and one of towed, the self-propelled guns allowing us to move quickly off the beaches in support of the tanks. Then as we progressed through France and Belgium and gained experience we added one troop of 6-pounders. The idea was that the 6-pounders and the Archers formed the front line anti-tank defence, and the 17-pounders, which took half a day to dig into a good defensive position, acted as the backstop for anything that got past the front line. We gradually got a mixture of Archers and M10s; the M10s were nice vehicles, roomy and reliable, but big, whereas the Archer may not have been so comfortable but it was nippy and easier to hide. We would find a nice ambush position, conceal ourselves and wait. We used to work out the distance to likely points in the field of fire; that tree was 500 yards, that gateway 750 yards and so on, so that when a tank appeared we had a good measure of its range without having to guess. But the 17-pounder shot pretty flat anyway, up to about a thousand yards, so range wasn't quite as critical as all that. And once a tank appeared you let it get as close as you dared before opening fire. One shot generally did the business, two if need be, and then it was time to get out of it to another position because you could bet that Jerry's forward observers had you spotted and somebody was working out his gun data before you got the engine started.

To the Soviets this was not a problem: all their artillery was multi-tasked, so any gun with a tank in its vicinity was automatically an anti-tank gun, provided it could depress its barrel sufficiently to take aim. In similar vein, their self-propelled artillery performed as anti-tank or field artillery as the situation dictated.

Soviet self-propelled guns appeared first as assault guns, not primarily for infantry support (as was the practice with comparable German equipment) but rather to beef up the deficiencies in Soviet armoured formations in 1942, when the T-34 tank was slowly coming into service but while there were still very large numbers of earlier, under-gunned tanks. The obsolescent T-70 two-man light tank was being mass-produced by one of the largest motor-car factories in Russia, so it did not affect the production of other tanks to seize on this, do away with the turret, lengthen the chassis by putting an extra wheel on each side, build up an armoured box at the rear, and mount a 76.2mm (3in) Model 1942 field gun in it. The result was the SU-76, which carried four men and 60 rounds of ammunition. Early experience was not altogether success-ful: the vehicle broke down too often and the open-topped barbette was unpopular with the crews who, like the Americans of 1944, fancied their chances at attacking tanks. A better engine and transmission cured the reliability problem, but the crews were told to pull their helmets over their ears and get on with it. The SU-76 served throughout the Second World War and for some years afterwards in the hands of satellite armies.

It was 1943 before the SU-76 reached the hands of troops in any numbers, and in that year the Germans introduced the PzKpfw V Panther tank, which could outrange any 76.2mm (3in) gun on SU-76 or T-34 with its powerful 75mm (2.75in) long-barrel gun. Something needed to be done, and done quickly, so a hasty modifica-tion was effected to the chassis of the T-34 tank. By this time the T-34 was coming off the production lines in quantity, so there was spare capacity to make the chassis with an armoured compartment over the hull in place of the turret. This was fitted with a powerful 85mm (3.35in) anti-aircraft gun in the front face: the driver sat on one side, the three other crewmen were in the same compartment together with 48 rounds of ammunition, and the whole thing was in production and into service as the SU-85 before the winter of 1943 set in. At the same time designs were drawn up to fit the T-34 tank with the same 85mm (3.35in) gun and make a few other changes, and once the T-34/85 went into production, manufacture of the SU-85 ceased as it was superfluous. Nevertheless, it served until 1945 and, like the SU-76, was handed out to various satellite states after that.

Once the T-34 had acquired the 85mm (3.35in) gun, it was obvious that the support weapon had to be bigger, and the easiest and quickest solution was to look round for what was available and adapt it to a suitable chassis. The most readily available gun was a naval 100mm (3.94in) weapon, and it proved possible to shoehorn this into the chassis of the SU-85. Thus production of the chassis continued and the new gun was fitted, the result being the SU-100. This proved more than enough to deal with any German tank which came in view and it was to remain in Soviet service until the late 1950s and even later than that with some of the satellite armies.

Why, one might ask, were anti-aircraft guns so popular for conversion to anti-tank guns? The answer lies in the fact that the two types of gun have two things in common: high velocity and 'fixed' ammunition. The anti-aircraft gun needs high velocity to get the shell high into the sky as fast as possible and thus cut down the distance the aircraft can move between firing and having the shell arrive: this reduces the amount of aim-off needed, and thus helps accuracy. The anti-tank gun also needs velocity, partly for the same aiming reason, partly to have the shot arrive at high speed and thus overcome the armour by its impact, and partly because high velocity means flat trajectory and thus less chance of missing should the gunner estimate the range wrongly. Fixed ammunition is ammunition in which the shell and cartridge are in one piece: this speeds the loading process as there is no need to put the shell in, then ram it, then load the cartridge behind it, and finally close the breech. The complete round is loaded in one movement, and the breech closed automatically behind it. This means a higher rate of fire, either to get more shells into the sky or to get off a quick second shot against a tank if the first failed to do the job. So starting out by taking an anti-aircraft gun meant that the basic design was done: all that was needed was to make a different type of projectile and make a new mounting and sights for ground shooting.

Reverting to the German development of tank destroyers, there is ground for making Hitler himself responsible for the critical step from assault gun (Sturmgeschütz) to anti-tank gun (Jagdpanzer). The German army had asked for an assault gun as early as 1936, and the response was to modify the PzKpfw III tank by taking away the turret and building a low armoured superstructure in its place, mounting a low-velocity 75mm (2.95in) gun. The first of these StuG III vehicles appeared in February 1940 and a number were used in the campaign in France and the Low Countries in the summer, as a result of which some modifications were made and mass production began. In September 1941, however, Hitler decreed that future models were to be given heavier armour and a more powerful gun. Since the gun was more visible than the armour, the StuG III received the long 75mm (2.95in) PaK 40 anti-tank gun, which gave it a very useful anti-tank performance, but the armour remained unimproved. This became the StuG III Ausf F (Assault Gun 3, Modification F), and 359 were built. There were subsequent modifications which saw the armour improved, but the gun remained the same for the remainder of the war and a total of 7,893 of the various models of StuG III were produced.

The success of the StuG III led to thoughts of using the PzKpfw IV chassis for something similar, and these thoughts were moved into action in December 1943 when a severe bombing raid on the Alkett factory in Berlin put a temporary stop to the production of StuG III. The simple answer was to take the hull of the PzKpfw IV and graft on the superstructure and long 75mm (2.95in) gun of the StuG III, thus creating the StuG IV. This went into production at the Krupp works at Essen and was so successful that Krupp gave up tank production and concentrated on making 1,139 StuG IV vehicles before production ended in March 1945.

By this time the role of the assault gun as an anti-tank weapon had made itself apparent. By this time, too, production of assault guns for their proper purpose as assault guns was running along quite smoothly and could cope with the replacement problem, so a decision was taken to redesign the StuG IV as a pure anti-tank machine, a Jagdpanzer (hunting tank). A prototype was produced in late 1943 and production, by Vomag of Plauen, began in January 1944. It used the running gear and chassis of the PzKpfw IV, but the hull was then built up into a low sloping superstructure with the 7.5cm (2.95in) PaK 40 gun mounted in the front plate alongside the driver. With 80mm of frontal armour, a height of only 1.85m (6.07ft) and capable of 40km/h (25mph), the Jagdpanzer IV was a nimble and powerful weapon. But by 1944 the 75mm (2.95in) gun, which had seemed so powerful in 1939, was no longer in the first division and in mid-1944 a third version of the vehicle was developed, basically the JPz IV with a new, longer and more powerful 75mm (2.95in) gun in the same mounting as before. As the Panzerjäger IV, this went into production alongside the JPz IV and in December 1944 replaced it as the standard self-propelled anti-tank weapon. By December 137 of the new PzJ IVs had been built and they were used to good effect in the Ardennes battle of that month, the 'Battle of the Bulge' in which Hitler made a desperate last attempt to break through to Antwerp and the coast of the English Channel. Production continued, and by March 1945 over 900 had been built by Vomag, while the Nibelungenwerk of Linz, Austria, produced about 280 of a slightly different version.

Good as this equipment was, however, it was felt that adherence to the original tank chassis tended to restrict ability, and that a completely fresh approach, using existing components where possible but not tied to a particular chassis, might produce something more versatile; and it would certainly allow the use of a heavier gun. And so in the middle of 1942 work began on the Nashorn (rhinoceros) gun carrier. The chassis was a lengthened version of the PzKpfw IV hull with the engine moved forward to a central position, so leaving a clear space at the rear for a floor. An open-topped superstructure of sloping armour was built around this, and into the front plate went the 88mm (3.465in) PaK 43 anti-tank gun. The result was an excellent machine with formidable anti-tank performance which rapidly made a name for itself on the Eastern Front, and just under 500 were built before the war ended.

The introduction during 1943 of the PzKpfw V Panther tank, with the long 75mm (2.95in) gun, led to suggestions that a useful tank destroyer might be made from this chassis once production of the basic tank had become well established. By October a mock-up had been made, mid-December saw the prototype demonstrated to Hitler, and production of the Panzerjäger Panther (otherwise known as the Jagdpanther) was under way in January 1944. As with the smaller designs, it was simply the chassis and lower hull of the Panther tank, built up into a closed armoured superstructure with the 88mm (3.465in) gun mounted in the front plate. First issues reached troops in June 1944, and 392 were built. At a weight of 46,750kg (103,065lb) with considerable height and width, the Jagd-panther was much bigger than any other tank destroyer of the period, and it put the fear of God into its enemies. There was no tank in existence that the Jagdpanther could not destroy at a range of 2,500m (2,735 yards), well before the other tank could make an impression on its 100mm of frontal armour.

In the early part of 1942, when the PzKpfw VI Tiger tank was under development, the designers were urged to make it carry the heaviest anti-tank gun then available, the

88mm (3.465in) L/71 weapon: this was actually a tank gun but its anti-tank performance was about the same as that of the PaK 43: it could penetrate 159mm of armour at 2,000m (2,185 yards) at 30° impact angle using an AP shell, and 184mm of armour under the same conditions using tungsten-cored shot. Unfortunately the dimensions of the turret would not permit this, and the Tiger went to war in the first instance with a 75mm (2.95in) gun, later being upgraded to an 88mm (3.465in) weapon, although one of lesser power. So in default of a powerfully armed Tiger, an assault gun variant was proposed in September 1942 and orders were given for 90 to be built. The result was Panzerjäger Tiger (P) Ferdinand, named not after the famous bull but after Ferdinand Porsche, the designer of the Tiger (P) tank upon which the assault gun was to be based.

The conversion was simple: the hull of the Tiger was flat-decked, so an armoured superstructure was built over the rear two-thirds of it with the massive 88mm gun planted in the front plate. Additional armour was bolted on to give a frontal and side thickness of 200 mm, and fifty of these monsters were issued in the late spring of 1943, just in time to partake in the momentous Battle of Kursk (July 1943) that decided the outcome of the war on the Eastern Front. There seems little doubt that anything which got into the sight of a Ferdinand gunner was doomed, but there is equally little doubt that unless the Ferdinand had a platoon of infantry around to watch its back, it was equally doomed. With the gun limited to 14° of traverse to each side of the centre-line, the only other armament a single forward-firing machine-gun, and the six-man crew minding their own affairs and watching their front for Soviet tanks, it was a comparatively easy task for a determined Soviet soldier to slip round the back and plant a charge on the engine compartment or track and immobilize the huge machine. The German troops stopped calling it Ferdinand and began calling it Elefant instead. The survivors were pulled out of the Kursk salient and late in the year were shipped off to Italy. There they were perhaps in less danger from suicidal infantrymen, but on the other hand Italy was not the best terrain in the world for a huge vehicle with a limited-traverse gun.

In January 1943, though, an improved Tiger tank had been ordered, and this time the designers took care to get it right and mount the long 88mm (3.465in) gun in the turret, so that now there would be a tank with the same firepower as Ferdinand the Elephant but with better mobility and no blind spots. The prospect of this Tiger II, which went into service in February 1944, led to suggestions that perhaps the assault gun to end all assault guns might be constructed on this chassis. Orders were accordingly given early in 1943 and a prototype appeared in April 1944, but technical problems with the suspension delayed production until July. The resulting Panzerjäger Tiger (otherwise known as the Jagdtiger) was a triumph of engineering: a hull with 150mm of frontal armour and a superstructure with 250mm of armour, mounting a massive 128mm (5.04in) gun capable of defeating 173mm of armour at a range of 3,000m (3,280 yards) with an AP shell weighing 28kg (61.73lb). The Jagdtiger was the monarch of the battlefield, but it still had a blind area behind it and a determined tank commander might be able to get round

The tank/anti-tank war began the moment the British Mark IV made its debut on the Western Front in 1917. Initially stunned by its appearance, the Germans quickly learned to exploit its sheer bulk and ponderous speed (4 mph/6.4k/ph) and to attack its thin 12mm (1/2 inch) armour with direct artillery fire.

The revolution in tank versus tank combat came in the early 1930s with the introduction of communication by radio telephone, which meant a single commander could order large tank units around the battlefield. Countries such as Germany, America and Britain were quick to realize that the only way to stop such a force would be to attack it with one of your own, and so throughout the 1930s manoeuvres like this one were held to work out battle tactics.

A column of German Panzer II tanks on the breakout from the Ardennes to the Channel Coast, during the opening moves of the invasion of France in 1940. Compared with later German tanks, such as the Tiger, the small 8.1 tonne (8 ton) Panzer II was very lightly armoured, with only 13 mm ($^1/_2$ inch) of steel plate on its turret and hull. This made it vulnerable to the light anti-tank guns of this early period.

Burning wood to defrost the frozen ground, Moscow's civilians dig makeshift anti-tank positions in November 1941. Only five months into their invasion of Russia, the German panzers were only 48km (30 miles) from the Soviet capital, and with the first frosts hardening the autumn mud, were ready to roll on right into the heart of the city.

The British PIAT was one of the crudest anti-tank weapons of the Second World War.
A simple metal tube held a large spring which drove a firing pin into the base of the 2.5 kg
(5.5 lb) bomb. This detonated a charge in the bomb's tail which blew the projectile
towards its target. Though the PIAT only had a range of 91 metres (100 yards),
the bomb proved surprisingly effective.

Loading the 2.36 in 'Bazooka' rocket launcher. The weapon being used here is
the first version of the bazooka, the M1A1, introduced into the US Army in 1942.
The rocket being loaded is only the blunt-nosed training round – the live
HE round could be identified by its pointed warhead instead.

The 'bazooka' being carried by the paratrooper on the right was America's first attempt to produce a rocket-propelled anti-tank weapon. Though it could punch a hole through 178mm (7 inches) of steel plate, the weapon's main drawbacks were that the rocket's low velocity restricted its effective range to 100 metres (109 yards).

A Soviet 76mm gun in action around the River Volga during the winter of 1942. Indicative of the robust adaptability of so much Soviet equipment, the 76mm gun, like most Soviet artillery, was meant to fulfill the roles of both field gun and anti-tank gun.

In July 1943, the greatest tank battle of the war was fought at Kursk. Nearly 5000 German and Soviet tanks were thrown into a titanic struggle which lasted eight days. The Soviets employed every anti-tank weapon they had in the defence of the salient, including this largely obsolete PTRD anti-tank rifle.

These German Tanks wait in the Brenner Pass in December 1943 on their way through the Alps towards the invading Allied forces in Italy. From its first introduction around Leningrad in September 1942, the Tiger's 100mm (4 inches) of frontal armour and formidable 88mm gun made it more than a match for any Allied weapon or tank thrown against it.

Opposite: A StuG III tank destroyer knocked out near the German town of Bourheim in December 1944. The StuG was first introduced in 1940 as a mobile assault gun for the infantry, but was upgunned in 1941 with the long 7.5 cm StuK40 gun. The StuG was extremely successful in its anti-tank role, over 7500 being produced from 1942 to March 1945.

Produced in the late 1930s as an anti-aircraft weapon, the German 88mm gun did not take on the anti-tank role until the Afrika Korps was forced to adapt it in 1942. Its range and hitting power soon proved lethal against every Allied tank sent against it. This example is in action in Russia in 1943.

British Royal Engineers operating in Italy in late 1943 prepare a road obstacle of Mark V anti-tank mines. A string of such mines would be unlikely to destroy a tank by themselves; they would, however, be quite capable of blowing off the tracks, thus stopping the tank and allowing anti-tank guns to finish off the job.

The Dragon anti-tank missile was developed in the mid-1960s as a replacement for the US Army's 90mm recoil-less rifle. Wire-guided and consisting of a tracker unit and separate missile canister, the Dragon has a range of 1000 metres (1090 yards) and its 2.5 kg (5.5 lb) warhead is too small to be effective against the latest types of main battle tank.

GERMAN HOLLOW CHARGE BOMB WITH PROJECTOR.

The German Second World War single-shot Panzerfaust fired a 3kg (6.6 lb) hollow-charge projectile. With a range of around 30m (96 ft), it could knock out just about any known Allied tank, providing the user could get within range.

The Soviet RPG-7 is one of the world's most widely used light anti-tank weapons. The RPG-7 launches a grenade using a recoil-less charge. The grenade travels several metres away from the firer before its rocket motor safely ignites, propelling the warhead out to ranges of up to 400 metres (430 yards), where it can penetrate up to 320mm (12 inches) of armour plate.

The American TOW missle. Since its introduction into the US Army in 1970 it has undergone several upgrades, which have steadily increased the size of its warhead and improved its penetrative power from 600mm 800mm (23 inches to 31 inches) of armour plate.

The MILAN is a wire-guided anti-tank missle system which consists of two units: the launch and guidance platform and the reloadable missle tubes. The missle when launched is propelled by a two-stage rocket motor and is guided to target by thin wires, which lead directly from the missle to the operator at the guidance platform.

The American M72 rocket launcher, like the Second World War German *Panzerfaust*, supplies the modern infantryman with his own one-shot anti-tank weapon. Though its sights are simple and the rocket is unguided, the M72 can penetrate nearly 200mm (7 inches) of steel plate at a range of 100 metres (109 yards).

The MILAN missle system in action with the French Foreign Legion during the 1991 Gulf War. Note the missle's enormous back blast, which makes its use from inside enclosed spaces like bunkers or buildings both impractical and extremely dangerous.

Above: Over the past ten years, the guidance systems of infantry anti-tank missles have progressed from wire-guided methods toward the use of lasers. One of the new generation of laser-guided anti-tank weapons is the TRIGAT. This missle, developed by a European consortium, is capable of firing three missles a minute up to a range of 2000 metres (2180 yards).

Main picture: An Iraqi T-72 tank becomes another Allied 'kill' statistic during the final stages of Operation 'Desert Storm', the 1991 campaign to liberate Kuwait. Consisting of a fin-stabilized bolt of tungsten or depleted uranium fired in a sabot, the APFSDS, flying at speeds of up to 1400 metres per second (4,590 feet per second), could penetrate even the best protected vehicles in the Iraqi arsenal.

Many believe that the future of anti-tank warfare belongs in air attack from helicopters such as the American AH-64 Apache. The main tank-busting armament of the Apache is the AGM-114 Hellfire missile. This is a 'fire and forget' weapon which once launched can fly up to 6 km (3 $\frac{1}{2}$ miles) to its target guided by a laser designator housed in the Apache's nose.

and take it in the rear if he was lucky. The initial order was for 150 vehicles, but in the event no more than 77 were made and only two combat units received them, putting them to use in the Ardennes and in the final defence of Germany in the west in 1945.

The Jagdtiger well illustrated the problem facing designers by 1944: to deploy a gun capable of devastating the opposition demanded a massive piece of equipment. This was a lesson the Allies were learning at the very same time. As noted above, both the UK and USA had developed heavy anti-tank guns; the British their 32-pounder gun of 94mm (3.7in) calibre, and the Americans a 105mm (4.13in) gun. Both now decided to put the weapons into tank destroyers.

The British machine was known as the Heavy Assault Tank A39, which was nicknamed 'Tortoise' probably because it had a thick shell and moved slowly. The hull and superstructure were of cast armour up to 225mm thick, proof against any known anti-tank gun, and the 32-pounder gun, which was really a worked-over 3.7in (94mm) anti-aircraft gun, was mounted in the front with the usual limited amount of traverse. The vehicle was monumentally heavy, and moved at a mere 19kph (12mph). Development began in 1944, but it was 1947 before the first vehicle was completed. Six were built, but, in the words of the War Office, 'the design will not be perpetuated'. After they had carried out a series of trials, which simply confirmed that they were too big to be of any practical value, four were scrapped and the other two relegated to museums.

The American venture was also called a tank, the Super

Heavy Tank T28, though it was in the same mould as the Jagdtiger and Tortoise with its heavily armoured hull and superstructure carrying the enormous 105mm (4.13in) gun mounted in the front plate. Armour thickness on the frontal area was 305mm, the vehicle was prodigiously heavy and moved at only 13kph (8mph), and in 1945 the 20° of gun traverse led to it being renamed the Gun Motor Carriage T95. Two were built for completion late in 1945: one caught fire during testing and was abandoned and, according to rumour, still lies forgotten on a deserted proving ground. The other was scrapped in the 1950s.

It was not entirely a waste, for much of the research work which had gone into the T95 was to be applied to the next generation of heavy tanks. But these three monsters certainly saw the end of the heavy self-propelled anti-tank gun, just as their towed counterparts had marked the end of the heavy towed gun. Towed or driven, these heavy anti-tank weapons were simply too cumbersome for the battlefield. Indeed, it could have marked the end of tank destroyer development altogether, since the experience of the war had shown that the tank destroyer concept, as originally envisaged, was obsolete. There were two areas where a lightweight tank destroyer still looked attractive, however, and this was for airborne operations and amphibious landings.

The development of American self-propelled guns after the Second World War falls into three distinct periods. The immediate postwar years saw much energy expended in producing enormous thickly protected vehicles capable of surviving a nuclear blast; then came the rush to air-portability, and self-propelled guns were stripped of all their armour and protection and given the lightest chassis compatible with actually firing a gun off them; and then came the present period of vehicles with adequate protection, some of which are capable of being lifted by very large aircraft.

Before the period of air-portable weapons, airborne troops were poorly served in the field of heavier weapons: there was no artillery capable of being air-lifted other than the venerable 75mm (2.95in) pack howitzer, and although this could fire a shaped charge shell it was no great bargain as an anti-tank gun. At the same time improvements in aircraft meant that quite heavy loads were now feasible. There had been airborne tanks during the Second World War, though little use was made of them since they could only be taken into action by gliders; with the better load-lifting capability of new aircraft, there seemed a chance that airborne armour might be possible. And since everybody knew that self-propelled guns weighed less than tanks, thought was now given to an airborne tank destroyer.

The result of this was the M56 Scorpion, which appeared in the early 1960s, and it could have been the stripped-down appearance of this equipment which caused a rethink of the entire self-propelled gun programme as the air-portable era dawned. For there was nothing more basic than this vehicle: a light tracked chassis with space for the driver alongside the engine, and on top a 90mm (3.54in) gun on a simple rotating mount with a tiny shield and two seats for the gunner and his mate. There was room above the tracks for a couple of boxes of ammunition, and that was that. The all-up weight was 7,020kg (15,475lb), speed 45km/h (28mph) and range 225km (140 miles) on a full tank, and provided it got its shot in first, the M56 could cope with most tanks of the period. But if the other side had anything heavier than a revolver it was in trouble, for apart from the skimpy shield on the gun there was no protection worth thinking about.

At much the same period, during the late 1950s, the US Marine Corps began worrying about getting anti-tank weapons ashore during the initial phases of an amphibious landing. By this time they were using the 106mm (4.17in) recoil-less rifle as their standard anti-tank weapon, and somebody had the idea of mounting a handful of these on top of an armoured vehicle. The prime disadvantage of a recoil-less gun is, of course, the back-blast as it fires, which precludes ever mounting such a weapon inside a turret like a conventional gun. So the result as reached by the US Marines was a small armoured vehicle, which bore no resemblance to any other vehicle in the US armoury, carrying six 106mm (4.17in) recoil-less rifles on brackets, three each side of the turret. This could revolve with the turret, which carried three spotting rifles: these were used to obtain the range and ascertain any corrections for wind or drift, after which the main armament was fired. The complete equipment was known officially as the Rifle, Self-Propelled, Full Tracked, Multiple, 106mm (4.17in), M50 but was more familiarly known as the 'Ontos'. So far as is known its only combat application came in the Dominican Republic in 1964, when it was used to demolish houses concealing snipers. It might be added that the US Marines had also experimented with an amphibious version of the M18 Hellcat, but this was less than successful and never went into service.

The Soviets might possibly have been watching all this activity across the Atlantic. In any event, they appear to have reached similar conclusions about supporting airborne troops and set about developing their own air-portable tank destroyer. This resulted in the ASU-57, a very light and lightly armoured open-topped box on tracks mounting the 57mm anti-tank gun in its front face. Unfortunately by the time this appeared in the early 1950s the 57mm gun was of very little practical value on the battlefield, and though the ASU-57 trundled round until some time in the late 1970s, its principal role would probably have been the reduction of pillboxes and field fortifications rather than serious anti-tank operations.

That the 57mm was obsolescent was quite obvious to the Soviet paratroops, and as soon as they were given the assurance of an aircraft capable of heavy lifting, they set about a replacement. This became the ASU-85, which went into service in 1960. Like so many other self-propelled guns, the chassis of this vehicle came from an existing tank, in this case the PT-76 amphibious light tank. On top went a covered armoured superstructure carrying the 85mm (3.45in) D-70 gun in the front face. The whole thing could be lifted by the Antonov An-12 'Cub' transport aeroplane, and the type became standard equipment of air assault divisions and remained in service until some time in the late 1980s.

In the Berlin Victory Parade of 1945 the Soviets revealed their Josef Stalin heavy tanks, which quite put the Western world in an uproar: these were big, they had well-sloped armour and rounded turrets from which shot was all too likely to bounce off, and they carried a massive 122mm

(4.8in) gun. Thereafter the biggest bogey for land forces was the Soviet armoured force which, at the drop of a hat, would come screaming through the Fulda Gap (or whatever was the locally favoured route) and demolish everything in its path. This led to some rethinking on the anti-tank question in the mid-1950s, when the West German army was reconstituted and admitted to NATO. The Germans, who had some experience of Soviet armour, were quite certain that they wanted a new equivalent of their wartime Jagdpanzer, and very rapidly organized a Swiss chassis mounting a 90mm (3.54in) gun in the front plate. This proved unsuccessful, but by this time work had begun on a chassis which could be adapted to various roles: as an APC, a rocket carrier, and now a gun carrier. Prototypes were built and tested during the early 1960s, and in 1965 production of the Jagdpanzer Kanone 4-5 began, a total of 750 being built.

The JPZ 4-5 is a low, tracked vehicle with the 90mm (3.54in) gun mounted in the front plate. It has a crew of four and can move at 70kph (43.5mph). The gun is actually the American 90mm (3.54in) M41 weapon, which fires HE, squash-head, shaped charge and APFSDS projectiles of German or American manufacture. The JPZ 4-5 is still in service with the German and Belgian armies, but during the past twenty years numbers have been withdrawn and their original guns replaced with various types of guided missile. In the early 1990s there were suggestions that the remaining gun vehicles might be refitted with 105mm (4.13in) or even 120mm (4.72in) tank guns, but nothing appears to have come of this.

There are two other nations deserving of mention for

having retained the tank destroyer in service, although their views on what constitutes a tank destroyer might be open to argument. Austria, for example, deploys the Jagdpanzer SK 105 and calls it a tank destroyer or a light tank according to whatever tactic they might require of it today. Known also as the Kürassier, the SK 105 was built by the Saurer company and based on a redesigned APC chassis. The hull is a straightforward tracked vehicle much like any other light tank, but the turret is a variation of a French design, licensed by Steyr-Daimler-Puch, which absorbed Saurer, and improved in some respects. It is an oscillating turret: the gun does not elevate within the turret, for the entire turret elevates and depresses, taking the 105mm (4.13in) gun with it. The advantage of this is that the gun, staying fixed in relation to the turret, can have a twin-magazine automatic loading system built behind it. An automatic loader does away with one crew man, and with a 105mm (4.13in) gun, makes life easier inside the turret: a 105mm (4.13in) gun cartridge is a bulky thing to heave around by hand in a confined space. Another point about the 105mm (4.13in) gun is that it provides enormous firepower from what might otherwise be considered as a light tank: it is actually the same gun as that fitted into the French AMX-30 main battle tank, and it can defeat 360mm of armour with its shaped charge and probably 400mm at a range of 1,000m (1,095 yards) with its APFSDS shot. As tank destroyers go, this is probably the best one in existence today.

The Japanese took an entirely different line. During the 1950s, as the Japanese Self-Defence Force began to take shape, the performance of American recoil-less guns in the

Korean War (1950–53) impressed many Japanese military observers. They therefore decided that since their demand was for a lightweight vehicle, recoil-less guns might prove the solution – and this all took place in the period before the US Marines produced their Ontos.

The resulting vehicle is quite unique. The Type 60 self-propelled gun, introduced in 1960, is a light armoured and tracked vehicle with two 106mm (4.17in) recoil-less rifles mounted side by side to the right of the centre-line. On their right is a raised portion of the hull in which the commander sits, with a hatch and periscopes. On the left side is another raised portion in which the loader sits. Travelling, the whole affair is quite low, but to enable them to fire the two rifles are raised hydraulically about 0.6m (2ft) so that they are higher than the raised hull sections and can traverse 30° either side of the centre-line. The commander, who acts as the gunlayer, has a range-finder and night vision equipment in addition to the usual aiming rifle, while the driver and loader attend to reloading the guns.

There is, in addition to these two vehicles, an enormous amount of equipment which their owners describe as tank destroyers, but upon examination they all prove to be the same thing: any vehicle carrying an anti-tank guided missile. And since guided missiles are considered in another chapter, such vehicles can be left to that point especially as, in the author's opinion, the installation of a TOW missile launcher (see page 176) on a Jeep does not make the Jeep into a tank destroyer.

CHAPTER FIVE

TANKS AGAINST TANKS

The possibility of direct combat between tanks was scarcely considered in the war of 1914–18. In the first place, the tank was intended to support the infantry during their assault by crushing wire entanglements, crossing trenches, clearing trenches by machine-gun fire, and using their heavier guns to deal with any surviving strongpoints. The instructions of the period went no further than this. In the second place the Germans never had more than a handful of tanks, which they viewed in the same way and used in an identical fashion. It was not until the postwar theorists began postulating fleets of tanks, cruiser tanks, tank marines, tank artillery and subjects of that nature that the question arose of what was going to happen when two opposing fleets happened to meet.

Nevertheless, it was at Villers-Bretonneux on 24 April 1918 that the first tank-versus-tank battle took place. By this time the Germans had managed to collect together thirteen tanks (some of their own and some captured from the British and painted with black crosses) and on 23 April they launched an attack against the British and Australian troops confronting them as part of their drive against Amiens. On the following day the Allied force counter-attacked with the aid of tanks, and three British Mk IV tanks met three German A7V tanks. Shots were fired: two British tanks were holed but not stopped, and after receiving three hits one German tank stopped and its crew dispersed. The other two A7Vs drew off in reverse, shooting as they went, and the British turned to aid their own infantry. A German warplane then intervened and near-missed one Mk IV, which steered itself into a shell crater and stalled. The other two had retired, and the stalled tank eventually hauled itself out of its crater to find a mass of German infantry waiting with explosive charges and other forms of destruction. At that moment, the proverbial eleventh hour, what should appear but seven British Whippet light tanks, machine-guns blazing, to disperse the German reception party. A German tank then appeared and wrecked one Whippet before both parties separated and the action died away.

In the aftermath of the war, British and French tanks were sent to Russia to aid the White Russian forces in their fight against Bolshevism, and after the Allied troops left Russia and the White Russians were gradually defeated, some of these tanks fell into Soviet hands. No tank battles had taken place, because the Soviets never had any tanks, but the ability of these vehicles to act as a 'force multiplier' for the White Russians made it plain to the Soviets that the tank was going to be a significant weapon, and that they should put their minds to its development.

A handful of light tanks saw action in the Gran Chaco War (1932–35) between Bolivia and Paraguay in the early 1930s. In 1933 a scratch collection of British light tanks in Bolivian hands attempted to support infantry operations, but on each occasion they discovered that light tanks in jungle were easy meat for short-range artillery and armour-piercing bullets from machine-guns, and the development of armoured fighting was scarcely affected by their activities.

More serious was the invasion of Abyssinia by the Italians in 1935, in which light tanks were extensively used to overawe the unsophisticated Abyssinian soldiery, though the Abyssinian soldiers soon became adept at shooting into the vision slits of the tanks. The outcome of the war was always a foregone conclusion, but it was a good deal more expensive than the Italians had bargained for.

Finally, as the curtain-raiser for what would become the Second World War, in 1936 the Spanish Civil War broke out, and the backers of both sides furnished them with tanks. The USSR sent over 700 T-26 and BT-1 light tanks to aid the Republicans, while Italy and Germany provided about the same number of PzKpfw I light tanks and Fiat CV-33 tankettes to the Nationalists. Though all of these vehicles were categorized as 'light', the Soviet tanks were somewhat less light than their German and Italian opponents, and carried respectable armament in the form of 37mm and 45mm guns, whereas the German and Italian tanks were less well armoured and carried nothing more than machine-guns. The tactical views of the two sides were also at variance: the Republicans, guided by their

Soviet 'adviser' General Pavlov, grouped their tanks into brigades, hoping to use them as an independent arm, but lack of training, lack of officers and virtual absence of communications meant that they had to be kept fairly close to the rest of the army. To make things worse the commanders were of the opinion that they could win battles by themselves and paid little attention to what the infantry and artillery were doing.

On the Nationalist side the chief 'adviser' was General von Thoma of the German army, a man who understood tanks as much as anyone did in those days, and who possessed a keen appreciation of their limitations. Von Thoma therefore kept them solely as close support for the infantry and avoided any grandiose theories of manoeuvre.

As a result of these two methods of employment, there were no major tank clashes during the Spanish Civil War, merely a number of minor skirmishes between handfuls of tanks, skirmishes which were usually settled by the intervention of anti-tank or field artillery on one side or the other. The two 'advisers' thus returned home in 1939 bearing different messages. Pavlov reported that independent action by tanks was out of the question and that the dreams of tank divisions and armies sweeping all before them were nonsense: according to Pavlov, therefore, the tank had to be operated at the most basic level and as a result, the Soviet army dismantled all its tank formations and parcelled out its several thousand tanks to infantry battalions as direct support weapons. This, coupled with the result of the Stalin purges in 1936–38, meant that any expertise in tank handling was lost, and the price for this had to be met in full during 1941.

Von Thoma went back and pointed out that the light tank was useless on the modern battlefield, that the anti-tank gun was virtually the master of the field, and that only heavily armoured tanks had any chance of surviving. This point of view was also accepted by most military observers, but as usual the realities of money supply ensured that light tanks were not removed from the inventory, and that not much effort was put into the provision of anti-tank guns or more heavily protected tanks.

And yet, on the eve of the Second World War came a major tank battle which went virtually unnoticed and which showed precisely how armour would eventually be employed.

The border between Japanese-occupied Manchuria and Soviet-dominated Outer Mongolia was defined by the Khalkin river in part and by an arbitrary boundary line in the remainder. In one particular spot there was a considerable difference between the line of the river and the boundary line in favour of Mongolia. In the early summer of 1939 the Japanese army, always keen to test the mettle of any potential enemy, decided to push the border down to the river, some 13 or 16km (8 or 10 miles) farther west, over a salient about 50km (31 miles) long. There was nothing new in this: both sides played the game in turn, and it was accepted that if one side tried it on and the other made a minor display of strength, the first retired gracefully, honours even, to await the attempt of the other side.

This time the Japanese did not retire gracefully but

pushed harder. Both sides began feeding in reinforcements and the affair began to escalate alarmingly. By early July the Japanese had in the field some 40,000 troops with 135 tanks and 225 aircraft, while the Soviets had about 12,500 troops, 185 tanks, 225 armoured cars and generous air support. Command of this force was now given to a little-known General Georgii Zhukov. This able officer confined his actions to repulsing the Japanese wherever they pushed, but each reverse suffered by the Japanese merely spurred them to greater efforts next time, until by August they had 80,000 men, 180 tanks, 300 armoured cars, three regiments of artillery and 450 aircraft involved in this 'border incident'.

Zhukov decided that there would be no end to this nonsense until the Japanese were taught a lesson even they could not ignore. He requested reinforcements, and on 20 August 1939 he fielded 35 infantry divisions, 20 squadrons of horse cavalry, 500 pieces of artillery, 500 tanks, 350 armoured cars and 600 aircraft. An air attack, followed by a two-hour artillery bombardment, opened the attack and the Soviet infantry marched into battle accompanied by tanks in the accepted manner. Zhukov now showed what could be done with armour, however, for despite the 'lessons' brought home from Spain by Pavlov, Zhukov sent two independent tank brigades around the flanks of the battle. They were accompanied by motorized artillery and truck-borne infantry, moved wide of the battlefield, drove into Manchuria, turned inwards and met at the village of Nomonhan to fall on the rear of the Japanese position.

The entire Japanese 6th Field Army was surrounded,

and Zhukov now set about exterminating it. With a ring of armour to keep in the victims and to keep out any possible reinforcements, the Soviets launched a systematic series of attacks by air and artillery, after which the armoured ring would move in and tighten, then pause for another round of bombardment, then another tightening move, and so on. As the circle shrank, so the Japanese were either killed or taken prisoner and shipped off to oblivion in Siberia. By 31 August over 50,000 Japanese had been killed or captured, and only about 10,000 Japanese troops managed to escape. It was the worst defeat yet suffered by the Japanese, and it went largely unnoticed: in the first place the Japanese were scarcely likely to announce such a defeat; in the second place the Soviets, being secretive by nature, were unwilling to announce such a sweeping victory and thus alert their potential enemies; and in the third place, while the Japanese were being annihilated the German army had struck across the Polish border and the eyes of the world were far away from the Manchurian theatre of operations.

Tactics aside, what had now become clear was that the outcome of tank battles was decided by the armament and armour of the combatant tanks. At Nomonhan the Soviets had fielded their latest BT-5 and BT-7 medium tanks armed with 45mm guns and armour up to 22mm thick. The Japanese used the Type 95 Light Tank with a 37mm gun and 12mm of armour, together with a handful of Type 97 Medium Tanks with a 57mm gun and 25mm of armour. On paper the Type 97 could see off anything the Soviets possessed, but there were not enough of them to make any impression; the light tanks were shot to pieces.

The rest of the world was arming its tanks in the same way: design the tank first and then see what sort of gun you could get into the turret, and this led to a generation of seriously under-gunned armour. Since it was uncommon to know what the other side was doing, the only criterion that could be applied was to look at one's own tanks, assume the enemy to have something similar, and settle for a gun good enough to penetrate one's own armour in the hope that the armour of the enemy's tanks would be no thicker. Moreover, finance demanded a degree of rationalization. If tanks and anti-tank guns were supposed to shoot at the same targets, then the two could be the same and save the expense of making a special gun for the tank. This, of course, placed a handicap on the anti-tank gun: instead of being as big as the gunners could manage to push around the battlefield, it was only as big as could be fitted into the turret of the contemporary tank, and that usually meant a good deal smaller than the gunners would have liked.

Between the world wars, British tanks were produced by Vickers and were armed with Vickers' own 3-pounder gun of 47mm calibre. The next generation of tanks, developed under War Office sponsorship in the rearmament period, were given the 2-pounder gun of 40mm calibre: this was a drop in size but a step-up in performance, since the 2-pounder gun had a higher velocity and better armour-piercing capability, dealing with 51mm of armour at a range of 915m (1,000 yards). The prime reason, though, was that the 2-pounder was the new anti-tank gun, so that there was a common supply of both guns and ammunition. The drawback was that the 2-pounder was simply an anti-tank gun, and as such was useless for anything else since it was never provided with an explosive shell. One was designed, but for reasons never really explained it was never put into general issue, and both tank and anti-tank shooting was done entirely with solid shot. So the tank was well able to fight other tanks, but had nothing other than a machine-gun with which to assist the infantry.

To solve this, though, the British earmarked a proportion of their tanks as 'close support tanks' and armed them with a 3.7in (94mm) mortar: this was generally the same as the 3.7in (94mm) mountain howitzer except that the barrel was in one piece and the breech mechanism was the same as that of the old 3-pounder gun so as to simplify training. This weapon had useful high-explosive and smoke shells, so that it could do whatever the infantry wanted in the way of removing obstacles or concealing their movement. If it encountered an enemy tank then there would no doubt have been an interesting confrontation, because a well-directed 3.7in (94mm) high-explosive shell would have ruined most tanks of the 1930s. This, at least, was the situation if the British tank got in its 3.7in (94mm) shot first, since the tank would have suffered from the anti-tank projectiles fired by the opposition.

Germany looked at things in much the same way. At the outbreak of war they had four basic tanks; the PzKpfw I, II, III and IV. The PzKpfw I was the light tank which had gone to war in Spain and which even the most rabid Panzer enthusiast now admitted was worthless, but it made up the numbers: it was armed with two 7.92mm (0.312in) machine-guns. PzKpfw II was considerably better and carried a 20mm gun. The PzKpfw III began with a 37mm gun but by the outbreak of war had a 50mm weapon. And the PzKpfw IV was the close support tank and carried a short 75mm (2.95in) gun. But the roles of these tanks were not so clear-cut as in the British army, since all three of the guns could fire a mixture of ammunition, armour-piercing or explosive, though the 75mm (2.95in) AP shell was more use against fortification than it was against tanks because of the low velocity of the short-barrel gun.

France had some peculiar ideas about the employment of tanks and their armament reflected this. The light tanks carried either the 25mm Hotchkiss anti-tank gun (also used on wheels as an anti-tank gun), or a 37mm gun specially designed for tanks, or the 47mm anti-tank gun that was another weapon removed from its wheeled mount to go into tank turrets. The heavy tanks also carried the 47mm gun in their turrets, but backed this up with a 75mm (2.95in) gun, a shortened version of the universal French field gun, in the front of the hull so that they were well provided either to fight other tanks or support the infantry. The light tanks were more or less considered as the replacement for cavalry: reconnaissance and pursuit of a beaten foe were their tasks, and the anti-tank armament they carried was appropriate for this role. The heavy tanks were officially designated 'infantry' tanks, and their role was simply to replay 1918 all over again, lumbering forward with the infantry, crushing the wire, sweeping the trenches and hammering the machine-gun posts: in this capacity the French heavy tanks can be regarded as the right tanks for the wrong war.

The USA had gone the same way as Britain. The

Americans had adopted an anti-tank gun and then used it to arm their tanks. The gun was a useful 37mm based on the Rheinmetall 1936 German pattern, and Rock Island Arsenal adapted it to the turret of the Medium Tank T5, which later became the Medium Tank M2. Production of the M2 began in August 1939, and, as might be imagined, the progress of the war (and particularly of the German armoured forces) in Poland and later in France and the Low Countries, was watched very carefully by those people in the US Army who were concerned with tanks. By the summer of 1940 they had reached the conclusion that a tank armed only with a 37mm gun was a liability. In August 1940, therefore, when a meeting was held to plan a new medium tank, a 75mm (2.95in) gun was demanded as the primary armament. But since little or no research had been done on mounting a gun of this size in a turret, it was decided to adopt an idea which had been tried some years before, that of putting the gun into a 'sponson' or half-turret on the right side of the hull. (In fact this was almost a reversion to the original tank armament of 1916, but instead of sticking out of the side like a bay window, it was blended into the front corner of the hull.)

This became the Medium Tank M3 General Grant (or General Lee to the British – there was a slight difference), and served valiantly in the Western Desert with the British and in North Africa in American hands. It still carried the 37mm gun in its turret, so that it had a 'pure' anti-tank gun, but the 75mm (2.95in) in the sponson was a versatile weapon which fired a 6.35kg (14lb) high-explosive shell or an AP shell or AP shot of similar weight: all of these were effective against tanks, and the HE shell, of course, was useful for supporting infantry or standing off and dealing with anti-tank guns while still out of their effective range. The drawback to all this was that in order to get the 75mm (2.95in) gun into action it was necessary to expose a large part of the tank. A favourite tank tactic is to drive up behind a rise in the ground until the turret is just clearing the crest, and then open fire. The bulk of the tank is thus concealed from the enemy's fire and the exposed turret is difficult to locate, provided the tank commander chooses his spot with some discretion. But heaving the larger part of the Medium Tank M3 over the crest in order to be able to bring the hull-mounted 75mm (2.95in) gun to bear was a proceeding fraught with danger, especially against an enemy as astute as the Germans proved themselves to be.

This, of course, had been foreseen. Even as the details of the M3 were being worked out, the designers were already applying their mind to the turret-mounted 75mm (2.95in) gun which would be the next tank, the Medium Tank M4 or General Sherman. This took rather more work than might be thought: there is more to putting a gun into a turret than boring a hole in the front. The gun has to balance so that it takes equal effort to elevate or depress, rather than having to heave and strain to elevate and then have the gun run away in depressing. This may mean having a lot of the gun inside the turret or having to design and fit some sort of spring compensation apparatus. The turret must also be in balance so that when rotating there is no unequal load on one side of the roller race on which it runs. Moreover, it must continue to balance even if the tank is tilted to one side, as it might be on the side of a hill, so that the effort of traversing 'uphill' is not excessive.

After all that is done, there still has to be room inside the turret for the gunner and the commander (and perhaps a loader as well) plus some ammunition, and a radio or perhaps two, and a machine-gun, and so on and on. So designing a turret is no longer quite such an easy task as the layman might imagine.

However, all these things were attended to, and the American designers also threw in something they considered entirely new and entirely attractive in the form of a stabilizing device.

There are (or were) two schools of thought on the matter of firing the main gun of a tank. The first school, to which the British have always adhered, is that one should shoot whenever the opportunity presents itself, whether the tank is moving or still. This, one supposes, stems from naval gunnery, and demanded considerable skill from the gunner to judge the interlinked movements of tank and target and fire at precisely the right moment so that shot and target coincided in time and space. The second school, to which various nations subscribed, was to stop the tank to make the shot, giving the gunner a better chance and, as a by-product, demanding rather less skill. The principal problem facing the shoot-on-the-move school was that of keeping the gun at the correct quadrant elevation (that is, the elevation demanded by the range and which referred to the ground as a horizontal plane) while the tank pitched and yawed as it moved across country. If the tank nosed down into a ditch, then the gunner had rapidly to elevate his gun; if it clambered across a rise, then he had to depress it.

A stabilizer is a device which cuts out this constant

hunting: once brought into operation, it keeps the gun barrel at the same quadrant elevation irrespective of what the tank does beneath it. For example, if the tank on level ground needs an elevation of 10° to hit the target but then dives 5° down into a ditch, the stabilizer will automatically elevate the gun by 5° so that the angle relative to the level is maintained. This device, stabilizing in elevation, was the innovation now added to the 75mm (2.95in) gun on the Medium Tank M4. It would be nice to be able to record a marked improvement in tank gunnery thereafter, but the bitter truth is that the device never worked as well as it was intended to, and it was invariably disconnected and ignored by the crews. It was to be another twenty years or so before stabilization became a working reality.

It is worth recording that, entirely independently, Soviet designers were working on precisely the same thing at the same time. In 1940–41 the T-34 tank, destined to be revolutionary in many aspects, was under development and elevation stabilization was among the innovations promised. But the Soviets had no more luck than the Americans, for while the idea was sound enough the required technology lagged far behind.

However, if they failed to stabilize their gun, the Soviets compensated for this minor setback by at least recognizing that it was size of gun that was all-important, and instead of making (as did most other European designers) a series of small steps in calibre, they took the plunge in the T-34 and moved directly from 45mm to 76.2mm (3in), mounting what appears to have been a shortened version of a 1931-vintage anti-aircraft gun. Provided with an AP shell, and later with tungsten-cored arrowhead shot, this proved a formidable weapon and it was instrumental in driving other designers to face the realities of tank fighting and begin to mount heavier weapons.

The UK, having gambled on the 2-pounder gun, was paying the price in North Africa by this time. Provided it could get close to a German tank, then a British tank stood a reasonable chance of doing some damage. But in the desert wastes it was a skilful tank commander who could get close, and in the majority of cases the German tanks armed with the 50mm gun could stay out of the lethal range of the 2-pounder shot and proceed to bombard the British tanks with high-explosive shells, which were sufficient to do some damage to the British armour of the period, even if it did not completely wreck the tank. (There are those who argue that non-fatal damage to a tank is more effective than totally destroying it, in the same way that wounding rather than killing a soldier is in many ways more effective in purely military terms: the wounded man or damaged tank takes up a disproportionate amount of manpower and logistic effort to backload and repair.)

In order, therefore, to decimate the British armoured strength, the Germans resorted to a simple tactical trick, which one cannot help but suspect was based on a shrewd psychological assessment of their opponents. German tanks would appear in the desert and thus attract the attention of their British opposite numbers, which would sally forth in pursuit. The Germans would stage a fighting withdrawal, the British would charge after them, and then the German anti-tank gun ambush would open fire and that would be the end of the action. Again, the limited capability of the 2-pounder gun meant that the British tanks could not do anything effective about the German guns; they had no high explosive, their shot was barely effective at the range at which a ground gun could engage, and their machine-guns were useless.

A replacement for the 2-pounder was available in the form of the 6-pounder gun of 57mm calibre, which had already appeared as a towed anti-tank gun. But it was impossible to shoehorn this into a turret designed around the 2-pounder: all the problems mentioned above, of balance and space, were too great to be solved. The 6-pounder gun had to wait until fresh designs of tank were made with wider turrets, and all this took place after the Americans and Soviets had shown that nothing less than a 75mm (2.95in) calibre was worth considering in future designs.

The Germans had also seen this particular point, and their later PzKpfw III and IV tanks were being equipped with 75mm (2.95in) guns: the PzKpfw III got a short-barrel gun and replaced the PzKpfw IV as the 'close support' tank, while the PzKpfw IV was given a longer 43-calibre 75mm (2.95in) gun which gave ample velocity to piercing projectiles and thus became the principal German fighting tank for the rest of the war. In addition, the shaped charge was now a practical if not perfected proposition, and this was also being provided for most tank, anti-tank and field guns in German service.

The appearance of the Soviet T-34 tank, with its wide tracks, sloped armour, powerful engine and 76.2mm (3in) gun, gave the Germans a terrible shock, and the heavier KV-1 with the same gun and up to 75mm of armour gave them an even worse one. General von Manstein's LVI

Corps reported that a large and impervious tank of unknown design had suddenly appeared across its supply route and for two days had defied every German attempt to drive it off, knocking out any gun or tank which came near it. It required a major diversionary manoeuvre by the Germans to lure it away and into an ambush where a battery of 88mm (3.465in) guns was waiting for it. This was their introduction to the KV-1.

At almost the same time the 17th Panzer Division reported on a low-slung fast tank of new design which appeared out of the bushes alongside the Dnieper river and charged straight into the German lines, shot bouncing off its sloped armour. It flattened an anti-tank gun beneath its tracks, destroyed two PzKpfw III tanks in casual manner and carried on in similar vein for about 15km (9 miles) before it was stopped by a shot into the engine compartment from a 105mm (4.13in) field howitzer it had inadvertently overlooked. That was the Germans' introduction to the T-34.

The German response was firstly to up-gun the PzKpfw IV yet again, to a longer 75mm (2.95in) 48-calibre gun (48 × 75mm = 3.60 metres, a convenient way of expressing the length of the gun). All things being equal, a longer barrel gives greater velocity as it allows more time for the propulsive gases to work on the projectile, so the longer gun improved penetrative power. The second step was to develop two new tanks, the Panther and the Tiger, and, into the bargain, make sure they were big enough to take some useful armament. The Panther received an even longer 75mm (2.95in) 70-calibre gun, while the Tiger was fitted with the formidable 88mm (3.465in) 56-calibre gun.

Both these tanks could now take on their heaviest Soviet opponents with confidence.

The Allies, on the other hand, appeared now to be locked into the 75mm (2.95in) calibre bracket due to their design policies. Although the Americans had developed a heavy tank (the M6) mounting a 3in (76.2mm) gun in 1941–42, their Armored Board had decided that there was no requirement for such a vehicle and stopped production after only forty had been made. Their arguments, which were persuasive, were that one M6 took up as much shipping space as two or three M4 mediums; that periodic modification would keep the M4 comparable with enemy developments; and that having only one main battle tank, in the form of the M4, meant simplification of the supply lines. So the heavy tank was dead so far as the US Army was concerned, and the Sherman would win the war. As an up-gunning measure it was proposed to put the 3in (76.2mm) gun from the M6 into the Sherman, but it simply would not fit, and therefore a new gun was designed, called the 76mm T1. It was lighter than the 3in (76.2mm) weapon, fired the same projectiles from a smaller cartridge, but nevertheless achieved the same muzzle velocity. When installed into the turret, however, the new gun was found to be unbalanced and to correct this 381mm (15in) had to be cut off the muzzle and the propellant charge redeveloped in order to regain the velocity lost with the shortening of the barrel. Twelve tanks were built, but after testing the Armored Board rejected them and told the Ordnance Department to think of a fresh design. A year had been wasted.

In 1943 the British fielded the Cromwell tank with the 6-pounder gun, and an improved version of the Churchill also with the 6-pounder gun, by which time the anti-tank gunners had the 17-pounder gun of 76.2mm (3in) calibre, so the tanks were lagging behind the anti-tank artillery. By this time too the tank soldiers had gained some experience with the American 75mm (2.95in) gun on the Lee and Sherman tanks, liked what they saw, and thought the 6-pounder less effective. So the British set about designing a similar weapon. This was of 75mm (2.95in) calibre but with similar external dimensions to the 6-pounder gun so that it could fit into turrets designed for the smaller weapon; the new gun was also chambered to fire the American ammunition and gave the same performance as the American gun. In late 1943 this was installed into Churchill and Cromwell tanks instead of the 6-pounder gun, which now declined in importance.

Vickers, which had foreseen the need to improve on the 6-pounder gun, had privately developed a 75mm (2.95in) high-velocity gun which it now offered to the army, but the army felt that a better idea would be to make it in 76.2mm (3in) calibre and thus be able to fire 17-pounder projectiles, albeit with a smaller cartridge case. The conversion was done, the result being called the 77mm (3.03in) gun even though it was of 76.2mm (3in) calibre, the difference in nomenclature being introduced merely to distinguish it from other weapons of the same calibre, and while it improved on the 75mm (2.95in) performance, it fell short of that of the 17-pounder. Moreover, it was not interchangeable with the 6-pounder/75mm (2.95in) family, and new turrets would therefore have to be designed and built. Indeed, a whole new tank had to be built since the new turret demanded a wider turret ring in the hull, and this led to the Comet tank. This, so far as the troops were concerned, was the first British tank which was both mechanically reliable and had something like equal gun strength to its German opponents, though this was only true of the PzKpfw IV; the Comet was sadly lacking when confronted with a Panther or Tiger. For the most part the British used the Sherman, as did the Americans, and thus they were under the same constraints.

Development, though, does not always move on the pre-ordained lines, for on occasion people get an idea and pursue it in the teeth of official opposition. The British tank troops felt that the 17-pounder gun might be a more effective weapon in the turret of the Sherman tank than the standard 75 or 76.2mm (2.95 or 3in) guns. The Ministry of Supply Tank Division rejected the idea as impossible, but the soldiers got the ear of the Director-General of Artillery, who directed his staff at Woolwich Arsenal to see if it was possible. It was, and on New Year's Day 1944 the first conversion was completed as the precursor of the Sherman 'Firefly' series. The Americans were told of this, and were offered 17-pounder guns to make their own conversions. But by this time the Armored Board was chasing a fresh hare and asking for the US 90mm (3.54in) anti-aircraft gun to be installed in the Sherman turret. The Ordnance Department pointed out that this would be too heavy, would protrude so far into the turret as to prevent it being used, and would totally unbalance the turret structure. The UK again pressed the 17-pounder conversion on them, offering 200 guns, but got no reply. The 76.2mm (3in) gun ruled the day in the minds of the Americans, and the Sherman would win the war.

Between 1920 and 1939 many theorists had expounded their views on the future of tank warfare, and one common theme was of fleets of tanks manoeuvring against each other in all-tank battles, rather like fleets of ships manoeuvring around the ocean. This theme tended to ignore the facts of geography: there are few places on the face of the Earth where great fleets of tanks can operate without getting themselves involved with towns, villages, canals, railways and other mundane obstacles. The North African desert was one such area, but the fleets which assembled there were relatively small: in spite of its strategic significance, the campaign here was strictly a side-show, and neither side put really large forces into it.

The steppes of Russia were another unobstructed area and here, moreover, were the two prime contenders facing each other with their main armies. This, surely, was the place for the fleet engagements. And so it was, but it took time for the fleets to emerge. In the initial German invasion of 1941 and subsequent operations into 1942 the Panzers, except for the occasional setback, had things much their own way. In the summer of 1941 Soviet tank organization was effectively non-existent. Due to the ill-digested lessons from Spain, Soviet tank strength had been frittered away in penny packets distributed down to infantry companies and there was no cohesive command organization capable of assembling a large tank force and wielding it as a single instrument. Thus the German armour, with superior command organization, was able to carve its way through the Soviets and defeat them piecemeal. Moreover, the greater part of the Soviet tank force in 1941 was obsolete or, if not obsolete, sufficiently obsolescent to be incapable of offering much resistance to the PzKpfw III and IV and the highly effective German anti-tank organization.

The T-34 and KV-1 tanks had been designed and proven, and were entering large-scale production, but the speed of the German advance overran most of the established tank factories. The machinery was removed as the Germans approached and shipped far enough east to be out of danger; there it was reconstituted into enormous tank arsenals which set to work to produce T-34 and KV-1 until somebody told them to stop. All this took time, however, and production was not properly under way until early in 1942. Crews had to be trained, regiments and divisions had to be organized, staff had to be found and trained, and all the while the Soviet army was standing-off the Germans to allow the build-up of the armoured force.

By 1943 this build-up had reached the point where some worthwhile numbers of moderately competent armoured units could be put into the field, and the Soviets looked around for some suitable place to challenge the Panzers.

The Germans were also looking for somewhere to make an impression on the Soviets, and both sides looked at the map and saw the same thing: a fat salient bulging out of the Soviet lines around Kursk. 'There', said the Germans, 'is where we will attack the neck of the salient from two sides, pinch it off and surround and crush the Soviets.' 'There', said the Soviets, 'is where the Germans are bound to mount a pincer attack, and we shall stuff the salient with tanks and anti-tank guns and annihilate them.' Thus it happened that the tank fleets would finally meet.

The German attack was originally planned for May, but was postponed twice in order to build up the tank strength.

Eventually, on 5 July 1943, with about 2,400 tanks and assault guns between them, two German armies struck simultaneously from north and south against the base of the salient. Awaiting them were 20,000 Soviet guns and 3,300 tanks. Despite initial heavy losses, the German 9th Army managed to preserve its northern half of the offensive until it was brought to a standstill by a defensive line about 15km (9 miles) into the salient. On the southern side the 4th Panzer Army broke into the salient and advanced about 10km (6 miles) before being brought up against another defensive line in which several hundred tanks had been driven into pits so that only their turrets showed above the ground. It made nonsense of the mobility of armour, but it proved an impenetrable barrier and the Panzers moved away, towards the village of Prokhorovka. This caught the Soviets on the wrong foot, and the Panzers made a spectacular advance, taking 24,000 prisoners, 1,800 tanks and 1,200 guns in a very short time. Faced with this near-disaster, the Soviets threw in their reserve, the 5th Guards Army and the 5th Tank Army, and on 12 July this massive force swept into the Prokhorovka district to do battle with the Panzers. Estimates vary, but it is generally agreed that about 1,500 tanks met head-on that day, to produce the greatest tank battle the world had so far seen. Across the open steppe, in clouds of dust and smoke, the two forces charged each other like medieval knights. To start with, some order could be seen as the Soviet attack sliced across the flank of the Panzer force, but within minutes all order had vanished as tanks began to select targets and manoeuvre against them; tanks roared back and forth firing at whatever enemy presented itself, crashing into each other, independent of their companions or higher command. The dust and smoke which rapidly arose prevented commanders from seeing how the battle was developing and it became a 'soldier's battle' in which individual tank commanders fought as best they could. In such conditions the better training and experience of the German Panzer troops gave them a degree of superiority which balanced the greater numbers of the Soviet force and the battle dragged on until dusk, after which both sides fell back to recuperate and count the cost.

That cost, though, is something we shall never know. The Soviets claimed to have destroyed 300 Panzers, but are silent about their own losses. German figures for the whole operation do not give a specific figure for the action at Prokhorovka. But whatever the figures, the conclusion remains that the Soviets, with their massive production and manpower pool, could afford them, while the Germans could not. On 1 July the Germans mustered 2,269 tanks and 997 assault guns on the Eastern Front. Their overall losses in the Kursk salient were 1,217 tanks and 350 assault guns: in other words the Kursk operation had cost the Germans 53 per cent of their tanks and 35 per cent of their assault guns. It marked the end of German encroachment into Soviet territory. On 10 July the Allies had landed in Sicily and Hitler called off the operation in order to reinforce Italy, and on 12 July, even as the battle raged around Prokhorovka, the Soviets launched the first of a series of counter-attacks. Germany had failed to recapture the strategic initiative on the Eastern Front, and for the rest of the war it was the Soviets who were in the driving seat.

The Soviet reaction to the events at Kursk was realization that the Panther and Tiger had the measure of the T-34 and KV-1, that the standard Soviet 76.2mm (3in) gun was now outclassed by the German 75mm (2.95in) and 88mm (3.465in) weapons, and that the armour thickness and disposition on the new German tanks had made them more difficult targets. A new turret had already been under consideration for the KV-1, mounting an 85mm (3.45in) anti-aircraft gun in much the same manner as the Germans had converted their 88mm (3.465in) anti-aircraft gun into a tank weapon. This 85mm (3.45in) weapon could defeat 100mm of armour at a range of 1,000m (1,095 yards) with a simple piercing shell, and the Soviets now copied the German tungsten-cored arrowhead shot and endowed the new tank gun with the ability to defeat 130mm of armour at a range of 1,000m (1,095 yards). As the Germans now had to abandon the use of tungsten in ammunition, moreover, the balance was more or less restored.

Now, in the wake of Kursk, the modification of the KV-1 was put into effect, and the T-34 was now modified to take the same turret and gun to form the T-34/85 tank. Armour was increased to 110mm on the front of the hull and 90mm on the turret; the larger turret allowed a three-man crew (commander, gunner and loader) leaving the commander to command rather than part-command and part-load the gun. And after getting all that under way in the factories, so that issues could commence in January 1944, the designers turned to think about the replacement for the KV-1.

By the summer of 1944 British tanks armed with the 6-pounder gun were issued with tungsten-cored APDS ammunition, which gave their elderly gun a new lease of life; similar ammunition was also to become available for the 17-pounder guns in the modified Sherman tanks, now known by the British as the 'Firefly'. Both Americans and British had their Shermans with 75mm (2.95in) or 76.2mm (3in) guns. The former was by this time rather dated – it was, after all, based on a design which originated in 1897 – but the 76.2mm (3in) gun was universally respected – or at least until it came to be used in anger.

On 6 June 1944 the Allies invaded Normandy and soon afterwards came face to face with the Panzers in Operation 'Goodwood', the British break-out from Caen. In simple terms the Allied strategy was to draw the major German armoured strength northward to Caen to facilitate the break-out of the Americans from the south of the beach-head to make a sweeping movement round the rear of the Germans and aim for Paris. The Germans were less than obliging about this plan, failing to be drawn northwards, and therefore a major British advance had to be made in order to force the Germans to react. The British 2nd Army therefore advanced southward from Caen, and the result was probably a tank battle more intense than that at Kursk, some 1,800 tanks engaging in a mêlée inside an area some 8km (5 miles) square. After the initial clash, further tanks were fed into the battle until seven Panzer divisions were embroiled. After three days of fighting the British had lost 300 tanks, while the Panzers had lost 60. As with Kursk, however, the real cost lay not in the relative numbers of tanks lost but in the ability of each side to replace its losses. By now the British had an excellent battlefield salvage system running and, for example, of 126 tanks of the 11th Armoured Division which had been immobilized, only 40 could not be repaired. The Germans, on the other hand, lost the field and their losses, repairable or not, were completely rather than temporarily lost.

Normandy was the scene of one of the most remarkable tank against tank battles ever fought, the one-tank crusade of Obersturmbannführer (SS Captain) Michael Wittmann. Wittmann had enlisted in 1934 and transferred to the Waffen SS in 1936. He began the war as an armoured car commander in Poland, served in Greece with an assault gun unit, then took part in the invasion of the USSR as an assault gun commander, winning the Iron Cross. After retraining on Tiger tanks, he commanded one during the Battle of Kursk and there, in one day, knocked out 30 T-34 tanks and 28 anti-tank guns. By December 1943 he had destroyed 60 tanks, and within a month increased that to 88 and gained the Knight's Cross of the Iron Cross. After more successes he took over command of his tank company and took it to Belgium as part of the 1st SS Panzer Division 'Leibstandarte SS Adolf Hitler'.

On 13 June 1944 the British 7th Armoured Division began an outflanking sweep which, if it worked, would prise the Germans loose from Caen. Soon after dawn the advance guard of the 4th County of London Yeomanry, 22nd Armoured Brigade, passed through Villers-Bocage and then halted on a road, well closed up nose to tail, to allow another unit to pass them and take up the lead. Sitting on a hill overlooking this scene was Wittmann in his Tiger. With no further ado, Wittmann burst from cover and swept the length of the column. His first shot blew a half-track across the road, preventing any further manoeuvres, after which Wittmann simply destroyed every vehicle in the British line, his tank apparently impervious to what little return fire there was, before turning off and vanishing back into the undergrowth. In five minutes of accurate shooting he had added 25 to his score and completely ruined the plans of 7th Armoured Division.

Wittmann was awarded the Swords to his Knight's Cross and promoted before the day was out. He was also offered an instructor's post at the tank school but declined. He was killed on 8 August 1944 when he met a 'Firefly'. His score at the time of his death is uncertain, but was over 140 tanks and roughly the same number of anti-tank guns, the highest score made by any tank commander in the war.

The biggest losses in the subsequent battles to break out of Normandy were largely due to anti-tank weapons, since the armour had to operate in very close country, the *bocage* area which was criss-crossed by embanked hedge-rows behind which Panzerfausts and anti-tank guns lurked and fired at ranges at which it was impossible to miss. By careful stalking it was possible for an Allied tank to get close to a German tank, close enough to kill with whatever gun it had, but by the same token it was a lot easier for a German tank to stalk and kill an Allied tank, simply because he did not have to get so close. Once the Allies broke through the *bocage* and out into the open meadow-lands beyond, things could only get worse for now the Panthers and Tigers could take up defensive positions hull-down and simply pick off the Cromwells and Shermans at ranges at which their 6-pounder and 75mm (2.95in) guns were harmless and the 76.2mm (3in) gun was outranged.

As reported in General Omar N. Bradley's *A Soldier's Story*, General Dwight D. Eisenhower, the Allied commander-in-chief, was furious. 'You mean our 76 won't knock those Panthers out? Why, I thought this was going to be the wonder gun of the war. Why is it that I am always the last to hear about this stuff? Ordnance told me this 76 would take care of anything the Germans had. Now I find you can't knock out a damn thing with it!' In real terms it meant that the Tiger could knock out a Sherman at a range of 3,500m (3,825 yards) while the Sherman had to get within 200m (220 yards) to do any damage to the Tiger with its 76.2mm (3in) gun, and with a 75mm (2.95in) gun would probably do no damage if he laid alongside the Tiger and fired.

What saved the day were two British vehicles which could take on the Tiger at its own choice of range and defeat it: one was the Archer self-propelled 17-pounder gun, and the other was the 'Firefly' conversion of the Sherman with the 17-pounder gun. At the start of the invasion the 'Fireflies' were few and far between, no more than 25 per cent of a British or Canadian armoured regiment, but production was rapid and eventually there were about 600 of them in action. The Americans now asked for them, but production was still insufficient to permit an official transfer, though many were unofficially loaned to American formations. An emergency palliative was the issue of tungsten-cored shot for the 76.2mm (3in) gun, and this improved its short and middle-range performance but did nothing to increase its reach against the Tiger. It was not until March 1945 that the US Army was able to withdraw 160 Shermans from battle and ship them back to England to be fitted with 17-pounder guns. By the time they were converted the war was over.

If the Germans were confident of gun superiority against the Allies in the West, they were far from being so confident in the East. By this time the Soviet designers had produced their replacement for the KV-1 in the form of the Iosif Stalin or IS-2, sometimes rendered Josef Stalin or JS-2. The basic KV-1 chassis had been thoroughly revamped, a new engine and transmission were fitted, and a new cast turret mounted the 85mm (3.45in) gun. This became the IS-1 and a small number was produced in the winter of 1943–44 for operational evaluation before the decision was made as whether or not to put the type into mass production. While this testing period was in progress, the designers thought again: they now saw little point in fielding a new heavy tank which carried the same gun as the medium T-34/85, so a second model was produced mounting a new 100mm (3.94in) gun. But still the designers strove, and in the spring of 1944 they got it right: they designed a completely new turret and managed to get a 122mm (4.8in) gun into it. This fired a massive 25kg (55.1lb) piercing shell which could penetrate 160mm of armour at a range of 1,000m (1,095 yards). Though this was less penetration than could be achieved with the 100mm (3.94in) gun firing tungsten-cored shot (180mm at 1,000m/1,095 yards) the target effect was infinitely greater; there is no comparison between a 25kg (55.1lb) shot arriving at speed and a 4.5kg (10lb) shot arriving at a somewhat higher speed. The heavy shot can literally lift a turret out of a tank when it strikes, whereas the lighter shot merely penetrates and makes a small hole. With this gun and turret combination replacing the earlier efforts, the Soviets arrived at the IS-2 that went into production during the early summer of 1944. The Panzers on the Eastern Front now discovered that the Soviets could destroy them at a range of 2,000m (2,185 yards), while the German shot was bouncing off the thicker Soviet cast and sloped armour.

In the postwar world the immediate Western reaction was to decimate its armoured forces, but this holiday lasted only a few years. With the outbreak of the Korean War (1950–53), in which tanks played a relatively small part, the West began to reconstruct its forces and the Cold War began in earnest. The development of tanks had never stopped, but it was now moved into a faster phase, although the actual progression was the same as it had always been, a continual improvement upon existing designs with very little real innovation. The Soviets had produced their IS-3 model as the war ended, a heavy tank which took the existing IS-2 and gave it sloped and rounded armour making it almost impervious to shot except at suicidally short ranges, and British and American designers simply took this as the standard to which they had to respond.

The UK made a quantum leap and developed a 183mm (7.2in) gun, but this was felt to be too much of a good thing and the Allies standardized on 105mm (4.13in) as their calibre, using APDS shot.

More unsettling, though, was the emergence of significant tank armies in the hands of smaller countries, some of whom were, to say the least, a trifle irresponsible in their international relations. The effect of this was seen in 1967 when, alarmed by a sudden build-up of Egyptian and Jordanian troops on their borders, the Israelis decided on a pre-emptive strike against Egypt and began the Six-Day War. The Egyptian army was well provided with Soviet T-54, T-55 and IS-3 tanks, all modern designs, while the Israelis had a mixed bag of 1,000 British Centurion, American M48 and French AMX-13 tanks. In addition the armies of Jordan and Syria added to the tank strength facing Israel. The Israeli strategy was to stand off the Jordanian and Syrian forces while launching a massive blow against the Egyptians, the most dangerous of their foes. By rapid manoeuvre they managed this difficult strategy, and by making the first move they got the initiative and retained it, harrying the Egyptian armoured forces all over the Sinai desert, never giving them time to assemble into major formations and using their superior training to engage and kill at ranges the Egyptian troops could not match. Within two days some 80 per cent of Egyptian armour was either wrecked or captured and the Egyptian army virtually immobilized.

The Israelis then turned on the Jordanians, who proved to be a rather more difficult target, but they eventually subdued them with the aid of superior air power. And finally came the turn of the Syrian army, which was emplaced on the Golan Heights. Here the action reverted to First World War standards, with the Israeli tanks punching holes in the defences and the infantry passing through. This led to a wholesale collapse of Syrian morale, and the war was over.

The Six-Day War might be said to be the last of the old-fashioned tank wars, because the 1960s brought the transistor and the electronic chip, and with them came all kinds of technical developments in fighting ability. Most of these were due to advances in sighting and computing technology. Hitherto the tank gunner took aim through an optical telescope, estimated the range or measured it by means of an optical rangefinder, applied the correct elevation, aimed off for movement by means of marks in the telescope crosswires, and fired. Now he received a ballistic computer which was programmed with the trajectory and velocity of the ammunition, was fed with wind speed, target movement, tank speed and similar factors, and produced an aim-off angle which, again, the gunner applied by using his telescope marks. This was an improvement but, as was showed by the tank battles between the Indian and Pakistani armies in 1965, manipulating this computer and feeding it with all the information took time, and a competent Indian gunner with an optical sight firing his Centurion's 20-pounder gun could often get a killing shot in before his Pakistani opponent in an American M47 tank had finished solving the ballistic equation.

The scientists moved rapidly. The speed at which new ideas reach fruition in computers is quite astonishing, and by the 1970s advanced fire-control systems were being developed in which a laser measured the range and continuously informed the computer, from which target speed and angle could be calculated; other sensors measured wind speed, ammunition temperature, tilt of the tank and other factors, and the computer reached an answer in a second or two. The sight was constructed with a projected aiming mark which the computer now moved in accordance with its calculations, and the gunner had merely to lay the gun until the repositioned aiming mark was again on the target, and then fire with a good assurance of gaining a first-round hit.

In order to make the most of the battlefield, night vision sights were developed. First came infrared searchlights mounted on the turret and used in conjunction with infrared telescopes in the sights. Then came image intensification, in which the existing light is electronically amplified some 20,000 times to produce a clear picture when the naked eye can see very little apart from the difference between ground and sky. Finally there emerged thermal imaging, in which the temperature difference between the target and its background is detected and converted into a video-like picture on a screen which is incorporated into the sight. The advantage of thermal imaging is that it permits observation when there is absolutely no light whatever, and it is also useful during the daytime for 'seeing' a hot target hidden behind bushes or camouflage.

Little of this, however, was available at the start of the Vietnam War, which involved the USA between 1961 and 1973, and ended with the conquest of South Vietnam by the communist forces of North Vietnam in 1975. Here the Americans fielded tanks against the North Vietnamese forces in small numbers at first, because the North Vietnamese were not using armour and Vietnam is not 'tank country', being largely jungle or swamp, or so it was believed. Studies eventually showed that this was not quite the case and that armour could be used in most of the country for most of the time. With no tank opposition, however, armour was confined to its infantry support role.

The next major tank combat came when the Egyptian

and Syrian armies managed to co-ordinate their action when they launched simultaneous attacks on Israel in October 1973 to start the Yom Kippur War. Syria and Egypt attacked from the north and south-west respectively, thus preventing the Israelis from standing-off one enemy while dealing with the other. In addition, the two Arab states had trained their armoured forces thoroughly and were confident of their ability to dominate the field with a massive superiority of numbers. The Syrian attack, with 1,500 tanks, initially rolled back the Israelis but then began to falter in the face of stiffening Israeli resistance. Finally the Syrian attack came to a halt against an Israeli defensive line in front of the River Jordan, and thereafter the fighting on the northern battlefield became positional warfare, with the Syrians trying to force a hole in the line and the Israelis sitting tight and picking off the attackers one by one by superior gunnery.

What also caused a good deal of damage to the Israelis was the arrival on the battlefield of the anti-tank guided missile (see below), which added to the casualties suffered by the Israelis until they realized what they were up against and were able to devise countermeasures. In four days the defending Israelis, who knew the terrain like the backs of their hands, were able to kill over 500 Syrian tanks.

Meanwhile reinforcements had been pushed into the Israeli lines and they were then able to deliver a counter-attack which drove the Syrians back, decimating them as they went and, almost incidentally, putting to rout a combined Iraqi and Jordanian attempt at a flank attack. Total Arab losses on the northern front were in the order of 1,150 tanks against only about 250 Israeli tanks.

On the southern front the story was much the same. Initially the Egyptians gained a number of successes against the Israeli defensive line on the eastern side of the Suez Canal, throwing bridges over the canal and then passing more than 2,000 tanks over them with anti-tank missile teams roving the front. It all looked very bad and the Israelis were 'bounced' out of their initial defensive positions. The Egyptians were slow to exploit the initiative, however, and the Israelis found that by the use of smoke and audacious manoeuvre they could confuse the Egyptian armour and anti-tank teams. While a screen of tanks kept harrying each portion of the Egyptian attack, for the Egyptians were attacking in small groups in an unco-ordinated manner, Israeli reserves were assembling in ambush positions behind the immediate front. Eventually the Egyptians organized themselves and began a major attack, spread out in six columns. Since their routes were fairly well constrained by the terrain, they moved straight into the prepared ambushes, where the Israelis shot them to pieces at short range. Within a day the Egyptian advance had been disrupted and the Israelis in their turn went over to the offensive, chasing the Egyptians back to the Suez Canal and trapping and destroying them there.

The result of this destruction was that the Israelis were across the Suez Canal and the road to Cairo lay before them, virtually unguarded. A ceasefire was hurriedly arranged and the Yom Kippur War was over.

The most recent activity in this part of the world has been the so-called Gulf War (1991) in which a coalition of forces under United Nations overall control successfully evicted the Iraqi forces that had invaded and occupied

Kuwait late in 1990. In reality this was no contest so far as armour was concerned. It involved the three most highly trained and highly technical armies in the world in combat against a rag-tag of half-trained and often unwilling conscripts operating weapons they could barely understand. Had there been no political constraints the destruction of the Iraqi army would have been total, but it would scarcely have been a battle. As it was the destruction visited on the Iraqis was enormous, but it was a one-sided affair.

One thing it did do was act as a proving ground for the most recent developments in tank armament. In the late 1960s the Soviets had caused something of a furore in the West by revealing that their latest tank gun was a 115mm (4.53in) smooth-bore weapon firing fin-stabilized ammunition. In those days whatever the Soviets did was automatically what the West had to do, for such was the fear of the Soviet military machine that a Soviet example had always to be followed. Several experienced artillery voices pointed out that this was not necessarily so, and that there were a few drawbacks to smooth-bore, like loss of accuracy compared to rifled guns, but this was to no avail. Work began on smooth-bore guns. The advantage, besides the very practical one of not having to undertake the long and expensive process of rifling the gun, was that absence of rifling for the projectile's driving band to engage meant absence of a great deal of frictional resistance, so that a heavier charge could be used and a much higher velocity attained. And a higher muzzle velocity means a higher striking velocity. The fin-stabilized discarding sabot (APFSDS) projectile which appeared with the smooth-bore gun had a long tungsten or depleted uranium rod penetrator which, because of its density and length, had enormous momentum and thus enormous penetrative power at the velocities of about 1,400m (4,593ft) per second it could achieve.

All this took time: as the experts had said, a simple smooth-bore gun is not as simple as it looks, though it was many years before the West discovered that. In fact, the early Soviet smooth-bore guns had been something of a technical failure and they had to be withdrawn and partially rifled in order to give the projectile some spin before they could hit the target at which they were aimed. By that time enormous energy and sums of money had been directed at the smooth-bore problem and solutions had been found, so that by the middle 1980s 120mm (4.72in) smooth-bore guns were being mounted in the newest American and German tanks. The UK remained aloof: it retained the rifled gun because it offered a greater diversity of ammunition types (including HE, smoke, squash head, HEAT and APFSDS) than a smooth-bore gun which was restricted to firing only HEAT and APFSDS ammunition.

The Gulf War proved the APFSDS in combat, as it also proved other technologies such as reactive armour and composite armour. They were all found to work reasonably well, but fine-tuning was obviously required to perfect them, now that experience had been gained. On the whole, however, it seems that tank armament has now reached a plateau similar to that being felt in small arms: technology has reached a point where the necessary degree of destruction is virtually assured. Any further advance will only be achieved at an enormous cost in development, and there is a maxim that the final 10 per cent of performance represents 60 per cent of the weapon's development costs. So a question that has to be asked is whether or not one is prepared to pay a very large sum of money and devote a very large research and development effort to gain a very small improvement in killing power.

Only time will tell.

CHAPTER SIX

THE SMART WEAPONS

In spite of what its practitioners preach, gunnery is not an exact science because once the projectile has left the gun muzzle the gunner has no further control over it. Vagaries of wind, air pressure, temperature and muzzle velocity can all affect the flight of the projectile so that the precise point of impact may well differ from the intention of the gunner, and that is even supposing that the gunner estimated or measured his range correctly, set his sights correctly and took a careful aim. And it must be recognized that most of those desiderata tend to be skimped when the target is an aggressive tank coming in your direction.

With this in mind, with a number of successful rockets in existence, and with the first stirrings of methods of guiding rockets beginning to make themselves felt, it is scarcely surprising that in 1944 a German scientist began looking at the possibility of directing a rocket-propelled missile against a tank.

Without going too deeply into the German missile programme, suffice it to say that development of the X-4 wire-guided air-to-air missile was started by the Ruhrstahl company in mid-1943, and prototype missiles were flown successfully from September 1944. Early in 1944 the German army, desperately seeking methods of countering the growing Soviet tank strength, had sent out distress calls to several companies asking for ideas, and the Ruhrstahl firm decided to adapt some of the X-4 technology to a ground weapon. The result was the X-7, also called 'Rotkäppchen' ('Red Riding Hood'), with a streamlined body carrying a 2.5kg (5.51lb) shaped charge warhead and propelled by a two-stage rocket. The stubby body had two wings, at the ends of which were two pods from which fine wires were paid out during flight; the ends of these two wires were connected to the ground control unit, and electrical signals were transmitted along them to steer the missile during its flight. There was a peculiar tail-fin stabilizer on a boom swept down below the rocket blast, but flight control was done by pushing 'spoiler' fins out into the airflow so as to drag the missile in the required direction. The weapon had a range of 1,000m (1,095 yards) and could penetrate 200m of armour at an impact angle of 30°. It has been claimed that a 'substantial number' of X-7 missiles was built during the winter of 1944–45 and that many of these were sent to front-line troops for test and evaluation in real combat, but no one has ever discovered any reports made by the soldiers who might have fired the weapon, and it therefore remains doubtful that any were actually fired. No complete specimen was ever discovered after the war, when Allied investigation teams turned the

German missile programme inside out, though there are records of successful test-firings in late 1944. So whether the X-7 was ever fired at a live enemy tank or not, it undoubtedly qualifies as the father of all the anti-tank missiles which have appeared since then.

The X-7 was the most successful but not the only German guided anti-tank missile under development in the closing stages of the war. The 'Pfeifenkopf' (pipe-bowl), also known as 'Pinsel' (paintbrush), was a missile using a television guidance system. Developed by BMW, it carried a super-iconoscope (a primitive TV camera) in its nose, which scanned spirally and signalled back an image of the target's contrast with its background by means of a wire link, and the operator, viewing this on a screen, could then command the missile to impact. It was tested late in 1944 with some success but appears not to have got any further than laboratory models. 'Steinbock' (Capricorn) was a similar missile but using an infrared homing device. The missile was initially guided by using a visual sight and wire control, after which the infrared detector picked up the heat of the tank engine and steered itself to impact. Like the 'Pfeifenkopf', it got no further than a laboratory model before the war ended.

Strange as it may seem, with all this experience to guide them none of the victorious Allies bothered to follow up these ideas after the war and so begin development of an anti-tank missile. It seems probable that expense was the deterrent: guns and rockets were relatively cheap, and in the aftermath of the war, with most people looking forward to peace, it seemed pointless to spend large sums of money on what was, after all, a relatively risky and

untested area of research. Moreover, the postwar enchant-
ment with nuclear weapons and big rockets effectively
prevented any spare cash seeping down to something as
humble as an anti-tank weapon.

It remained for the French to take an interest. They had
little or nothing of their pre-war armoury left, and what
they did have was worthless, so new designs were impera-
tive and they decided that they might as well take the
plunge and see what missiles could do. Work began in the
Arsenal d'Aéronautique in 1948 and moved along slowly
but steadily until 1954, when this arsenal and others
became part of the Nord-Aviation group. By this time the
design was almost complete and in 1955 it was offered for
sale to interested parties. It was a compact missile using a
two-stage rocket behind a powerful shaped charge warhead, supported by four wings in cruciform array. Guided
by wire, it was launched from a simple box and, by
present-day standards, was ridiculously cheap: about £350
for the missile and just over £1,700 for the control unit.
Known as the Nord SS10, the missile made its combat
debut in 1956 in the hands of the Israeli army, when units
equipped with the SS10 effectively destroyed the Egyptian
tank strength in the first Arab-Israeli war. The weapon
was then hurriedly bought, albeit in small numbers mainly
for evaluation, by almost every army in the world, but was
then adopted by some of these armies and remained in
production until 1962, by which time almost 30,000 had
been made.

The SS10 had a maximum range of 1,600m (1,750 yards),
and the reaction of the French and other armies was
'Great, but we want more range...' So in 1953 Nord-

Aviation had begun a more powerful model which doubled the range and speed but also doubled the weight. This became the SS11, which was simply an enlarged SS10 but with a warhead capable of penetrating over 600mm of armour, a quite phenomenal performance for the time. As it stood, it was too heavy to be an infantry weapon, but it was successfully installed on French army tanks (a completely new idea), on ships and, later, on helicopters. A completely new factory was built, and by the late 1970s over 180,000 missiles had been built and supplied to thirty-five armies from Argentina to India and Peru to Norway.

Firing the SS11 was easy, but guiding it was something else. The gunner had to have a steady hand on a joystick to correct the missile's course without overdoing it and swerving it off so far that it could not be brought into line before it reached the end of its range. The missile carried a flare in its tail, and the gunner's job was to have this flare lined up with the target every inch of the way: various arcade-game style simulators were made to give him lots of practice before he was allowed to try it with a real and therefore expensive missile, but skill came hard.

In the late 1950s another French company, SAT, looked hard at this and saw a way of making life easier for the gunner. An infrared detector was built into the sight and connected to a computing scanner. This 'saw' the infrared flare in the tail of the missile and measured its deviation from the axis of the sight. The computer then generated a correction which would steer the missile back into the sight axis line. All the gunner had to do now was keep his sight aligned on the target, and the infrared system would do the rest.

The French called it TCA (Télé-Commande Automatique) but it has since been standardized as SACLOS (Semi-Automatic Command to Line Of Sight), the original system being classed as MCLOS (Manual Command to Line Of Sight).

Among the customers for the SS11 was the USA, since it had no comparable weapon of its own. The US Army had been one of the armies which had bought the SS10 for evaluation purposes, and decided that the SSM-A-22, as the SS11 was known, would be followed by an American weapon whose development was initiated in the early 1950s. The result was the SSM-A-23 Dart, a large missile which was fired from a launcher mounted in the bed of a truck. A heavy and large weapon, it had four wings and four tail fins, a two-stage rocket motor and a 14kg (31lb) shaped charge warhead capable of wrecking any tank in existence to a range of 2,745m (3,000 yards). A large amount of money was poured into the programme, but eventually the US Army realized that a 1.5m (5ft) long missile with a wing span of 1.2m (4ft) was not the most ideal weapon to fire into any terrain except a desert, and the programme was terminated in 1958. After that the US Army affected to be happy with the 106mm (4.17in) recoilless gun and the SS11, but in 1959 the Missile Command began a most audacious project, nothing less than a missile which could be launched from a tank gun. This was a few years after the discovery of the transistor and the early days of solid state circuitry, and the prospect of building a missile which would withstand being fired from a gun was ambitious, to say the very least.

It was soon apparent that the M13 (later MGM-51)

Shillelagh, as the gun-launched missile was designated, was going to be difficult, and in the early 1960s the Hughes company began working on a guided missile capable of being brought into action by infantry, as a replacement for the 106mm (4.17in) recoil-less rifle. They decided that it would be Tube-launched, Optically tracked and Wire guided, so it became known as TOW and proved to be the most successful anti-tank guided missile so far made.

The BGM-71 TOW missile has been periodically upgraded, but its basic form has remained the same. It is a cylindrical missile delivered in a sealed tube, which is simply clipped on to the rear of the launcher tube. The tripod-mounted launcher carries the sight and most of the SACLOS guidance system, and the missile carries a hefty shaped charge warhead and in its original form had a range of 2,750m (3,000 yards). It went into service in 1970, was soon bought by Israel for very successful use in the 1973 Arab-Israeli War, and was then adopted by almost every European and Scandinavian country as well as by Middle and Far Eastern armies.

A helicopter-borne version was developed, and a series of improved warheads and other modifications mean that the current TOW-2A has a tandem shaped charge warhead capable of dealing with explosive reactive armour, and TOW-2B is designed for top attack, against the thinner upper surfaces of the tank, and carries special sensors and shaped charges which fire downwards as the missile passes over its target.

Excellent as TOW is, even its best friends must admit that it is a cumbersome piece of equipment, impractical for being carried by a man in combat. To supplement TOW, once its size became apparent, the McDonnell Douglas company developed Dragon. This is a quite unique system: the soldier carries a substantial sealed tube and a sight unit. In firing position, he unfolds a pair of legs on the front of the tube, squats down, puts the rear end of the tube over his shoulder and lets the front legs support most of the weight. He clips on the sight, takes aim and fires. A recoilless charge launches the missile out of the tube, after which thirty pairs of miniature thruster rockets dispersed around the body of the missile proceed to fire in turn. These are angled so as to combine lift and thrust, and which pair fires is decided by a computer, since the missile is rolling as it moves forward. To maintain flight, a pair of rockets is fired as they are exactly beneath the centre-line of the missile. The guidance is SACLOS, so the gunner merely keeps his sight aligned and the computer does the rest, and in this case it calculates which rockets to fire in order to make a steering correction as well as give the necessary lift and thrust. The whole thing sounds most unlikely and in defiance of gravity, but it works well and Dragon has been in service since 1973, is used by several armies besides the US Army and, like TOW, has had a series of upgrades which have kept it a viable weapon system even against improved tanks.

What of the UK, meanwhile? The British were going their own inimitable way, beginning by totally ignoring the anti-tank missile. By 1955, however, with a number of missile programmes being pushed in various countries, private enterprise decided it was time to take a hand and the Pye Company, who were better known for radios and record-players (Hi-Fi By Pye was their slogan in the

1950s) developed the Python. This was a nice design, somewhat heavy but suitable for mounting on armoured cars, and was tested in 1957. The War Office was not interested, though, and Pye dropped the idea.

The reason why the War Office was not interested in Python was that it was waiting for the completion of an Australian design called Malkara, which had been begun in 1951 and was by 1955 showing considerable promise. The only drawback to Malkara was that it was massive: almost 2m (6.5ft) long and weighing 94kg (206lb) at launch, it carried a 26.1kg (57.5lb) squash-head warhead guaranteed to demolish any tank in existence at a maximum range of 1,830m (2,000 yards). Wire-guided, it was an MCLOS device which therefore demanded a high degree of skill from its operators, and the size ensured that it had to be mounted on a vehicle.

The Malkara went into service with the Australian and British armies in the late 1950s, mounted on armoured scout cars in pairs. It was a formidable weapon, but not something that the infantry could use.

Seeing this, the Vickers-Armstrong company set about developing, as a private venture, a missile suitable for the foot soldier. This became Vigilant, designed in 1956, first fired in 1958, and subsequently adopted by the UK and a number of Middle Eastern countries. Vigilant was very advanced for its day, weighing only 14kg (31lb) as a result of the use of lightweight composite materials, and carried a 6kg (13.2lb) warhead which could defeat over 220mm of armour. It was an MCLOS system, but used an unusual control system which ensured that once the operator had steered it to one side it would automatically pick up a parallel course to its original flight when he released his control: this did away with the looping and swooping swings which an ordinary MCLOS steering system imposed on the flight and made Vigilant much easier to control than any other contemporary system.

This successful private design appears to have stimulated the War Office to 'do something', whereupon it issued a specification and gave a contract to Fairey Aviation to build a missile code-named 'Orange William'. (There was a fashion for coloured names at the time: 'Blue Water', 'Blue Streak', 'Red Planet', 'Red Dean' and 'Blue Boar' were all missile projects, most of which went down the drain.) Fairey struggled with this for some time until it was cancelled in 1959, whereupon Vickers took up the gauntlet. For some time it had been contemplating a bigger missile than Vigilant, but one which would be more practical than Malkara, and taking over most of Fairey's experimental results it set about developing another unusual missile, Swingfire.

Swingfire was specifically intended for use on a vehicle, preferably armoured, though an infantry version was later developed. It was launched from a sealed box, and this could be displaced for some distance from the operator if the tactical situation demanded. The operator would locate his launcher vehicle in a suitably concealed spot, then move, with his observing sight, to an observing position. The launcher's computer was then fed with data on the separation of launcher and sight, direction of fire, and height of the concealing crest in front of the launcher. The observer picked his target and fired, whereupon Swingfire launched itself from the vehicle's box, swooped over the intervening crest and automatically flew into the field of vision of the observer's sight. The observer then 'gathered' the missile into his control. Swingfire had two gyroscopes inside it, keeping it stable in flight: to steer, the operator thumbed a joystick in the required direction, and the further he moved the stick the faster the missile responded – what was called 'velocity control'. As soon as he released the joystick the missile took up its former direction, having simply moved itself laterally rather then swerving off on to a fresh course. All the operator had to do was keep the missile between his eye and the target until it struck. On impact, the 7kg (15.5lb) warhead could defeat any tank then known, and Swingfire had a maximum range of 3,660m (4,000 yards), well above any other missile then in existence.

Swingfire went into British service in 1969 and was initially issued to Royal Armoured Corps units, though in the late 1970s, with reorganizations, it was reallocated to the Royal Artillery, which used it on the Striker armoured reconnaissance vehicle. A highly effective weapon, it subsequently went into service in Belgium and in several Middle Eastern and African countries. Various improvements in sighting and control have been incorporated, and a SACLOS upgrade, which allows four missiles to be tracked simultaneously, has been developed but not, apparently, adopted.

By 1960 it had become obvious that the expense involved in developing a modern missile was getting beyond anything that a single company could provide out of its own funds, and extracting development funds from government sources was slow and painful. The only way to develop a missile appeared to lie in the direction of international co-operation, and in 1961 Nord-Aviation of France and Bölkow of Germany got together and formed a new company called Euromissile to develop missiles of various sorts. Euromissile's first venture was an anti-tank weapon to replace the first-generation MCLOS SS10 and SS11. The basic design was completed by 1963 and the perfected missile entered French and German service in 1972 as MILAN (Missile, Infanterie, Légère, Anti-char, or infantry light anti-tank missile). The consortium was later joined by British Aerospace when the British army adopted MILAN, and production is divided between the three countries. The missile has been taken into service by most of NATO, South Africa, India and various Middle Eastern and African countries.

MILAN consists of a launcher firing post and the missile which is prepacked in a sealed tube. This tube is clipped to a supporting tray on the firing post, and automatically connected. The gunner takes aim on his target and fires. The missile is flung from the tube by a small ejection charge and, once clear, the rocket is ignited and the missile accelerates toward its target. A flare in the tail is detected by the sight, its displacement is measured with reference to the sight axis and corrections are automatically sent down a guidance wire. All the gunner has to do to ensure a hit is to keep his sight lined up with his target.

Since its initial appearance a number of improvements have been made to MILAN, and the current production is known as MILAN 3. The missile is fitted with the MILAN 2T warhead, a tandem type which carries two separate shaped charges. The 'precursor' charge is in an extended

TANKKILLING

probe in front of the main warhead, and on impact this blows away any reactive armour or other shielding which may be in front of the main armour of the target. Microseconds later the main shaped charge detonates and now has a clear path to the main armour; and this main charge has been shown to be capable of going through over 1m (39.4in) of solid steel armour plate.

The launcher unit of MILAN 3 has been greatly improved: it now has a night thermal imaging sight as well as its daytime sight, and this thermal imaging unit can also be useful in daylight to 'see' the heat emitted by targets concealed from view by camouflage. The pyrotechnic flare in the base of the missile has been replaced by a flashing Xenon lamp. One of the drawbacks to the standard infrared detection sight was that should the missile fly past a fire – say, a tank on fire – or a pyrotechnic flare on the battlefield, there was a grave danger that the sight would forget the flare in the missile's tail and lock on to the bigger heat source of the blazing tank or flare. As a result the gunner would lose command and the missile would simply fly off into the distance.

In MILAN 3 the Xenon lamp flashes in a coded pulse, and every missile differs in this code. Connecting the missile to the launcher and switching on the power allows the missile to 'tell' the firing post what its code is. When the missile is fired, the sight recognizes only a light source which flashes the appropriate code. It will thus ignore burning tanks, rockets, flares or any other source of light or infrared which may come into its field of view. As a further insurance the firing post computer takes a 'snapshot' of the scene at the moment the gunner presses his trigger, and this snapshot is constantly compared with what the sight is currently seeing. Should a pyrotechnic flare be fired by an enemy tank in order to confuse the gunner or the missile, the computer sees the difference between the present scene and the 'snapshot' scene, and suppresses the image of the flare in the computer circuitry so that as far as the correction computer is concerned the flare does not exist.

MILAN is an infantry missile. It can be carried by two men, set up in a few seconds and as rapidly removed.

Once they had MILAN well on the way to completion, the Euromissile consortium turned to a heavier weapon for vehicle mounting. Studies began in 1964 and mass production began in 1977. Known as HOT (Haut-subsonique Optiquement Téléguidé Tiré d'un Tube (high subsonic, optical remote-guided, fired from a tube) the missile can be thought of as the European equivalent to the American TOW and about as widely distributed around the world.

In broad terms, HOT is an enlarged MILAN: the principal operating difference is that since it is carried on top of an armoured vehicle there is no need for a small ejecting charge to boost the missile out of the tube and clear of the operator before the rocket fires, and HOT ignites its rocket in the tube and launches under full power. The greater size allows a more powerful sustainer rocket, which burns longer, and thus the maximum range was increased to 4,000m (4,375 yards). The warhead is also bigger, weighing 6kg (13.2lb) and capable of penetrating 250mm of armour when striking at 60° impact angle. As with MILAN, periodic improvements have been made, and the most recent version has adopted the Xenon lamp tracking system of MILAN 3.

The foregoing might be said to be a recitation of mainstream missile development in the form of those which were significant and which have survived as major contenders. There was also a good deal of development outside this main stream. Germany produced the Cobra in 1957, a first-generation MCLOS weapon which was adopted by some eighteen countries, and followed it with the Mamba, an improved version with a better rocket motor, but by the time this was ready for sale MILAN was under way and eventually pushed Mamba off the stage.

The Italian subsidiary of Contraves of Switzerland produced the Mosquito in the late 1950s: this was a lightweight infantry MCLOS weapon with good performance, but it was only ever used by the Italian army and was replaced by MILAN in the middle 1970s. Bofors of Sweden produced the Bantam in the late 1950s as a very light missile using plastic folding wings so that it could be carried in a small container. It was a MCLOS system, wire-guided and with a range of 2,000m (2,185 yards). Adopted by Sweden and Switzerland in 1963, it went out of service in the early 1980s in both countries, the Swiss adopting the American Dragon and the Swedes taking an entirely new design from Bofors, the Rbs 56 BILL.

The BILL (Bofors, Infantry, Light and Lethal) broke entirely new ground. By the middle 1970s it was apparent that the tank designers were catching up with the missile makers: new types of composite armour, reactive armour, and the mystique of 'survivability' (by means of shaping armour to deflect attack, making the tank silhouette lower and more difficult to see and hit, and making tanks more agile) were all factors that were making the target harder in every respect. The Bofors scientists took a fresh look at the problem and decided that the weak spot of the tank lay in the upper surfaces. Since the greatest attack threat almost always came from ground level, the front and sides of the tank and turret were the most vulnerable areas and therefore they were the most heavily protected. Attack from the air was, at that time, a secondary and relatively minor threat, so that the upper surfaces of the tank (the engine decking and the turret roof and hatches) were less well protected. The Bofors scientists therefore decided to create a missile that would attack these vulnerable upper surfaces.

It would be possible to fire a missile high up into the air and then angle it steeply downward so that the shaped charge would fire through the top of the target, but this would demand some very precise range-finding and some alarming aerodynamics. Bofors therefore chose a different solution, and equipped the missile with a warhead pointing obliquely downwards, fitted it with a proximity fuse, and programmed it to fly 75cm (29.5in) higher than the line of sight.

The gunner takes aim at the turret/hull joint and fires; the usual booster pops the missile out of its container, then the rocket ignites and the missile accelerates away. The gunner keeps his eye on the target, the sight keeps its eye on the flare in the tail of the missile, and the computer issues commands down a wire link to keep the missile on course at its designated height above the aiming point. As the missile closes with the tank the proximity fuse senses the presence of the target, analyses it, decides when it is at the correct distance to give the best effect of the shaped charge, and detonates the charge. This fires downward into the top surface of the tank, carving through the thinner armour to do the maximum internal mischief. A recent variation on the standard warhead has a tandem charge, the first to dispose of any reactive armour and the second to penetrate the main armour, and there is also a version with a swivelling warhead which can be programmed to attack the turret in the normal way or, if there appears to be too much additional armour or reactive armour on the front upper surfaces, to overfly the tank and then fire the shaped charge backwards into the rear of the turret or the engine covers of the tank.

While all this was going on more or less openly in the West, there was a good deal of activity going on out of sight on the other side of the Iron Curtain. Just when the Soviets began work on anti-tank missiles is not known, but their first to see service was 'Schmeyl' (bumblebee), known to the West by the NATO reporting name of 'Snapper'. This first became common knowledge when it was used by the Arab armies in the 1967 Arab-Israeli (Six-Day) war, and after a number had been captured by the Israelis and examined, it became obvious that it was more or less copied from the French SS10 missile. An MCLOS pattern, optically tracked and wire-guided, it was invariably mounted on a vehicle and controlled by an operator off to one side.

'Snapper' was followed by 'Swatter', a much more advanced design. This latter began life as an MCLOS system, optically tracked but controlled by radio signals rather than the usual wire link. It was then modified to a SACLOS system, and the final version has both systems available, the operator being able to change from one to the other, even after the missile has been launched. This may seem to be a superfluous option, but it does have its uses if the SACLOS system gets confused by a flare or fire and loses control of the missile: the operator can switch over to MCLOS and steer the weapon back on track, though with a flight time to the maximum 2,500m (2,735 yards) of about 15 seconds, he does not have a great deal of time for fine-tuning his aim.

The third Soviet missile to make an appearance, and the one which caused the most concern, was 'Sagger'. This was first seen mounted on armoured personnel carriers in the annual Red Square parade in 1965, but during the 1973 Yom Kippur War it appeared in a man-portable form. Arab soldiers with what looked like suitcases dispersed themselves across the battlefield, opened the cases and proceeded to launch small but destructive missiles at Israeli tanks with great effect. In its original form it was an MCLOS wire-guided missile, but in the late 1960s it was upgraded to SACLOS configuration and, like 'Swatter', was then given the option of either system. Weighing only 11kg (24.25lb) at launch, 'Sagger' had a range of 3,000m (3,380 yards) and a 120mm (4.72in) diameter shaped charge which was highly effective. The sight was a simple peri-scope which was fitted to the lid of the carrying case and simply planted on the ground near the launcher; a couple of connecting wires and the whole thing was ready, and so small as to be easily hidden in a fold of the ground.

After the appearance of 'Sagger' there was a long silence

from the USSR. Rumours of a full-SACLOS system were heard, but it was not until 1980 that hard information began to appear via military journals in Warsaw Pact countries. The new weapon was called 'Spigot' which, upon closer examination, proved to be a close approximation to MILAN. (So close, indeed, that India, which later acquired a number of these systems, was able to modify them to fire the MILAN missile.) 'Spigot' is mounted on a tripod, has a maximum range of 2,500m (2,735 yards) and is claimed to be able to defeat 600mm of armour, which seems a reasonable claim for a 120mm (4.72in) shaped charge warhead. A similar missile is used with a different launcher for fitting on to armoured vehicles, when it becomes 'Spandrel'.

The most recent Soviet design to be made public is 'Saxhorn', a short-range man-portable weapon similar in intent to the American Dragon. A one-man device, it can if necessary be fired from the shoulder provided the range is short enough to permit the operator to stand long enough to control it to impact. Wire-guided, and with a SACLOS system deriving information from a flare in the tail of the missile, 'Saxhorn' appears to have entered service some time in the early 1980s.

The only other shoulder-fired missile (as opposed to simple rocket) is the French Eryx. Developed in the mid-1980s and brought into service with the French army in 1991, Eryx is wire-guided to its maximum range of 600m (655 yards), a distance which it covers in 4.2 seconds. This obviously leaves no time for the gunner to make any manual corrections, and the entire process is automatic. He takes aim and fires: the missile is launched at low speed (allowing it to be launched from inside a building with no fear of back-blast problems) and then accelerates. Guidance is by wire, the corrections being made by a computer using the same Xenon lamp system as used on MILAN 3: the missile sight reads the position of the flashing lamp, ignoring any other source of heat or light, and corrects the missile on to the line of sight. All the gunner has to do is hold his aim for four seconds and success is assured. The 160mm (6.3in) diameter shaped charge warhead is capable of penetrating almost 1m (39.4in) of armour.

What comes next? So far as NATO is concerned, the next missile to appear will be 'Trigat', so-called because it has been developed by a three-nation effort between the UK, France and Germany. Trigat will appear in two forms, medium- and long-range. The medium-range version will be laser-guided: after launch the firing post will generate a 'guidance tunnel' of circular shape inside which the missile will fly. Fitted with a rearward-facing laser detector, the missile will automatically locate itself in the axis of this tunnel and fly along it, correcting any deviations from its ordained line. So long as the gunner keeps his sight aligned on the target, Trigat will fly along it to impact. In general form and size, medium-range Trigat will be similar to MILAN, with a maximum range of 2,000m (2,185 yards).

Long-range Trigat will be a totally different weapon for mounting on helicopters or armoured vehicles, and is to have a third-generation guidance system. MCLOS was the first generation: the gunner physically steered the missile to the target. SACLOS was the second generation: the gunner maintained his aim and the missile automatically conformed to the line of sight. The third generation is the 'fire-and-forget' missile: the missile locks on to the target before launch and then retains that lock, steering itself to the target without the need for any further attention from the firer, who can either take cover or go looking for a new target. This, of course, demands some very clever circuitry so that the missile locks on to what is wanted and ignores anything else.

At the time of writing (1995) there is no certainty over the guidance system to be used. The two options under test are an infrared system or millimetric-wavelength radar, and it will be some time before confirmation of which system has been chosen. Medium-range Trigat, it is hoped, might be in service by the year 2000, and Long-range Trigat by 2005.

In the USA the third-generation system currently under development is Javelin, a joint venture by the Texas Instruments and Martin Marietta companies to meet the requirements of the US Army's AAWS/M (Anti-Armor Weapon System/Medium) programme. Javelin uses an imaging infrared seeker head which is locked on to the target before launch. Once launched, it steers itself to the selected target and then adopts a top-attack mode. And that, plus a weight of about 16kg (35.25lb) and a range of 2,000m (2,185 yards), is as much as has been publicly admitted about Javelin.

With the story of the missiles brought up to the present day, it is worth backtracking to 1959 to take up the story of Shillelagh, the American gun-launched missile, and see where that led. This began as a project to arm a new tank, the air-portable M551 Sheridan. In order to keep the weight down some original thinking had to be done on the armament, and it was decided to develop a 152mm (5.98in) cannon capable of firing conventional ammunition and also of launching a missile. This was a considerable challenge to the state of the art as it then stood: the whole of the missile had to be packed into a cylinder of small diameter and kept short enough to be loaded into a gun inside a tank turret; it had then to stand up to the shock of being fired out of a cannon at several thousand *g* and still collect its wits in time to be guided to the target in some way or another. (It is worth adding that the late 1950s were vintage years for development engineers biting off far more than they could chew. The 1955–65 decade was strewn with futuristic projects which collapsed under their own weight.)

To be fair, the Shillelagh programme did not collapse, but it took a great deal more effort than had been foreseen before the missile system could be made to work, and it was commendable that the Americans actually got the missile into limited production by 1964. Testing and modification took another three years, and it was formally accepted into service in 1967, after which some 13,000 missiles were made at a cost of about $14,000 each.

The Shillelagh was a remarkable weapon. Loaded into the gun like a shell, and fired by the usual sort of propellant charge, it left the muzzle at about 396m (1,300ft) per second, after which the rocket ignited and accelerated the missile to the speed of 4,185kph (2,600 mph). The gunner held his aim on the target and the missile automatically gathered itself into an infrared beam projected by the sight. Guidance signals were sent down the IR beam, and the missile had a maximum range of 5,200m (5,750 yards). The warhead was a 7kg (15.5lb) shaped charge and the results at the target were very satisfactory.

The problem lay in getting the warhead on to the target. When the equipment actually got into the hands of troops, it became obvious that development had been more concerned with making the system work than making it reliable. The Sheridan tank itself produced a variety of mechanical failures, and the missile system proved to be a lot less reliable in service than it had been in the laboratory. The entire equipment was withdrawn from service for extensive modification and it was not until the early 1970s that it could be called anything like combat-worthy. Even then, the gun-launched missile never lived up to its promise and by the early 1980s had been withdrawn, leaving the Sheridan with a conventional shaped charge shell as its armament. Shortly after that the vehicle itself was largely withdrawn, remaining only as the fire support vehicle for the 82d Airborne Division, and that only because there was nothing that could replace it.

So the gun-launched missile appeared to be an expensive mistake and was written off as a good idea that was impractical. But at the same time that the Americans were giving up on the idea, the Soviets were beginning their own development programme, and towards the end of the 1970s brought into service the Kobra gun-launched missile, which is better known in the West by the US reporting designation AT-8. Kobra was fired from the 125mm (4.92in) gun of the T-64 and later tanks: it was fired at low velocity from the gun, after which the rocket ignited and accelerated the missile towards the target. The gunner kept his sight aligned with the target and the sight computed the position of the missile and sent radio correction signals to steer it into the sight line. With a maximum range of 4,000m (4,375 yards), Kobra carried a 7kg (15.5lb) shaped charge warhead.

After some experience with this missile a fresh design, the 9M119, was developed. This uses a laser beam projected from the tank's sight to control the missile by coded laser signals. The most important difference between this and the earlier design is that the missile does not carry a rocket as it is, in fact, a steerable artillery shell. Four fins in the nose extend after launch and these perform the steering function, as determined by the sight and ordered down the laser beam. The absence of a rocket motor means that there is room in the missile for a large shaped charge, and with a maximum range of 4,000m (4,375 yards), the 9M119 is claimed to be able to defeat over 700mm of explosive reactive armour.

Similar missiles, though rocket-boosted, have been provided for the 100mm (3.94in) and 115mm (4.53in) tank guns in Soviet (now Russian) service. All have the same 4,000m (4,375 yard) maximum range and use shaped charge warheads. The only thing remaining to be determined is whether these missiles are, in fact, as accurate and effective as their producers claim. They were never allowed to be exported from the USSR, and therefore were never provided to any Arab or other nation, so that there has never been any chance to evaluate their use in combat.

It is apparent, when one thinks about it, that all the missiles so far described have one thing in common: they are all line-of-sight weapons. They all require that the launcher and the targets must be within sight of each other.

The minor exceptions in the case of missiles capable of being launched from behind cover do not really invalidate this classification, since the observer has to be in sight of the target and the missiles cannot be more than a few metres away.

The other point to note is that none of these missile systems can deal with an enemy until he is within 4,000m (4,375 yards). There are good technical reasons for this: the signal systems (wire, laser or radio) are rarely capable of transmitting information over greater distances than this. But there is a better and more practical reason, in the simple fact that there are few occasions on which one can see a target as far away as 4,000m (4,375 yards). This may be possible in the desert or the Arctic, but in the more common terrain of most of the world it is highly unlikely as trees, hills and buildings tend to get in the way.

Nevertheless, it is always preferable to deal with an enemy as far away as one can, keeping him at arm's length and preventing him from using his own weapons first. Thinking along these lines brought the final groups of smart munitions into existence.

It seems probable that the origin of the 'Improved Conventional Munition' (ICM) lies in the development of cluster bombs for aircraft. These bombs are mere casings, containing a number of 'submunitions' or bomblets. They are dropped from the aircraft and a timing device or height-sensitive fuse then opens the casing and allows the bomblets to fall free, scattering themselves along the path of the bomb. The bomblets land on the target area and either detonate, giving a wide pattern of destruction, or lie there armed, waiting for somebody to come and move them, whereupon they detonate. For this reason they are often called 'area denial munitions', since a couple of containers emptied across an airfield or similar target area can effectively deny this area to the movement of men and matériel until the bomblets have been carefully removed.

For many years artillery weapons had been firing projectiles broadly classed as carrier shells: these contained smoke canisters, or flares, or parachute flares, or even propaganda leaflets. Whatever the contents they were ejected from the shell by a time fuse at the appropriate point on the trajectory. It now occurred to an American ordnance engineer to tie these two together and put bomblets into an artillery shell.

The first ICMs were filled with anti-personnel bomblets which hit the ground, bounced, and then detonated so as to fill the area with flying fragments. Then came small shaped charge bomblets which would detonate and penetrate any hard target upon which they landed, as well as flinging anti-personnel fragments in all directions. After this came small anti-personnel mines which would scatter across the ground and await detonation by an unwary foot, and then came larger anti-tank mines which, likewise, would lie around until some unwary tank drove over one.

The soldiers contemplated these and agreed that they all had their uses, but, if the ICM engineers were really interested, then they ought perhaps to concentrate on anti-armour payloads: the prospect of putting an enemy armoured column out of action before it was within 25 or 15km (15.5 or 9 miles) of the front was highly attractive. If one could thin the number of the enemy's tank force before it got into action, one gave one's own direct-fire weapons and missiles fewer targets to confuse and distract them.

Bomblets, while effective, were only effective against thinly armoured vehicles: most bomblets could penetrate only about 60mm of armour if they got a fair hit, but this was not really enough to guarantee putting a main battle tank out of action. It followed that fewer but more powerful bomblets would be the better answer. Compared with missiles, ICMs were relatively cheap and several could be fired for the cost of a missile, so even if only three or four bomblets were contained in each shell, the weapon would be cost-effective.

It is obvious that this sort of projectile is impractical in small calibres, and much of the initial American work was done for the 8in (203mm) howitzer. By the late 1970s the concept was proved workable, but it was then decided that the more commonly used 155mm (6.1in) howitzer would be a better vehicle. Eventually the 155mm (6.1in) Shell XM698 SADARM (Seek And Destroy ARMor) was perfected, and production of this weapon is to begin in 1996–97.

SADARM contains two submunitions, each with a parachute. A time fuse blows off the base of the shell at the target and releases the two devices: their parachutes deploy and they begin to fall through the air, slowly spinning. As the parachute opens, so a set of sensors (two millimetric-wavelength radar and one infrared) begin to scan the ground beneath. The spinning of the submunition slows, so that the sensors scan a gradually decreasing circle; they are programmed to recognize a tank and, once they have identified one beneath the descending weapon, they keep track of it until the sensors determine that the munition is close enough to take effect. At that point the explosive charge is detonated. At the bottom of the munition is a heavy metal plate which is now converted, by the force of the explosion, into a slug of metal and propelled at high velocity downwards at the top of the tank. This 'Explosively Formed Penetrator' is quite powerful enough to go through the top armour of any tank.

Bearing in mind that this is fired by a 155mm (6.1in) howitzer and thus has a maximum range well over 20km (12.5 miles), it is obvious that tanks are now at risk long before they arrive at their forming-up points, let alone the front line. A similar projectile, known as the Smart 155, is made in Germany and, to illustrate the amount of technology which has gone into this sort of munition, it is worth quoting the manufacturer's data sheet:

The sensor fuse system is based on gun-hardened processing electronics, comprising a multi-channel infrared and millimetric-wave sensor system, a digital signal processor and a power supply unit. The sensor system receives signals radiated from or reflected by the targets and the surrounding background. These signals are processed using an algorithm which ensures reliable detection of armoured targets even under adverse weather and background clutter conditions, and with a high level of false target rejection. The power supply unit is activated only after the level of spin and unit deceleration has fallen below certain limits while the infrared sensor unfolds only after the vertical spinning descent stage has commenced.

The lethal mechanism consists of an explosively formed

penetrator warhead and the safety and arming unit. The penetrator has high behind-armour effectiveness and outstanding armour penetration capabilities.

All that, or rather two of all that, is inside a shell 155mm (6.1in) in external diameter. Similar projectiles have been developed in France by Thomson-Brandt and in Sweden by Bofors, and both are currently under evaluation by the French Army.

Of course, the Soviets were not far behind. A 152mm (6in) ICM containing 42 dual-purpose bomblets appeared in the 1980s, and was copied in Czechoslovakia, Romania and Yugoslavia. This was followed in 1993 by the news that development of a SADARM-type 152mm (6in) projectile was under way, though beyond the fact that it is to carry two submunitions and use millimetric-wave sensors nothing has been released.

Having provided the artillery with a means of engaging tanks at a distance, the inventors then turned to look at the infantryman's 'private artillery', the mortar. This is a weapon of smaller calibre than the heavy artillery, and one which has to be hand-loaded via the muzzle, so size becomes an important factor. Mortar bombs in 120mm (4.72in) calibre containing submunitions have been developed in Spain and Greece, but the size of the bomblets is such that they can only be really effective against armoured personnel carriers and similar lightly protected vehicles: a bomblet weighing 285g (10.05oz) and no more than about 30mm (1.18in) in diameter is not going to damage a main battle tank seriously.

To give the mortar some effect against armour it needs

to have a dedicated bomb. A shaped charge bomb would be simple enough to design, but the accuracy of mortars is not exactly pinpoint, and attempting to attack a distant tank using conventional mortar techniques would be a slow and wasteful business. So the bomb needs to have some sophistication.

The first organization to examine this closely was the German army, which asked for a feasibility study on a terminally guided mortar bomb in 1975. From this beginning arose the Bussard (buzzard) 120mm (4.72in) guided mortar bomb. The bomb is loaded and fired like any other mortar bomb, but performs quite differently after leaving the muzzle. Once the bomb has reached its vertex (the highest point of the trajectory) and begins to descend, four wings open to stabilize the flight, a gas generator begins to function so as to provide power, and a laser recognition system in the nose of the bomb is switched on. The selected target has to be illuminated by a ground observer using a laser target designator. This instrument directs a laser beam at the target: some of this laser energy is reflected skyward and is detected by the seeker in the nose of Bussard. The signal is processed, steering commands are given to the wings and tail unit, and the bomb is then steered into impact with the target.

Alternatively, designs have been drawn up for seeker heads using millimetric-wavelength radar or thermal imaging, either of which would remove the need for the ground observer and his designator and turn the system into a fire-and-forget weapon. At the present time the system is under evaluation by the German army.

Doubtless stimulated by reports of the German research,

two similar projects were begun in Sweden and the UK. The Bofors company has developed the 120mm (4.72in) Strix mortar bomb, while British Aerospace has developed the 81mm (3.2in) Merlin bomb. Development of the Swedish bomb began in 1984 by FFV aided by Saab Missiles, FFV being taken over by Bofors in 1990. The Strix is completely self-contained, requiring no laser illumination of the target, and is fired just like any conventional bomb, except that it has a special tail unit which carries the usual type of propelling charge and then separates from the bomb after leaving the muzzle. The bomb then follows a normal ballistic trajectory, which can be extended by means of a rocket booster if required, and not until the final stage of the downward flight does the infrared target seeker and guidance mechanism come into action. The seeker detects a suitable target and then steers the bomb into impact on the top surface of the tank. The rear section of the bomb is filled with a shaped charge which thus has the length of the bomb acting as the stand-off distance, allowing the penetrative jet to develop fully and reach maximum velocity before striking the tank's armour.

The Merlin bomb is, of course, a good deal smaller, since the standard British army mortar is of 81mm (3.2in) calibre. Nevertheless, inside this diameter is a millimetric-wave radar seeker driving the guidance mechanism and a shaped-charge warhead. The bomb is fired in the conventional manner. After leaving the muzzle six rear-mounted fins are deployed to provide basic aerodynamic stability, and four canard fins spring from the nose to give directional control. The seeker is switched on as the bomb crosses its vertex, and the seeker searches first for moving or, if it finds none, for stationary targets. The seeker carries out a search over an area about 300m (330 yards) square, and having acquired a target it provides the necessary error information to the guidance system which then steers the bomb to impact. The Merlin's effectiveness has been fully demonstrated, and it appears that only financial restraints are delaying its adoption into British service.

In the late 1980s the Boeing company in the USA had a promising programme to provide a guided bomb for the US services' 107mm (4.2in) mortar. Boeing's approach was somewhat radical: the bomb had a television camera in the nose and deployed a fibre-optic cable as it flew through the air, so that the mortar operator could literally see where his bomb was going. The fibre-optic cable also carried command signals from a control unit at the mortar, allowing the operator to steer the bomb on to his selected target. Just as things seemed to be going well, the US Army decided that the 107mm (4.2in) mortar had had its day and that a 120mm (4.72in) weapon would henceforth be the standard heavy mortar, so Boeing had to start all over again. The company demonstrated the feasibility of the project with a number of firings and then extended the project to cover the 81mm (3.2in) infantry mortar. Work is still in progress developing the 120mm (4.72in) FOMP (Fiber-Optic Mortar Projectile) and the 81mm (3.2in) IPAW (Infantry Precision Attack Weapon), and there is every possibility that they will result in effective anti-armour rounds much cheaper than the complex fire-and-forget guided bombs.

But assessment of these smart weapons puts one on

difficult ground, since only a few have been actually proven in conflict. The Israeli army conclusively proved that TOW would stop a Soviet-made T-72 tank, and the Arabs also proved that the Soviet missiles could stop Israeli tanks. Both sides also proved that a short, sharp burst of machine-gun fire over the head of the missile operator (assuming one could find his position) could usually put him off his aim for long enough to result in the missile swerving off harmlessly. The British army in the Falklands managed to use MILAN as a demolition device for machine-gun posts, a rather expensive way of removing a machine-gun, but found no employment for the weapon in the anti-tank role. There appears to have been little, if any, use of anti-tank missiles in the Gulf War, though some experimental SADARM rounds are said to have been fired, and certainly the bomblet-filled 155mm (6.1in) shell was used as an anti-personnel device, earning it the sobriquet of 'Steel Rain' from its unfortunate victims. But beyond that we are in the realm of experimental firings, demonstrations and manufacturers' claims.

CHAPTER SEVEN

OUT OF THE SKY

The aeroplane and the tank both made their military debut in the First World War, but there seems to have been no formal attempt to use the aeroplane as a weapon against the tank. It is important to stress the word formal, for while there was never any organized move towards the task, there appears to have been a handful of individual German pilots who attacked British tanks with machine-gun fire in 1917 and managed to immobilize one or two. This seems never to have gained any official recognition and was generally forgotten in the postwar years. In those years the only employment of an aeroplane, so far as soldiers were concerned, was either to drop ammunition to them, direct artillery fire or make machine-gun attacks on marching columns.

The first serious use of aircraft against tanks came in the Spanish Civil War. Here, as noted in an earlier chapter, Germany, Italy and the USSR supplied equipment of all types, including aircraft, to their ideological comrades, and in the battle for Guadalajara (March 1937) both these elements were used to the full. Italian troops forming part of the Nationalist forces launched an attack towards Madrid supported by about 65 CV-33 and CV-35 tankettes. The Republicans mustered about a hundred fighters, principally Soviet-supplied Polikarpov I-15 biplane and Polikarpov I-16 monoplane types. Each type was armed with two of the formidable ShKAS 7.62mm (0.3in) machine-guns, each capable of firing at 1,800 rounds per minute, and this concentrated blast of armour-piercing bullets severely damaged a number of the Italian tanks. The Italians were disorganized by the aerial attack and were thus in no fit state to withstand a subsequent Republican counter-attack by ground troops, and the advance on Madrid came to an inglorious halt.

This incident, and one or two others, persuaded the Soviet 'observers' who accompanied their equipment into action that a dedicated tank-attack aircraft would be a valuable asset. The Soviet aircraft designers had developed a number of ground-attack machines for the attack by gun and bomb of troops on the ground, and they had, in the late 1920s, attempted to develop a recoil-less gun which could be carried by an aircraft to provide a heavy projectile for the destruction of pillboxes and simple field fortifications. This came to nothing, however, for the experimental weapons had a distressing habit of bursting when fired, and when they did work successfully the velocity was insufficient to produce accurate fire. Stalin, who had been fascinated by the promise of these weapons, had the designer sent to a labour camp and disbanded the whole project.

In 1936 design work began on an anti-tank ground-attack aircraft by the Polikarpov design bureau. It was envisaged as a twin-engined monoplane carrying either four 37mm cannon or two 37mm and two 20mm cannon in the wings but, as is so often the case, other agencies got a finger in the pie and the design was cancelled in favour of a multi-purpose machine capable of being employed as an air fighter as well as a ground attacker. Then the specification was changed again to adapt it to the dive-bombing role, after which the whole project fell victim of its own inertia and died.

While this Polikarpov design was being batted to and fro, a second design bureau was instructed by the Soviet air force to begin design of an anti-tank machine, this time as a result of field experience in Spain. Specifications were given to the Ilyushin design bureau in late 1937, resulting in the BSh (Bronirovannii Shturmovik, or Armoured Attacker) which first flew in December 1939. A low-wing monoplane, armed with two 20mm ShVAK cannon and two 7.62mm ShKAS machine-guns in the wings, with racks for eight 82mm (3.2in) RS-82 rockets and four 100kg (220lb) bombs, the type entered production as the Il-2 and became the premier tank attack aircraft of the Second World War and is generally believed to have been produced in greater numbers than any other wartime aircraft: something in the order of 36,160 were constructed.

The original Il-2 was a single-seater, with almost 700kg (1,543lb) of steel armour protecting the pilot and engine. It was found that the pilot, intent upon his ground targets, was vulnerable from the rear and in 1942 a two-seat version with a more powerful engine became standard, the rear observer having a machine-gun and taking care of the pilot's back.

When the German army invaded the USSR on 22 June 1941, the Soviet air force had only 249 Shturmovik aircraft, of which only 70 were in service. The first unit to use the aircraft in combat was the 215th Assault Aviation Regiment, in the Veliki Luki area. Warned of a German armoured column which had broken through the Soviet lines, a flight of seven Shturmoviks (the only aircraft ready for service) attacked the column with bombs, flew off, swung round, and made a second attack with rockets and cannon. Several tanks and trucks were destroyed and the German advance was stopped.

Similar attacks were made over the following weeks, but the price was high. Most of the Soviet pilots had very little experience with their new aircraft before taking them into action; they had never had any training in ground attack tactics and were having to work them out as they went along; they had little or no radio equipment and were thus unable to make concerted plans once in the air; and the rockets and their associated sighting equipment were still in the development stage and only reliable at suicidally short range.

The Germans reacted rapidly to the new threat, providing light anti-aircraft guns on mobile mountings to accompany armoured columns and quickly producing new single-gun 37mm and four-gun 20mm equipment which could put up a dense barrage of projectiles in a very short time. This, and increased attention devoted to the Shturmovik by German fighters, made life difficult and generally short for the Soviet pilots: any who survived ten operational missions were automatically awarded the 'Hero of the Soviet Union' decoration. The situation was eased slightly when the two-seat Shturmovik appeared in 1942, giving the aircraft a degree of all-round defence, but it remained a precarious business until the production of Shturmoviks was capable not only of replacing losses but actually of increasing the strength. Once that point was reached in 1943, it became the same story as every other Soviet war initiative: swamp the enemy with numbers. The actual tactics of the Shturmovik pilots never reached a very sophisticated level – indeed, there can be nothing very sophisticated about flying at low level into the teeth of concentrated anti-aircraft fire and launching a salvo of rockets against a group of tanks – but once the attackers began to outnumber the defenders the success rate had to rise.

On the German side of the front there had been less haste in bringing aircraft into the anti-tank business, largely because the initial opinion was that the Panzers and anti-tank artillery were capable of dealing with anything the Soviets were likely to produce. This idea was rudely shattered by the appearance of the T-34 and KV-1 tanks, and, fortunately, aerial support was available.

The German pilots and observers who had gone to Spain with the Condor Legion had taken some of Germany's newest warplanes with them and put them through their paces. Among these was the machine which was later to become a legend, the Junkers Ju 87 'Stuka' dive-bomber. Put into production in 1937, pre-production models had already been tested in Spain and production models were sent to stiffen up the numbers. The purpose of the Stuka was simply to carry a single large bomb on a launching cradle between the undercarriage legs. Upon seeing a likely target the pilot went into a near-vertical dive, took aim, released his bomb and then pulled out and regained altitude before returning home for another bomb. Among other things it was discovered in Spain that the *g* force on the pilot as he pulled out of the steep dive frequently blacked him out and he then lost control and either crashed or had a very close escape. As a result of this an automatic device was fitted which, in the event of the pilot passing out, would pull the machine up and fly it to a safe altitude, giving the pilot time to recover.

The Stuka terrified ground troops and civilians in Spain, and its fame and terror spread further in 1939 in Poland and in 1940 in France and then Britain. But it gave less rise to terror among fighter pilots and anti-aircraft gunners, both of whom found it an easy target, and was eventually only used in areas where Germany had air superiority. One of those areas was the Eastern Front in 1941–43, and it was to this theatre that most of the Stuka force gravitated.

The original offensive armament of the Stuka was two forward-firing machine-guns, a 500kg (1,102lb) bomb amidships, and possibly eight 50kg (110lb) bombs under the wings with a smaller bomb under the fuselage; the defensive firepower amounted to a single rearward-firing trainable machine-gun. This armament was later modified, the centre-line bomb increasing to 1,800kg (3,968lb) under exceptional circumstances and various combinations of machine-guns being tried. For the task of tackling tanks, however, it was obvious that something better was required: a 1,800kg (3,968lb) bomb would shred the strongest tank, but hitting such a small target was another matter.

As with the Soviets in Spain, so with the Germans: they had also seen the possibility of an aerial tank-destroyer, and it should be borne in mind that the Luftwaffe was primarily in existence in order to provide support for the army's ground operations. After one or two false starts, the German air ministry issued in 1938 a specification for a close support and ground attack aeroplane, the result of which was the Henschel Hs 129. This was a single-seat monoplane with two engines, heavy armour around the pilot (the bulletproof glass in the cockpit was 76mm/3in thick), and self-sealing fuel tanks. The first models were drastically underpowered and were given to the Romanian air force; then the machine was redesigned using French Gnome-Rhône radial engines, which improved matters, although not to a truly effective degree, and the definitive version of the Hs 129 appeared on the Eastern Front early in 1942.

Armed with two 20mm cannon, two 7.92mm (0.312in) machine-guns and two 50kg (110lb) bombs, they were adequate ground attack machines, although the fields of vision for the pilot were very poor and the aeroplane flew like a powered brick, but their effect against tanks was nothing to write home about. The Hs 129 had a very strong airframe, however, and proved to be an excellent vehicle on which the German gun designers exercised their talents. By 1942 the Luftwaffe were beginning to have their doubts about the 20mm cannon as a weapon against bombers: at the combat speeds of the time, and the rates of fire of the contemporary guns, it was rarely possible to get more than a handful of rounds into the target, rarely proving lethal. In reply to this observation Mauser had developed the 30mm MK101 cannon: four 30mm shells filled with aluminized explosive could totally destroy any four-engined bomber.

Such projectiles could also severely damage a tank. While one 30mm projectile would be relatively unnoticed, a stream of them could devastate the upper surfaces of a tank, wrecking all the vision devices, cooling fans, hatch covers, engine covers, exhaust systems and external fuel tanks frequently found there, and a side-on attack could wreck the suspension of most tanks. With little delay, therefore, the 30mm MK101 was adapted to a streamlined 'pod' which fitted beneath the Hs 129 and Stuka in replacement of the central bomb. Most experts agree that an Hs 129 on the Eastern Front was the first aircraft to fire a 30mm cannon in combat in May 1942, when the first machines into combat were effective in stopping a break-out by Soviet armour from a bridgehead on the Donets river.

Though a continuous stream of 30mm shells did damage, it did not 'kill' the tank: it certainly took the vehicle out of action, but also left it fit to be repaired. What was needed was a weapon powerful enough to remove the tank from battle on a permanent basis. Some degree of improvement was achieved by the production of tungsten-cored projectiles capable of defeating 75mm (2.95in) of armour at 300m (330 yard) range, but the shortage of tungsten put an end to that fairly quickly. The obvious solution was to fit a bigger cannon, but none existed and thus the next solution was to take a standard anti-tank gun and put it into an aircraft.

Bearing in mind that the recoil of an anti-tank gun demanded a heavy carriage and recoil system to control it, the installation of such a weapon into an aircraft was not easy. Work began on adapting the 5cm PaK 36 gun, but as an interim measure the 3.7cm FlaK 36 anti-aircraft gun, an automatic weapon, was suggested. Large numbers were available, since they had been replaced in ground service by a newer model, and after some modification the 3.7cm Bordkanone appeared, one fitted beneath each wing of a Ju 87 Stuka. Trials showed it to be a practical weapon and quantity production began late in 1942.

A number of 5cm PaK weapons had been modified into 5cm Bordkanone and fitted to Hs 129 aircraft by mid-1943: little is known about these, since they appear to have been no more than a step on the road to larger things. The 5cm gun was all very well, but it had more or less been replaced as a ground anti-tank gun because the projectile was not sufficient to do severe damage to the Soviet tanks, and the 7.5cm PaK 40 was the preferred weapon. It therefore became necessary to fit this 75mm (2.95in) weapon to an aircraft, a slow and difficult business. Trying to hang this underneath a Ju 87 was found impossible and a new vehicle, the Junkers Ju 88 twin-engined bomber, was adopted as the basis for the conversion. Mounted inside the machine and pointed slightly downward, the cannon installation was proved workable, but expecting a crew member to crouch behind and load it while the pilot threw it around the sky was impractical, and there was a further delay while a 12-round magazine and an automatic loading mechanism were perfected. The gun and its loader and ammunition were then packed into a streamlined pod which could be fitted underneath the aircraft, with explosive bolts so that the whole affair could be jettisoned in an emergency. By late 1942 the conversion was approved and in production, but by early 1943 the increasing weight of Allied bomber attacks meant that most of the Ju 88 airframes available for conversion were taken for use as night-fighters, and only a relatively small number actually went into the anti-tank war. Those that did go into action soon showed that although it was an excellent gun carrier, the Ju 88 was not sufficiently agile for low-level ground attacks. The Ju 87 was too slow, which left only the Hs 129 and even that was considered on the slow side and sadly lacking in manoeuvrability. So the Hs 129 now became the target for the gun designers, and late in 1943 work began on mounting the 75mm (2.95in) gun into the Hs 129, using the same sort of underslung pod arrangement.

This final version of the Hs 129, of which only twenty-five were made because of the limited supply of guns, appeared in action in July 1944 and proved highly effective against the Iosif Stalin 1 heavy tank. This had hitherto resisted most forms of aerial attack, and indeed was the principal driving force behind the adaptation of the 75mm (2.95in) gun to the Hs 129.

While these German developments had been in progress, the Soviets had not been standing still. In the first place their continuous action against German armour soon led to improvements in their tactics and more skill in their attacks. The RS-82 rocket was improved in velocity and accuracy, better sights were developed, shaped charge bombs were taken into use for better armour penetration, and a certain amount of experimental work was done on fitting heavier guns to the Shturmovik. The 23mm Volkov-Yartsev VYa-23 cannon was the first choice: for its day this had the unusually high muzzle velocity of 905m (2,969ft) per second, fired at 750 rounds per minute and proved devastating against light armour though it was less effective against the heavier German tanks. Further development work went on, and in 1943 the 37mm Nudel'man-Suranov NS-37 cannon was perfected. Though heavier than the 23mm weapon it was a less cumbersome design and fitted neatly in place of the 23mm guns. The velocity was slightly less at 865m (2,838ft) per second, and the rate of fire a good deal less at 350 rounds per minute, but this was no great disadvantage and the target effect was vastly improved.

There were, however, some drawbacks to this installation. The 23mm gun was gas-operated, whereas the 37mm was recoil-operated; this meant that much more of the recoil force was transmitted to the aircraft, and as the 37mm was an extremely powerful cartridge this meant a very high stress on the airframe. Moreover the two guns, unless they fired in complete synchronization, which was rarely the case and impossible to control, tended to give the aircraft a lateral swing, scattering the rounds away from the target. As a result the 37mm was not popular with pilots and relatively few were ever fitted. The optimum results were achieved by Shturmoviks mounting four 23mm VYa-23 guns, and this remained the principal Soviet tank-destroying aircraft until the end of the war.

The German designers had reached the end of the line with the 75mm (2.95in) gun: there was no way they were ever going to get a heavier weapon into an aircraft and still have a practical ground-attack machine. They therefore began to consider rockets, having seen what the Soviets had been able to do with this weapon. Their other line of development concentrated on improving aircraft performance. While the Hs 129 was an efficient tank-killer, it was a slow and vulnerable target once it had expended its tank armament and was returning to its base. A demand therefore arose for use of the much faster Focke-Wulf Fw 190 fighter-bomber in this demanding role. Though in its standard form the Fw 190 was useless as a tank-killer, were it given the necessary armament, its performance meant that it could at least take care of itself at other times.

Experiments with the 3.7cm Bordkanone on the Fw 190 ran into the same trouble as had the Soviets with their 37mm gun on the Shturmovik: the firing of recoil-operated guns mounted in or under the wings set up a wobble which spread the shots all over the place, and no amount of redesign of the mountings could cure it. And as a result, the two lines of development (rockets and fast aircraft) finally came together.

Though the Germans had been among the pioneers of rocket armament, they had entirely ignored them as an aircraft armament, and thus when the need to combat tanks arose, they had no suitable 'off the shelf' weapon. So, in a considerable hurry, they came up with a remarkable adaptation: they took the infantryman's Panzerschreck shoulder launcher, the weapon which had been copied from the American Bazooka, and strapped it in pairs under the wings of the Fw 190. By October 1944 this had been tested and put into service: it fired a shaped charge bomb capable of defeating most Soviet tank armour, though the range was somewhat limited. The normal fighting range, when fired on the ground, was 150m (165 yards), and this was slightly extended by altitude and the forward velocity of the aircraft, but the pilot had to get within 250m (275 yards) of his target before he fired if he was to have any chance of a hit.

At this time the R4M air-to-air rocket was under development as a potent anti-bomber weapon for the Messerschmitt Me 262 jet fighter. By some means, a number of the prototype rockets were 'acquired' and fitted with shaped-charge warheads. A firing rack was designed and fitted beneath the wings of the Fw 190, and early in 1945 a ground attack squadron on the Western Front received the aircraft and their new armament. But by that time the fuel shortage was so critical that the aircraft were rarely able to fly sorties and reliable reports of the use of this combination in combat are unknown.

Meanwhile the 'lunatic fringe' of weapons designers, always active in Germany, had come up with Förstersonde as the ultimate anti-tank weapon. Förstersonde was a clutch of four or six steel tubes mounted almost vertically (they had a slight backward tilt) in either the fuselage or the wing roots of the aircraft. Inside was a recoil-less launching charge and a rocket-boosted shaped-charge projectile, pointing downward and slightly to the rear. An electric firing circuit was connected to a magnetic anomaly detector. The pilot merely had to switch this device on and then fly at full speed across the battlefield: the magnetic field of the tank would trigger the anomaly detector, which then fired the propelling charges. The recoil-less effect allowed gas to vent upwards as the projectile was discharged downwards, thus relieving the aircraft of any stress, and the rearward tilt compensated for the speed of the aircraft. The rocket-propelled bombs struck the top surface of the tank and they were sufficiently powerful to defeat almost any tank they were liable to encounter.

The final trials of this device took place in January 1945, when some reassuringly accurate and destructive results were achieved against captured Soviet and American tanks. By that time, however, the problems of getting such a weapon into production and into combat were enormous, and the war ended without Förstersonde getting very much further.

The British development of aerial anti-tank weapons began, like so many British developments, as a private venture by an armaments manufacturer. In 1938 the Vickers-Armstrong company were concerned that there seemed to be no official work being done on developing heavy weapons for aircraft and, together with Rolls-Royce, the company set about designing an airborne 40mm gun which became known as the Vickers 'S'. The design was completed and tested in 1939 and went into limited production early in 1940, but later in that year the Air Ministry decided that there was no requirement for such a heavy weapon as an air-to-air gun, but that there might be a place for it as an anti-tank gun. The investigation of an anti-tank aircraft was placed on very low priority (as was anything to do with air support for ground troops at that time) and it was not until early in 1941 that tests of the

40mm 'S' gun were carried out. Orders were given for a hundred guns to be made by Vickers for delivery late in 1941, but the sudden appearance of the German army in North Africa made everybody think again.

By September 1941 two guns had been fitted under the wings of a Hawker Hurricane fighter, the only fighter aircraft then available which was robust enough to carry weapons of this size. Even then, the wings had to be strengthened to withstand the additional weight and the recoil forces, and with these modifications the anti-tank version of the Hurricane fighter became the Hurricane Mk IID. In April 1942 the first production aircraft were delivered to Egypt, where they were used to re-equip No.6 Squadron, who immediately began training in low-flying tank-shooting tactics.

On 26 May the German forces in North Africa made a feint towards Gazala but then swung southward with the intention of making a looping encirclement through the desert to come up and take the British positions in either the rear or flank. They had, though, overlooked the Free French garrison at Bir Hacheim and were halted by this strongpoint. There being no Allied tanks in the area to assist the French, the services of No.6 Squadron were demanded, even though the squadron had not completed its planned course of training. On 2 June three Hurricanes swept past Bir Hacheim and found a group of German tanks which they promptly attacked, leaving two tanks, two trucks and the vital refuelling tanker in flames. A second attack on the same day was less successful, one Hurricane being shot down by the alert German anti-tank gunners, but another tank and more trucks were destroyed.

Subsequent attacks in the following days soon impressed certain facts on the pilots of the Royal Air Force: that hitting a tank did not necessarily mean killing it; that reports of armour in a certain place, received from other aircraft or from ground observers, had to be followed up rapidly since, after all, tanks were mobile and by the time the aircraft arrived they could well be miles away; and that the initial issues of 40mm ammunition were far from reliable, guns often failing to fire. All these problems were cleared up, and the Hurricane Mk IID rapidly became the scourge of Rommel's armour. But there was always a degree of reluctance on the part of the RAF higher command to disperse aircraft in direct support of the army, and it is remarkable that after the British break-out at El Alamein (November 1942) and during the subsequent pursuit of Rommel's Italo-German forces across North Africa, the tank-killers of No.6 Squadron were expressly ordered not to harass the retreating German columns; instead they were ordered off to the south of the Allied front to fly anti-tank sweeps in a region where there were very few tanks.

When the locus of the war moved to Tunisia, it was the turn of the Allies to be surprised when a number of German Hs 129 machines appeared and began attacking Allied armour. This led to No.6 Squadron being hurriedly moved into Libya in March 1943 and launched against German armour in the vicinity of the Mareth Line. The squadron was then to remain in action until the Axis forces finally surrendered Tunisia in May. During this period the German Tiger tank made its first appearance against the Western Allies, and it was rapidly seen that the 40mm gun was making very little impression on this monster. Fortunately, a fresh weapon was already being prepared.

In the early 1930s the UK had developed a solventless cordite propellant explosive which could be extruded to any length and shape desired, and somebody realized that it would make an excellent rocket propellant. Work began on developing 2 and 3in (50.8 and 76.2mm) calibre rockets (governed by the maximum diameter of cordite that could be extruded) for anti-aircraft use. These proved successful, and since the rocket motors were simply steel tubes filled with cordite, with fins at one end and a simple joint at the other, it proved very easy to develop different types of warhead to fit on to these standard motors. Since the submarine was a serious threat, a 76.2mm (3in) rocket with a 11.3kg (25lb) armour-piercing head was designed to be fired against submarine pressure hulls. In 1942 it occurred to somebody that this same thing might do very well against tanks.

Six Hurricane Mk II fighters of a trial flight were equipped with launch rails, trials were carried out, and in November 1942 the aircraft were sent to North Africa. Shortly after their arrival they attacked a group of Tiger tanks, and to everyone's surprise the Tigers survived, virtually unscathed. The 11.3kg (25lb) armour-piercing warhead might perform well on firing ranges, but in the field it was worse than useless: it did not have sufficient striking velocity to do any worthwhile damage to the Tiger's armour.

Another rocket development, taking place in an entirely different field, was 'Lilo', which was the marriage of the 3in (76.2mm) motor to a 27.2kg (60lb) high-explosive warhead for use by infantry to defeat Japanese bunkers. Since the AP warhead seemed not to be doing much good, a few 27.2kg (60lb) HE warheads were sent out to North Africa and fitted, some trials were made to ascertain how they flew and what changes had to be made to the sights, and then they were tried out 'for real'. The new weapon proved fatal to any tank: it could blow in engine covers, lift turrets off, mangle suspension, and blow tracks to shreds. So the 11.3kg (25lb) AP warhead went back to making holes in submarines (which it did very well) and the 27.2kg (60lb) HE warhead became the preferred anti-tank weapon. One might ask why a shaped charge warhead was not developed: the answer is that one was indeed developed, but that there were grave problems in devising a suitable fuse, and once the plain HE warhead was seen to be successful, work on the shaped charge was stopped.

The end of the African campaign almost spelled the end of the 40mm gun in RAF use. While the weapon itself was effective enough, the need to fly in close to the target and thus run the gauntlet of the German anti-aircraft artillery had led to a high casualty rate in both men and machines in North Africa. The particular requirements of the war in Burma gave a reprieve to the type, however, and in this theatre the Hurricane Mk IID was also successful to a later date. The rocket, on the other hand, had a motor which had been designed to push a 13.6kg (30lb) warhead up to an altitude of 3,650m (11,975ft), so even with a 27.2kg (60lb) warhead it was capable of reaching out from beyond light anti-aircraft range and dealing a killing blow. The only problem lay with aiming the rockets, since, being finned, they tended to turn into any wind that might be blowing. Pilots soon learned to check on wind speeds before they took off and how to judge the direction of ground wind from trees, smoke and other indicators. That, and improved sights, soon made the aircraft rocket a truly formidable weapon.

When the Allies set out to invade Normandy in 1944, air support was vital and aerial defence against tanks was high on the priority list. By this time the attitude of the RAF towards ground support had changed somewhat, and steps were taken to develop a new ground support aircraft. In 1937 the Hawker Typhoon had been designed as a future replacement for the Hurricane. It went into operational service in 1941 and, like so many aircraft and tanks rushed into service before full trials were done, it proved to have its own peculiar teething troubles. But by 1943 most of these had been cured and the Typhoon was a popular fighter-bomber, capable of carrying considerable weights of armament, with a top speed of over 645kph (400mph) and a fixed forward-firing armament of four 20mm Hispano cannon in the wings. The Typhoon proved itself capable of catching the fastest German aircraft, and was a rock-steady gun platform for the ground attack role. Now it was given eight rocket launching rails under the wings and in the summer of 1944 set about making itself a legend. Nothing moved in France without being pursued by a Typhoon: trains, trucks, tanks and whatever else moved on the landscape was a target. Persistent attacks by Typhoons prevented the German 21st Panzer and 12th SS Panzer divisions from reinforcing the battle lines in Normandy immediately after the invasion and when the remains of the German 7th Army and 5th Panzer Army were trapped in the Falaise gap, Typhoons killed 175 German tanks in a single day.

American development of tank-killing aircraft can be dealt with fairly quickly, since the Americans avoided most of the blind alleys and were wise enough to profit from the experience of others. In the late 1930s they flirted briefly with cannon-firing fighter aircraft, notably the Bell P-39 Bell Airacobra which was radical in having the engine behind the pilot and a 37mm cannon firing through the propeller hub, an idea adopted from the French Dewoitine D.500 and D.520 designs. It also carried two 12.7mm (0.5in) and four 7.62mm (0.3in) Browning machine-guns. The P-39 was widely used during the first part of the war, but not as a tank-killer since the idea of devoting a specialized aircraft to this role appears never to have raised much enthusiasm in the US Army Air Force: the aircraft was then maintained in production largely for delivery to American allies, and many of the aircraft delivered to the USSR were finally used in the ground attack and tank-killing roles for which it was best suited.

The Americans concentrated on the all-purpose fighter-bomber as its chosen ground support warplane. Perhaps the most famous and certainly the most effective of these was the Republic P-47 Thunderbolt. This enormous machine entered service in 1942 and soon became invaluable as an escort fighter, after which its talents as a ground attack machine were revealed. Its armament was eight 12.7mm (0.5in) Browning machine-guns, but when the RAF began mounting rockets for the attack of tanks the USAAF took note and set about a similar development for the Thunderbolt. Here they were aided, like the British, by the fact that a ground bombardment rocket was available for adoption. This was the 114.3mm (4.5in) rocket, which differed from British and Russian rockets by being spin- rather than fin-stabilized. The tail end of the rocket was closed by a plate perforated with a number of obliquely drilled holes, so that the rocket blast emerged at a tangent to the axis of the rocket and thus span it as well as driving it forward. This did away with the problem, inherent to finned rockets, of turning into the wind, and it made the 114.3mm (4.5in) rocket supremely accurate and steady in flight. Six rockets were fitted beneath the wings in simple three-tube clusters and fired electrically, and the P-47 was as effective as the Typhoon in north-west Europe in 1944–45.

The Americans succumbed to the attraction of a heavier weapon for tank killing by mounting a 75mm (2.95in) field gun into a North American B-25G Mitchell medium bomber in 1942. The idea was sound enough, but the aeroplane was not well suited to the high-speed manoeuvres demanded in the anti-tank role and it was soon earning its keep as an anti-submarine and anti-ship weapon, especially in the south-west Pacific theatre.

So all in all, the only real American tank-killing aircraft of the war was the Thunderbolt, and that was merely part of its role as a ground-attack machine.

In the years immediately after the war there appears to have been little attention paid to the 'pure' anti-tank aircraft, the role being generally subsumed into the general ground-attack role, as in the case of the Thunderbolt. When the Thunderbolt was phased out of service in favour of faster jet aircraft, there was a considerable gap in the

American tactical line-up, and this made itself apparent in the Korean War (1950–53) and the Vietnam War (1961–73). Here the high-speed jet fighters were pressed into ground support tasks to which they were entirely unsuited. In the opinion of the author, in his capacity as a forward observer, a high-speed jet was usually moving too fast to see the target properly and ended up scattering the area with bombs, whereas the older propeller-driven machines being operated by the Royal Navy and US Navy were slower, took their time about aiming, and put the rocket or bomb precisely where it was needed. As a result of this sort of comment from the people on the ground, and in view of the threatening preponderance of armour in the Warsaw Pact *vis-à-vis* NATO, the US Air Force sat down in the early 1960s to develop the ultimate ground support machine: something with massive firepower, plenty of speed and manoeuvrability when needed, and sufficiently well armoured to be impregnable to casual small-calibre fire from the ground. At the same time General Electric was approached to design a suitable gun.

General Electric had come into the gun business almost by accident. In 1944 somebody had remembered the Gatling Gun of the 1880s, had taken one from a museum, connected an electric motor instead of a hand crank, and delivered a rate of fire of 5,000 rounds per minute. Since the heart of the matter was obviously the electric drive, after the war had ended General Electric was invited to develop a 20mm cannon on the same lines and by 1956 they had produced the 20mm M61 Vulcan six-barrel gun for aircraft armament. In response to the USAF request it then produced a 30mm seven-barrel gun firing standard

Oerlikon KCA ammunition at either 2,000 or 4,000 rounds per minute.

The aeroplane which resulted from the request became known as the Republic Fairchild A-10 Thunderbolt II and went into service in 1975. This looks a trifle ungainly, sufficiently for unbelievers to call it the 'Warthog', but once in action all doubts are dispelled. The 30mm General Electric GAU-8/A Avenger cannon lies in the bottom of the fuselage, beneath the pilot's feet, with the enormous 1,350-round magazine behind him. (A total of 1,350 rounds, though 1,174 rounds is the more standard load, may sound a lot compared to the wartime machines which went up with 12 or 20 or so rounds on board, but at 4,000 rounds a minute 1,174 rounds give only about 30 seconds of actual firing.) The ammunition developed for this gun is either high explosive/incendiary, largely for softer targets, or armour-piercing shot with a core of depleted uranium. This last not only has excellent armour-piercing properties but is also pyrophoric: fragments of the depleted uranium, sliced off by its passage through the armour, spontaneously combust and thus start fires inside the target. A single round of this ammunition might not defeat a modern tank, but some sixty-five or so arriving in each two-second burst have a cumulative effect which literally chews its way through armour and inflicts appalling damage inside the tank.

Upwards of 700 of these machines were supplied to the USAF in the 1980s, and they are most certainly the most effective anti-tank aircraft in existence, and equally certainly the only fixed-wing anti-tank aircraft.

Other air forces appear to place their reliance upon what

are called 'multi-role fighters', but if history tells us anything it tells us that tin-openers are better than Swiss army knives for opening tins.

For the anti-tank role, however, the fixed-wing aeroplane has generally been elbowed aside in the past fifteen years by the rise of the combat helicopter. The helicopter first saw combat service in Korea, where it was largely used for casualty evacuation. After the introduction in 1955 of the turboshaft engine, which finally provided an adequate power-to-weight ratio by comparison with the air-cooled radial piston engines used up to that time, and with the almost simultaneous solution of various other technical problems, the number entering service rose dramatically. The first demonstration of its military potential came in Vietnam, when the helicopter was used to move troops rapidly enough to frustrate operations by the Viet Cong guerrilla forces and then was equipped with machine-guns to become a roving fire platform with far more agility than any tank. This role of giving the infantry more mobility seemed to be all that could be expected of the helicopter, but in the early 1960s some pioneers began experimenting with mounting pods carrying small rockets for ground attack tasks, and a few years later began fitting wire-guided anti-tank missiles on to the weapon pylons.

The wire-guided air-to-ground missile made sense on a helicopter, which could remain more or less stationary while the missile flew and which gave the firer an unprecedentedly clear view of the target. At the same time, of course, it gave the enemy an unprecedentedly clear view of a stationary target and invited him to do something instead of merely sitting there watching the missile getting closer. So while the soldiers had to agree that a helicopter-borne missile was theoretically a 'good thing', they were not slow to point out that in practice it was likely to prove disastrous.

The experimenters responded to this by demonstrating that a skilful pilot could easily stalk his enemy by keeping behind hills or trees, popping up to take a quick look and popping down again to make another move, until he had the enemy where he wanted him, looking the other way while the missile was launched and guided. Practical trials then showed that this was indeed feasible and that a tank crew, locked inside a noisy iron box and with restricted vision, was unlikely to detect an approaching helicopter unless the pilot actually flew it across their path.

What finally clinched it was the invention of the 'mast-mounted sight' in the late 1970s. The refinement in electro-optical sights and miniature video cameras made it possible to place a sight unit on the rotor mast above the helicopter's main rotor assembly and transmit the picture digitally to the pilot or gunner inside the cabin. Now the helicopter could hover, hidden behind trees or terrain, with only its mast-mounted sight above the cover. Once a target had been detected, the pilot could manoeuvre his machine into the best firing position without coming into view, and then rise above the cover to launch his missile. And if he could be given a fire-and-forget missile, then he did not have to stay above the cover for more than a few seconds. Instead he could be down and off to find another target, leaving his missile to find its own way.

The fire-and-forget missile has already been discussed within the context of infantry missiles. The helicopter can carry greater weights than an infantryman, however, and thus the restraints on size were less important. This made it possible to develop a suitable missile for helicopters, even though they were not yet technically feasible for infantry use. Development of the AGM-114 Hellfire (an acronym developed from 'Heliborne fire-and-forget') began in the USA during 1976 for a future attack helicopter which eventually became the McDonnell Douglas AH-64 Apache. Weighing 43kg (95lb), the Hellfire uses semi-active laser guidance and can be launched either directly at the target or indirectly, climbing over the intervening screen or cover and seeking out its own target.

Conventional wire-guided missiles, such as HOT, TOW and MILAN, are also widely used on NATO helicopters, while the Soviets have adopted their own equivalents. But with the general adoption of anti-tank missiles came various defensive systems which look likely to even the contest. In the first place came the rise of combat helicopters, machines with air-to-air armament which could be used to seek and destroy opposing anti-tank helicopters. Machine-guns, air-to-air rockets and missiles, and Gatling-type cannon and/or machine-guns can all be found on combat helicopters, as well as anti-tank missiles, and the helicopter is therefore emulating the fixed-wing aeroplane in becoming a multi-role machine, capable of taking on a wide variety of destructive tasks.

Moreover, the tanks and ground troops are now beginning to take notice and develop their own forms of defence. Anti-aircraft guns are now optimized for shooting at helicopters, and development has been completed of special proximity fuses which, unlike early fuses, are not confused by the multiple returns arising from the turning rotors and which can ignore the tree-tops and pick out the helicopter from its background. The most recent anti-helicopter measure is a proximity-fused shell that can be fired by the tank's main armament against the tank hunter once he has been detected by radar or thermal imaging sights.

The jury is still out in the case of the helicopter versus the tank. Experience in the Gulf War, the only real experience of modern helicopter and missile technology against armour, was so one-sided that it really produced no useful lessons. On the face of it, it would seem that the missile-armed helicopter would be a decisive weapon against the tank. But they said that about the anti-tank gun and the wire-guided missile, and they were wrong. However formidable a weapon may seem to be, one can be assured that the antidote will not be long in appearing.

CHAPTER EIGHT

MINES, TRAPS AND BARE HANDS

It is very reassuring, when confronted by an approaching enemy tank, to know that across one's shoulder is the most modern shoulder-fired rocket in existence; or that the man a yard or two away is diligently tracking the tank through the sight of a MILAN or TOW missile; or that the approaching thunder is an approaching A-10 'Warthog' and its 30mm Gatling gun. But there are times when none of these comforts are within reach, and one has to do the best one can with what is available, and that may not be much. One is, in effect, in the position of the first German soldiers confronted with the tank in 1916.

The soldiers who went to war in 1914, many of whom survived to see the first tanks, had received a long, slow, peacetime training that covered many subjects which, even then, were somewhat obsolescent. Engineers and pioneers were well versed in the finer points of fortification and could speak knowingly about redoubts and bastions, tenailles and hornworks. One of the oldest offensive methods against a fortified place was mining – digging a tunnel underneath and packing it with explosives to collapse the castle wall or whatever. Coast defences used fixed mines; these canisters of explosive were moored in the protected area and connected with a 'mine room' in the fort. When cross-observation located an enemy ship above one of these mines, a switch was closed and the enemy ship was, literally, blown out of the water. And those who had not had a formal education in fortification theory had sufficient experience of trench warfare to know that the spade was a vital weapon of war. So after the tank had appeared and the initial shock of its capabilities had died down, it was scarcely surprising that one of the first ideas that sprang to many minds was the use of mines.

The first mines were very simple affairs: holes dug in the ground under cover of darkness, packed with blasting explosive and linked to a forward trench by an electric wire. If a tank came in the right direction and passed across the mine, then the sentry in the trench would close the switch and the mine would be detonated beneath the tank. As a hurried response it was reasonable, but more considered thought brought about the idea of firstly thinking about where tanks might come (what was the best ground for them, how they would avoid obstacles too big to crawl over, and where they might attempt a covered approach) and put mines there. Simply putting mines in front of the front-line trenches meant that several tens of thousands of mines would have to be made and laid, and the odds were that very few of them would ever be needed. And so the 'tactical minefield' came into existence, even if it did not get that name for a long time afterwards.

With such a minefield it was scarcely practical to wire each one and have somebody sitting with his finger on the switch all day, every day. This led to the invention of 'contact' or 'pressure' devices, which would be activated by the weight of the tank or the pressure of its tracks and fire the mine. Bear in mind that nothing of this sort was on the quartermaster's ledgers: there was no chance of going to the nearest ordnance store dump and asking for two dozen mines, for such weapons simply did not exist as formal munitions, and had to be manufactured (or bodged up) on the spot. As a result, some of these firing devices were primitive and hazardous. A favourite German method was to dig a hole, and place upright a 150mm (5.91in) artillery high-explosive shell. The fuse was removed and, with care, opened so that the safety devices could be removed; the fuse was then replaced in the shell and around the shell were packed a few cases of blasting explosive. The hole was then carefully filled in with earth, and a plank laid across the top of the shell fuse, held clear of the fuse by packing up the earth around it. Any tank which rolled across the plank would press it down into the earth, thus pressing down on the fuse striker and firing the shell, which, in turn, fired the blasting explosive to produce a very satisfactory anti-tank measure.

No sooner were anti-tank minefields invented in this manner, of course, than the great bugbear of minefields made its appearance. The sequence of events went something like this: Company A of the 99th Infantry would lay a minefield. Some days or weeks later it would hand over its section of the front to Company C of the 156th Infantry, and carefully point out the minefield. But Company C never had cause to use the mines, and when it was relieved, it forgot to tell Company H; the result was one lost minefield. When elements of the American Expeditionary Force attacked the Hindenburg Line in September 1918 they lost ten tanks by running over a forgotten minefield that nobody knew about.

The other classic fortification solution was the obstacle, but when one remembers that the tank was specifically designed to cross trenches, flatten minor defensive works and squash barbed-wire entanglements, it becomes obvious the obstacle had to be something of considerable size. In fact it is doubtful if any extemporized obstacle which might have been thrown up hurriedly ever discommoded any tank in 1917–18. What did cause problems was the existence of large man-made or natural obstacles – canals, railway cuttings, marshes, thickly wooded areas, none of which could be called into existence at a moment's notice by threatened troops. Moreover, the tank people were prepared for the worst: as the war ended the British were already experimenting with a bridge-carrying tank for crossing canals and rivers.

There are no records of work done on the development of anti-tank mines in the decade after the First World War; doubtless there were some experiments and trials, but it was not until the middle 1930s that the subject appears to have been given any serious thought and that designs began to appear. For the most part, the resulting weapons were simple devices: tin-plate canisters containing a small quantity of high explosive and fitted with a simple pressure-sensitive fuse capable of being activated by the weight of a vehicle but not by the weight of a man. The fuse was usually surmounted by some sort of plate, spreading the sensitive area to offer a better chance of being run over. But in general, it seems that the consensus of opinion was that the siege-like impasse of the Western Front of 1915–18 was unlikely to be repeated, that mines were essentially a defensive device, that mobile and fluid warfare would henceforth be the general rule, and that mines would therefore rarely be required.

The obstacle, though, was well in favour. The tanks of the 1930s were not the ponderous monsters of 1916, and they were more susceptible to being stopped by ingeniously designed obstacles. Wherever there was a likelihood of having to stop an armoured onslaught, then obstacles appeared in the forms of the Maginot Line in France, its Czech equivalent on the border with Germany, and in the Low Countries. These 'Dragon's Teeth' defence lines were constructed with simple concrete blocks about 1m (3.25ft) high and of roughly pyramidal shape, planted into the ground in rows across likely tank routes, and the rows repeated until they were six or seven deep. Such a collection would stop any tank, bellying it if it attempted to cross and thus presenting an excellent stationary target for the anti-tank guns which were covering, or in war would cover, the obstacle. Where roads or railways passed through these zones, gaps were left in the Dragon's Teeth and arrangements were made to block these gaps, usually with steel girders upended into prepared holes in the road. Although hundreds of thousands of tons of concrete must have gone into these defensive belts, there seems to be no record of their ever having stopped a tank, and the only wartime pictures generally show tanks cruising through the gaps unhindered by any portable obstacles.

While all this concrete was being planned and poured, the Spanish Civil War (1936–39) broke out. German, Italian and Soviet tanks were provided, plus a few home-brewed Spanish designs, and the soldiers of both sides were back in the 1916 situation: confronted with tanks and with precious little means of retaliating. Lack of formal equipment, however, was no novelty to the Spaniards, most of whom were irregulars of one sort or another and most of whom had been improvising all their lives. Miners with access to explosives cobbled makeshift mines and some unknown genius invented the petrol bomb, simply a glass bottle of petrol with a petrol-soaked rag wrapped around its neck. The rag was lit and the bottle thrown at the tank, preferably the engine cover, whereupon the burning petrol spread through the ventilators to the engine compartment and generally set the tank on fire. Since most of this activity appears to have originated with the Republicans, their targets were the light and vulnerable Italian and German tanks, which burned quite well.

The threat of mines and petrol bombs soon undermined the morale of the tank troops on both sides, once these practices spread to the Nationalist side as well. This was so much the case that another inspired Spaniard found that if he simply laid a few upturned dinner-plates across a road in something of a pattern and then scattered dust on the top, it was enough to halt an armoured vehicle until somebody plucked up courage to crawl up and examine the mysterious threat. These 'mines' were of course covered by rifles and machine-guns, so a major delay could be imposed for the price of a handful of crockery.

Just how much of this extemporized anti-tank warfare actually took place in Spain is open to question. That petrol bombs, soup-plates and dynamite bombs were made and used is attested to by contemporary newspaper reports and pictures, but the memoirs of participants rarely mention their use. Such devices were to play their peculiar part in the Second World War (1939–45), as we shall see, but otherwise the greatest enemy of the tank in Spain was the anti-tank gun.

The next confrontation between men and armour took place in Finland during the 'Winter War' of 1939–40, when the Soviets decided to rearrange their frontier with Finland and the Finns objected. It was this brief but bitter campaign that gave birth to a legend.

The Finns were not well provided with the armaments necessary to repel the Soviets, but they managed to give a good account of themselves, and one of their tactics, particularly useful in the forested areas, was to ambush tanks by pitching petrol bombs at them. At the time, the Soviet air force was strewing the country with a new type of aerial weapon, a bomb in the form of a large container which, after being dropped, split open to shower dozens of incendiary bombs on the target beneath. The Finns christened these 'Molotov's bread-baskets' (Molotov being the Soviet foreign minister), and some newspaper reporter, stirred by this levity, promptly christened the petrol bombs 'Molotov cocktails'. The name has stuck ever since.

In May 1940 the German army struck across the Belgian,

Dutch and French borders, a manoeuvre which neatly by-passed most of the Dragon's Teeth and traps prepared in the Maginot Line defences by flanking them through Belgium or by driving through the Ardennes, an area which the French considered impassable to tanks. Once again, what damage was done to German armour was done by anti-tank guns or artillery, and there was little or no call for any other techniques. Late in the same month, the German army came up to the Channel coast and looked across at England.

The threat of invasion concentrated minds wonderfully. The British army began to reorganize itself after the débâcle of Dunkirk, and able-bodied members of the civil population flocked to the Local Defence Volunteers, or LDV. It was then discovered that LDV also stood for Look, Duck and Vanish and overnight the LDV became the Home Guard. And one of the things which worried the army and the Home Guard most was the prospect of German tanks coming ashore and administering a Blitz-krieg in England. So in August 1940 there appeared *Military Training Pamphlet No.42: Tank Hunting and Destruction*, giving precise instruction in the various ways that tanks could be attacked.

It is very hard for people in the 1990s to understand the frame of mind that the events of 1940 had created in the English people. Things which were taken seriously then frequently appear ridiculous when viewed with hindsight. This is nowhere more evident than in one of the opening paragraphs of *Military Training Pamphlet No.42*: 'Tank hunting must be regarded as a sport – big game hunting at its best. A thrilling, albeit a dangerous sport, which if skilfully played is about as hazardous as shooting tiger on foot, and in which the same principles of stalk and ambush are followed.'

Not many of the British population had much experience of shooting tigers on foot in 1940. But never mind, said the good book: 'Every soldier and every member of the Home Guard should be trained in the methods of tank hunting and in the use of special anti-tank weapons. The lessons of Spain and Finland confirm that tanks can be destroyed by men who have the bravery, resource and determination to do so.'

The 'lessons from Spain' were being assiduously propagated throughout the Home Guard by a school of instruction set up in Osterley Park, outside London, and manned by ex-International Brigade members, most of whom appear to have had a good line of bluff but very little actual combat experience to back it up. Some of their instruction was sound, but some of it came straight from the *Boy's Own Paper*, and this latter included their tank-hunting team.

The team was to consist of four men, who would be equipped with a length of railway line (though where they were to acquire this was never explained), a blanket, a bucket of petrol and a box of matches. They would position themselves up an alleyway or alongside a house on the route expected to be taken by the enemy tank. Two men held the railway track, with the blanket draped over the end of it. As the tank passed their lair, these two charged out and rammed the track into the tank's suspension so that it jammed the driving sprocket and track. Number Three then threw his bucket of petrol over the blanket, now tangled in the track, and Number Four struck the match and threw it at the petrol-soaked blanket.

Alternatively, should there be a local shortage of railway track or petrol, one took up one's station in a first-floor room with a hand grenade and a hammer. As the tank passed beneath, one leaped from the window onto the tank and pounded on the turret hatch with the hammer. When the tank commander opened the turret to see what the commotion was about, one dropped the grenade in and slammed the hatch back down.

These were actually taught as practical anti-tank methods, and were actually practised as such.

What of the 'special anti-tank weapons' of which the pamphlet spoke? These, it turned out, consisted of the anti-tank rifle (confined to the army), a variety of grenades, and flame traps.

The simplest of these grenades was simply called the 'hand percussion grenade': as yet no official number had been allotted, though it later became the No.73, more commonly called the 'Thermos Bottle Grenade' because its shape and size was roughly the same as a one-pint Thermos flask. A thin metal casing filled with TNT and carrying an all-ways fuse, this was simply held along the forearm and thrown at the tank. The resulting explosion was enough to damage severely any light tank. The No.74 grenade was the infamous 'sticky bomb', a glass sphere filled with nitroglycerine and coated with an exceptionally tenacious adhesive. A handle attached to the sphere carried a lever and pin similar to those of an ordinary hand grenade, and there were two metal hemispheres around the sticky sphere to allow it to be boxed and carried safely. To use this weapon, one pulled out a pin which allowed the metal hemispheres to fall free, then a second pin which unlocked the firing mechanism. Then, if one was sufficiently bold, one ran at the tank, jammed the sticky part firmly on to the hull, released the lever and finally threw oneself clear; alternatively, and perhaps more wisely, one threw it at the tank. Either way the detonation of about a pint of nitroglycerine was very satisfactory. The only drawback was that one needed to be very circumspect when rearing back to throw, ensuring that the sticky part did not come into contact with any part of one's clothing or equipment.

The No.75, or 'Hawkins', grenade was actually a small mine: rectangular, about 150mm (6in) long and 75mm (3in) wide, it held just over 0.45kg (1lb) of blasting explosive and had a plate on top, beneath which one inserted a chemical igniter. One then pitched this so that it skidded in front of the tank's track: as the tank crushed the plate, this in turn crushed the igniter, which released acid on to a sensitive chemical and this detonated the charge. One could also bury it as a mine, and its dimensions were such that it fitted neatly into the web of a railway line and could be used to blow a gap in the track.

Finally the No.76 grenade, the 'SIP' or Self-Igniting Phosphorus bomb. This was an institutionalized Molotov cocktail in the form of a half-pint beer bottle containing a mixture of petrol, benzene, water, white phosphorus and a strip of latex rubber. This was sealed with the usual sort of cap. There was no pin, no safety device, and nothing to do except throw it. On hitting a hard surface the bottle broke and the phosphorus, exposed to the air, spontaneously ignited and lit the rest of the mixture. The burning liquids melted the latex rubber which added stickiness and thus kept the blaze on the tank.

These were, of course, all short-range weapons: one needed to be within a few yards of the tank to guarantee a hit. To do this one could conceal oneself in a trench or pit, wait till the tank rumbled past (or over) oneself, then pop up and throw the grenade at the rear, where the armour was thinner and the engine compartment offered a good target.

Doubtless the British defenders would have tried it had the situation demanded and numbers would have succeeded. For in the following year the German army drove into the USSR and Soviet soldiers were using just these tactics to stop Panzers. A few years later the Germans themselves were advocating similar tactics in their vain effort to stop the hordes of Soviet tanks coming westward, though they had somewhat more sophisticated equipment. Instead of sticky bombs, they used magnetic bombs carrying a shaped charge: three magnets would clamp the bomb on to the tank, placing the shaped charge at the correct alignment and distance to penetrate whatever armour it struck. In default of this the Germans would take half a dozen grenade heads, lash them to a single stick grenade, and throw it as a 'bundle charge' which, if it lodged under the rear overhang of a T-34 tank's turret could severely damage the turret training mechanism. However, the basic premise was still that of the man in a hole, waiting until the tank had gone past him. The war diary of 101st Rifle Regiment, 18th Panzer Division illustrates the point:

Renewed Russian tank attack. A KV tank steam-rollered over our anti-tank barrier but got stuck . . . Sgt Weber leapt to his feet, Cpl Kuhne followed suit. They ran toward the Russian tank regardless of its machine-gun fire [until] they managed to get into the dead angle of the machine gun. They had tied hand grenades together to make heavy explosive charges. Weber threw first, then Kuhne. They flung themselves down. The upper part of Kuhne's arm was torn open . . . but the turret mechanism of the KV had been damaged and it could no longer traverse its gun.

Lt Kreuter jumped up on to the tank and dropped a hand grenade down the barrel of the gun, leapt down and rolled over. Like a clap of thunder came the burst of the hand grenade and a moment later that of the shell in the breech of the gun. The explosion must have blown the breech-block into the turret, for the hatch flew open. Cpl Klein, with great presence of mind and even greater skill, threw in an explosive charge from 8 metres distance . . . the turret was blown 3 metres into a field . . .

The devices which, perhaps, would have been most effective were the various flame traps which were carefully set up in selected places. In a sunken road, or one with obstacles alongside it which would confine the tank to the road, an oil reservoir was set up to one side and pipes led through the ground to the road surface. In some cases motor pumps were concealed to deliver the fuel, a mixture of 25 per cent petrol and 75 per cent gas oil. *The Training Pamphlet* gave precise instructions: 'Fuel is required on a scale of 2 gallons per square foot per hour. Thus to cover an area of road 50 feet long by 20 feet wide requires 200 gallons for every 6 minutes burning. To sustain a fire of great intensity a head of oil of only a few feet is necessary and a pump is not an essential.'

Even more effective were the 'petard flame traps', brutal in their simplicity. A 182 litre (40 Imp gal) barrel of petrol/oil mixture was buried in the ground alongside the road, with a small guncotton charge beneath it. This was fired electrically so as to blow the barrel into the air and drop it on to the tank, where the impact would burst it and release the contents, which were then ignited by a well-aimed flare pistol or a phosphorus grenade.

As the threat of a German invasion died down in England, the war began to move in North Africa, and here, at last, the mine came into its own. In the emptiness of the desert, with only some parts of it impassable to tanks due to the softness of the sand, it was obviously impossible to put a solid line of men halfway across the African continent. Minefields, therefore, were laid to keep the enemy out of various sectors, to channel him into other areas where anti-tank guns and tanks lay in wait, to make an attack difficult by slowing it down and thereby giving time for reinforcements to be assembled, or simply to give the enemy a hard time wherever he chose to go. Both sides used mines in profusion, and, of course, in the haste of some of the operations the records got lost or the precise co-ordinates were wrong, so that whole minefields disappeared into the desert sand and were frequently discovered by the wrong people – the ones who had laid them in the first place.

The mine is an anti-tank weapon with a drawback: a tank attacked by a gun or a missile or even a man with a grenade cannot do much about it once the missile is in flight. He can shoot up the gun before it fires, or the missile launcher before it launches, or the man with the grenade before he throws it: but once the missile is released, the tank is simply a target. The crew can try evasion and fire off smoke screens, but there is no way it can take direct action against the weapon. With a mine, the whole picture changes. It is there, dormant, lying in wait for the tank, and with a bit of skill and luck the tank operator can find it, neutralize it and thus win the contest. There is also another unique feature of the mine: it is the one weapon you tell the enemy about. Those laying a minefield wire its perimeter and put up notices such as DANGER MINEFIELD or ACHTUNG MINEN, with a skull-and-crossbones sign.

One might ask what is the point of these warnings, which give away to the enemy not only the presence but also the location of the minefield. The answer is twofold: in the first place, one has to let one's own troops know where it is, and you cannot offer every soldier a map; and in the second place, one does not necessarily have to be all that honest, for a roll of wire and some signs are cheaper than a thousand mines, and the enemy cannot be sure until he has crawled all over the area making sure that one is not running a double bluff on him. Mines, even the mere threat of mines, have a powerful psychological effect.

The first mines put to use were those which had been developed in the 1930s as metal canisters full of explosive and fitted with a pressure-sensitive fuse. At first the only way to discover such mines was to crawl along slowly, prodding the ground very gently with a stiff wire or a bayonet and examining the ground to see if there were any traces of it being disturbed. It was a slow business, but the only way of being absolutely certain, and clearing a route for a tank meant three or four men abreast crawling and prodding, marking each mine they found with a marker, crawling on, leaving the mine to be dealt with by a second crew coming along behind. The men of this second crew would carefully scrape away the earth, uncover the mine, put in a safety pin, then lift the mine from the ground. Another detail with white tape would mark the edges of the cleared area.

Of course, the people who put the mines into the ground had an interest in making them hard to find and hard to make safe. Thus the mines could be booby-trapped. A mine would be buried, and fitted with a different type of fuse, one using a pull mechanism. A string from this was tied to another mine, laid on top. The finder scraped away the dirt, made safe the top mine's fuse, lifted the mine out, and in the process pulled the release fuse of the bottom mine, blowing himself up. The German Teller (plate) mine was actually made with a second fuse cavity in the bottom, so that a special booby-trap fuse could be fitted when it was laid. As long as the mine was not disturbed this fuse remained dormant, but any attempt to lift the mine caused this fuse to function and detonate it.

Soldiers got wise. They uncovered the mine, tied a rope to it, went off to one side and hid behind a tree or in a convenient slit trench, and pulled on the rope so that the booby trap went off but did not hurt anybody. After a while somebody did this, tied his rope on, looked round, saw a convenient trench, hopped in ... and landed on an anti-personnel mine planted there for that very purpose. It all became very unpleasant as each side tried to outwit the other.

By the middle of 1941 things were looking up. The Polish army had begun working on a mine detector in early 1939. It was not ready when war broke out but the drawings and models were taken to the UK, research continued and eventually the Polish mine detector became standard issue and forefather of all the hobby metal detectors which abound today. It relied on the fact that the metal of the mine could be detected by a magnetic field and would distort that field, so giving an electrical indication, in this case a note sounding in an earphone.

This made life rather easier on the mine-hunter: he now walked rather than crawled, and simply scanned across his front with the detector, leaving a marker wherever he got a signal. The actual uncovering and lifting of the mine was the same, but the whole job was speeded by the quicker discovery. But it really was not quick enough: if one was suddenly given the opportunity to attack an enemy, it was no use at all if the start of the operation had to wait four or five hours while groups of men scanned, crawled and dug up mines. What was needed was something fast, something effective enough to carve out a track for a tank or a group of men or vehicles as quickly as possible.

As with so many ideas, it had been thought of many years before and an answer produced. In the early 1920s the British army had rigged a heavy roller suspended from a girder in front of a Mk V tank, so that as it went forward the roller was dragged along the ground in front of the tank and its weight fired any contact mines buried beneath the ground. This was a cumbersome device, however, and every time a mine went off the roller was blown loose and had to be re-rigged before the tank could proceed. It turned out to be slower, and harder work, than crawling along the ground with a bayonet.

In 1937, however, the idea was revived and a Covenanter tank was fitted with sprung rollers ahead of the tracks. These detonated mines, and the explosion simply blew the roller up against its spring, after which it rebounded down again to the ground and the tank carried on. This became the AMRA (Anti-Mine Roller Attachment), and various models were produced to fit different British tanks. It was this which now made an appearance in the North African deserts, slowly carving out routes through German minefields.

In 1937 experiments had taken place using a number of agricultural plough blades mounted on a framework ahead of the tank and supported by rollers. This, it was hoped, would allow the tank to plough up the ground in front of it and thus dig up any mines. It worked, in a limited fashion, but the power demanded to propel ten blades through heavy ground was too much for the tanks of the day and the idea was given up. It was revived in 1942 and a variety of plough devices was designed and tested. They worked rather better in the soft ground of the desert and with more powerful tanks doing the ploughing, but they were still not particularly effective.

What made this search a little more than normally intensive was the fact that the German army had got wise to the Polish mine detector and had begun making mines from wood, glass or earthenware which, of course, offered no magnetic field distortion to the detector. It was therefore back to crawling and prodding unless a better mechanized solution could be found. The final solution began with an idea from a South African army engineer officer. He attached a cross-shaft, rotated by the tank's engine, on a framework in front of the tank, and to this shaft he attached lengths of chain. As the shaft revolved, so the chains lashed the ground beneath in an ever-changing pattern which made sure that every inch of ground beneath the shaft was covered. No mine could stand up to that sort of treatment, and when one was detonated, the worst it could do was snap one of the chains, and that did not happen often. Thus the 'Flail' tank was born: it was to go through some improving modifications before it was perfected, the principal change being to give the cross-shaft drive an engine of its own, fitted into an armoured cover on the outside of the tank. This left the tank's own engine to its own job of propelling the tank without having to share out a considerable proportion of its power to the flailing mechanism. Attached to various makes of tank (it eventually settled on the Sherman) it was to flail its way through German minefields for the remainder of the war.

The Germans also experimented with a variety of mine-clearing devices, principally various arrangements of roller fitted to different tanks, but none of them was ever put into service. There were, though, some very ingenious ideas: as early as 1939 a radio-guided miniature tank which dragged a set of toothed rollers behind it was developed and tested, but the development then went off on to a different set of objectives and ended up as a radio-controlled demolition vehicle, a sort of miniature tracked box with electric drive, packed with explosive, which could be directed against a pillbox or other obstacle. The original mine-clearing purpose was forgotten.

Far more ambitious was the Krupp Raumer-S (from 'raumen' – to clear away). This was a gigantic 130-ton armoured box sitting on four 2.7m (8.85ft) diameter wheels. It was articulated in the middle, each pair of wheels was driven by a separate Maybach engine, and the front and rear tracks were different so as to cover as wide a patch as possible. This vehicle was to be driven along, and its sheer weight and bulk and strength made it totally impervious to any normal anti-tank mine. Unfortunately it also made it somewhat difficult to move about: not many bridges can carry a 130-ton vehicle, and this was still being pondered when the war ended and the solitary prototype was discovered in a Krupp testing ground.

Throughout the war there was little real advance in mine technology, apart from changing the material from metal to non-metallic and some attempts to better the chance of having the tank hit the mine by changing from the original round shape to a long, thin shape which, stretched across the enemy's line of advance, made it more likely to be run across. It was not until late in 1944 that a new approach was made, in Germany, where an engineer named H. Schardin began experimenting with shaped charges. It was known that a shaped charge required a short distance in which to allow the explosive jet to form and gather velocity (usually about two to three times the diameter of the charge). Schardin began to look at the possibility of using a large charge and allowing the jet to travel some distance before it hit the target. If the charge was big enough, it seemed probable that there would still be sufficient energy in the jet to defeat a tank's armour over a gap of several feet.

In the process of his investigation Schardin found that if he altered the shape of the charge, making the face of the explosive a shallow dish, and lined this with a thick steel plate, the detonation would blow the plate off at high velocity. He made a charge about 300mm (12in) in diameter, set it up some 50m (55 yards) in front of a Panther tank, and fired it. The result was a one-foot hole in the front plate of the Panther and a staggering amount of damage inside it. Schardin had invented what is now called the 'off-route mine'. Instead of planting it in the ground and waiting for the tank to step on it, one planted the mine at the side of the track and fired it as the tank went by. But by the time Schardin had worked it all out, the war was over.

Nothing new was to appear for some years after the war ended. Some experimenters toyed with Schardin's ideas, but nobody seemed to be able to get the same results against armour, and the principle was eventually applied to an anti-personnel mine, using several hundred small fragments of metal embedded in a curved dish of explosive, so that the detonation of the mine spread a fan of fragments towards the enemy. This became the Claymore mine, which first appeared in American hands in Vietnam in the 1960s.

What concerned armies more than the actual mechanics of the mine was the business of laying them. As the Cold War grew in intensity, so the threat of the vast Soviet armoured force became uppermost in NATO minds, and the problem was how to get a minefield across their path in time to stop them. It was impossible to sow a belt of mines across German farmland in peacetime, so the mines would have to be laid after the balloon had gone up. The existing system of having hundreds of men with shovels was scarcely practical given the probable time available. Work therefore began on methods of laying mines mechanically and at high speed. And since the Warsaw Pact appeared to have the same fears as NATO, but in the opposite direction, it too was in the race.

The solution was much the same wherever it appeared: a trailer, designed to be towed behind a vehicle carrying the mines, with a chute down which men in the truck slid the mines. On the trailer was a ploughshare which carved a furrow in the ground, into which the mines were dropped, at intervals, from the chute. On the chute was some mechanism for arming the mine fuse as it was laid, and as the trailer moved on a blade and roller turned the earth back over the mine and levelled it. With a well-drilled team on the truck, 600 mines could be laid in an hour by the British Barmine Layer, aided by the fact that the mine was no longer the round canister of Second World War vintage but an entirely new elongated mine. This was due to the wartime realization that long mines gave a better chance of intercepting a tank than did circular mines, and also because a long mine could carry more explosive than a circular one while remaining convenient to manipulate.

The quantity of explosive had become critical. During the war 5kg (11lb) of explosive detonated under the track were usually enough to put the tank out of action for a long time, if not permanently. But tanks grew bigger and eventually all 5kg (11lb) of explosive achieved was the breaking of a track, something which could be repaired relatively quickly. Two solutions were offered: bigger mines with more explosives, and changing the point of attack. Instead of aiming for the track (because, after all, that was the part that would actually step on the mine) go for the belly, usually thinner than any other part and in some designs not even particularly well armoured. Moreover, a successful attack against the belly would do severe damage to the occupants of the tank and its mechanical features.

The difficulty was that, for the purposes of ground clearance and cross-country performance, the belly of the tank was some distance off the ground, and simply banging off a few kilograms of explosive underneath might give the tank crew a surprise but was unlikely to do much else. Increasing the size of the mine to the point where a naked explosion could do some internal damage led to totally impractical mines. It therefore seemed better to adopt some form of 'projected' attack, and the obvious choice was to put a shaped charge in the mine so as to deliver its jet upwards as the tank passed across it.

The drawback with the shaped charge is that the jet is relatively fine and it is not impossible to fire one up through the floor of a tank and pass clean through the vehicle and out of the turret or top surface without actually hitting anything vulnerable. By making the angle of the shaped charge a shallow one, however, it is possible to develop a much broader explosive jet, though one with less penetrative ability. This was acceptable against the soft underbelly of a tank. And in the course of work on this idea, the concept of Schardin's plate charge was revived. This promised to blow a massive hole in the bottom of the tank and carry all before it, but for one small drawback. Because the mine was buried, when the plate came out of the ground it was carrying a large pile of earth on its face, which tended to inhibit the action of the plate in cutting into the armour. This was eventually solved by using a small 'clearing charge' which fired microseconds before the main charge and shifted away the overlying soil.

The problem with all types of belly attack mine is, however, the question of firing them at the correct moment. Mines intended to attack tracks are obviously easy to fire: when the track fires the mine it is precisely placed to receive the benefit. But how to fire a mine which is 0.6m (2ft) beneath the nearest part of the tank and 1m (3.25ft) away from the track? Various fuses appeared to solve this problem: the tilt fuse, which relied upon a vertical antenna rod which would be pushed by the body of the tank and thus release the firing mechanism of the mine; and the tentacle fuse, a rubber hose filled with hydraulic fluid and stretched out each side of the mine, so that when both sides were squashed by the tracks, signalling that the tank was straddling the mine, the fuse was fired (squashing only one side of the tentacles – indicating that the tank was off to one side of the mine and not astride it – failed to cause the initiation of the mine). Other systems, of which very little has been made public, involve acoustic detection of the tank's noise, sensing the ground vibrations, picking up the magnetic field of the tank hull or detecting the warmth of the engine compartment.

With Schardin's plate charge under revival, it was not surprising that his original idea of an off-route mine was brought out and dusted in the 1970s by the French. In

1980 they announced MICAH (Mine, Anti-Char, Action Horizontal, or horizontal-action anti-tank mine) which was a cylindrical mine on a tripod, with a Schardin plate in the business end. This, it was claimed at the time, would defeat 70mm of armour at a range of 40m (45 yards), although it was generally thought at the time to be a bit of Gallic understatement and that the MICAH was probably capable of defeating twice that thickness. It could be fired remotely, by electrical impulse; or it could be connected to an electrical proximity sensor which would detect the presence of the tank and fire the mine automatically at the correct time.

One or two other nations have developed similar off-route mines, but in general they have been overshadowed by the application of shoulder-fired rocket launchers in this role. As previously mentioned, a number of these (the British LAW80, the French Apilas, the German Panzer-faust 3) can be fitted to a simple tripod mount and connected to a variety of sensors. They are then sited close to a likely tank route and left to their own devices. When the sensor detects a tank, it measures the target's speed and course and then, at the optimum moment, fires the rocket at the tank. It is also possible to instruct the sensor to ignore one or two vehicles and fire at the third, so permitting any reconnaissance vehicle to pass through unhindered before one of the following battle tanks is hit. A recent French design allows the launcher to be reloaded and used again up to five times, or, if it is in a position where reloading is impractical, then it can be instructed to destroy itself once the rocket has been fired, so as to prevent reuse by the enemy.

The other side of the coin is, of course, the problem of removing these mines and clearing a route for the tank. The flail tank had fallen into disuse: experience showed that while it was effective, it kicked up an immense cloud of dust and debris and frequently had to stop because neither the driver nor the commander could see where he was going. In the desert this had been countered by using a compass, but in the confined conditions of Europe, this was of little use. Ploughs and rollers were still being brought out, tested, adopted, abandoned, changed for new designs; there was no end to it, but none have ever been really satisfactory.

Mine detectors are still widely used, though the manufacturers of mines have almost entirely forsaken metal in their construction: a new French anti-tank mine actually does without any sort of casing by incorporating glassfibre with the explosive so that the explosive itself is strong enough to retain its shape and resist weather and damp ground without deterioration. Other techniques such as ultrasonics and microwave radar have been explored and may, for all one knows, be in use.

The alternative is to forsake trying to find every individual mine and simply apply brute force to detonate everything. This form of attack began by pioneers using the 'Bangalore Torpedo' to clear mines. The Bangalore Torpedo is simply a length of pipe packed with explosive; the ends are threaded and capped, and by removing the caps it is possible to screw several together to produce a long explosive charge which, in its original intention, can be slid underneath a barbed wire entanglement and then fired to blow away the wire and leave a gap. Some unknown genius reasoned that if the blast went up and shifted wire, it would probably go down and detonate any mines in the area, and the technique was adopted with some success to this other task.

The Bangalore Torpedo was then followed, in the British army, by the Snake, a canvas hose which was launched across a minefield by a small rocket. It fell to the ground and was then connected to a pump and filled with liquid nitroglycerine. Once filled, the pump was disconnected, a remote fuse attached, everybody withdrew and the Snake was detonated. The blast wave from this would spread down and sideways and detonate any mine within about 3m (10ft) of the hose; it also made a nice mark on the ground which indicated where the safe area was. The only problem with the Snake was the business of sitting in the middle of a battlefield pumping nitroglycerine into a hosepipe. It was hazardous, to say the very least.

Eventually an improved Viper version was developed. This consists of several hundred yards of hose pre-filled with plastic explosive and connected to a powerful rocket, all carried in an armoured trailer which can be towed along behind one of the leading tanks in a column. Should an enemy present himself, the trailer can be instantly jettisoned and the tank left free to operate in the usual manner. But if a minefield is encountered, then the tank commander simply aligns his tank and trailer with the proposed route and fires the rocket. This tows the hose out and drops it a short distance ahead of the tank in a more or less straight line. A delay fuse goes into action as the rocket comes to the end of its flight, and after the hose has lain on the ground for a few seconds the fuse detonates the explosive and the result is a long strip of ground cleared of mines. If this is of sufficient length to cross the mined area, the leading tank goes ahead and the remainder follow; if not, then a second tank/Viper combination takes up the lead to the end of the cleared area, and then fires a second rocket to clear the rest.

The drawback to this system is that only a single track is cleared, and the tanks have to move along it in single file. At the best, two or three parallel tracks can be cleared, but the tanks still have to move along them behind each other, which is a gift to the enemy manning anti-tank guns or missiles to cover the minefield. The optimum solution is to set off all the mines in the field at once, and it has been suggested that a fuel/air explosive (FAE) might prove to be the solution to this. FAE is a combination of some inflammable substance which is dispersed into the atmosphere and, combining with the natural air, becomes an explosive. When suitably ignited it explodes to generate a pressure pulse in all directions which is slower than a detonation wave but which is capable of exerting a strong push, sufficient to overcome the pressure plate fuses of contact mines. As an example, FAE bombs consisting of coal dust were tested during the Second World War: fine coal dust, dispersed in the correct proportions throughout the interior of a building and then ignited, will explode and simply push the building apart. The trick, of course, is to get the dust or other substance distributed correctly and in the correct proportions. In theory, an FAE bomb dropped over a minefield and ignited should exert sufficient pressure to blow all the mines over a considerable radius. To the best of the author's knowledge, however, no one has yet been able to solve all the problems of distribution, proportion and ignition sufficiently well actually to detonate a minefield.

The use of traps has more or less fallen into abeyance; the only large-scale use of traps since 1945 was on the inner German border between the former states of East and West Germany, as part of the infamous 'Wall'. Here a deep and broad anti-tank ditch formed part of the compound of fences, minefields and booby-traps designed to keep the inhabitants of the Warsaw Pact countries from contamination by capitalism.

In place of traps, many continental countries have prepared chambers beneath roads and bridges into which explosive charges can be placed should hostilities break out. For example, anyone driving across the Swiss border will see a number of square plates let into the road surface some distance into Switzerland: these cover small mine chambers which can either be used to lie in wait for tanks or can be detonated to crater the road and render it impassable. It is noticeable that these plates are always in a defile or some position where it is impossible to leave the road and drive around them.

Other countries rely upon providing some quick-fix explosive kit which will allow a road to be cratered. The French army, for example, has what it calls a 'ground drill' consisting of a light tripod, a 7kg (15.4lb) shaped charge, and three 12.5kg (27.5lb) cylinders of high explosive. To render a road impassable to tanks, three kits are used. The tripods are set up across the road, 2.5m (8.2ft) apart, and the shaped charge units hung from them about 0.5m (1.6ft) above the road surface. These three are then fired downwards to make three bore-holes about 3m (10ft) deep.

Three cylindrical charges are then lowered into each hole, some earth tamped down on top, and then these three sets are detonated simultaneously. The result is a ditch across the road about 15m (50ft) long, 3m (10ft) deep and 10m (33ft) wide. No tank is going to get across that without engineer assistance.

As for bare-handed attack by the individual soldier, this is largely taken care of by the many shoulder-fired rockets already discussed. There is still one area in which every soldier, not just those carrying a rocket launcher, still has a chance against armour: this is the grenade.

The use of hand grenades has completely died out for anti-tank use. It is now recognized that no hand grenade is likely to do much damage against a modern armoured vehicle, and the chances of the soldier getting close enough to use one are slender. But the rifle grenade is still considered a practical weapon, not perhaps against the heavily reactive-armoured main battle tank but certainly against armoured personnel carriers, infantry fighting vehicles and similar lesser-armoured threats.

The first anti-tank rifle grenade appeared in the British army in 1918 as a simple canister of explosive on the end of a thin rod. The rod was inserted into the barrel of a rifle, a blank cartridge loaded into the breech, the rifle rested against something solid and the trigger pulled. This grenade would undoubtedly have blown a hole in any tank of the period, but by the time it was tested, approved and put into production the war was in its final days, and it was never actually put to use.

In 1940 a Mr Fonberg appeared before the Ordnance Board in the UK to demonstrate his new invention, a rocket-boosted anti-tank grenade. In the report of the board it was noted that: '. . . observing that the firer wore a steel helmet, lay face down, buried his face in one arm, and fired the rifle by means of a lanyard at arm's length, the Board opine that the chances of hitting are remote, and recommend No Further Action.'

With the arrival of the shaped charge a number of rifle grenades appeared in the course of the Second World War. The British No.68 was the first, but there were many others in German and US service. The Germans even went as far as to manufacture a tiny shaped charge projectile to be fired from flare pistols, with a range of about 75m (82 yards) and a claimed penetration of 80mm, though the author rather suspects that this was steel plate rather than armour. There are very few records of these devices being used in action, and even then they appear to have been principally used to blow holes in pillboxes and buildings.

In 1946 a new device appeared as the Energa grenade: though promoted at that time by a Swiss firm, it seems to have been a Belgian invention, and it rapidly became popular with several NATO armies. It was an over-sized shaped charge grenade which slipped over the muzzle of a rifle, or over an adapter attached to the muzzle, and was fired by a blank cartridge. With a 65mm (2.56in) diameter charge it had a range of about 250m (275 yards) and could defeat over 200mm of armour. In the 1950s it went into service and could, at that time, have given a main battle tank quite a surprise, but tanks grew thicker and harder and the Energa grenade went out of fashion in the 1980s, though some countries who are unlikely to encounter very heavy armour still use them.

The Energa grenade was superseded by a variety of other rifle grenades, utilizing modern shaped charge techniques using improved high explosives and wave-shaping internal construction which manages to develop very good penetrating power in a small-diameter package. Luchaire of France, for example, produce a 40mm (1.575in) diameter grenade which can be fired from any assault rifle, will go to 350m (385 yards) and can penetrate 200mm of armour, and similar grenades are made in Belgium, Israel, Italy and Spain.

The 40mm (1.575in) grenade launcher developed in the USA in the 1960s, and now widely used by several countries around the world, and equally widely copied by several others, is also furnished with a number of shaped charge grenades, but these are so small that penetration rarely exceeds 50mm of armour. Almost all of them are 'dual-purpose' designs, generating anti-personnel fragments as well as an anti-armour effect, and like most dual-purpose devices they do neither of their tasks particularly well. Many rifle grenades are also being developed along the dual-purpose path, which will inevitably reduce their armour-piercing performance, and, on the whole, one hesitates to agree with this. It is far better to give a soldier a grenade and say, 'This is a good anti-personnel grenade and you can also use it against light armour if pushed to it', than to try and kid him that a rifle grenade will stop 'all known tanks' as the old instructional phrase had it. Today's soldier has a wide variety of anti-tank tools at his disposal, and he soon gets to know which work and which do not.

Taking one thing with another, from the rifle grenade at

one end of the scale to the A-10 Thunderbolt II with its 30mm cannon at the other, the modern tank is not going to have an easy ride. Many years ago an instructor was lecturing a class on a new type of anti-tank mine and as the author has suggested above, finished with the contemporary phrase of reassurance: 'This mine will stop all known tanks.' He noticed that a soldier at the back of the class did not appear to be very happy. 'What's the matter, Jones?' the instructor asked, 'don't you believe me?' 'Oh, I believe that bit about stopping all known tanks,' replied Jones. 'What worries me is the unknown buggers.'

And who knows what might be over the next hill?

INDEX